# BLISS + BLUES = BIPOLAR

# BLISS + BLUES = BIPOLAR

## A MEMOIR OF MY UPS AND DOWNS LIVING WITH BIPOLAR DISORDER

Jason W. Park, Ph.D.

**2021**
**JJ Magik Publishing**

To the best of my ability, I have re-created events, locales, people and organizations from my memories of them. In order to maintain the anonymity of others, in some instances I have changed the names of individuals and places, and the details of events. I have also changed some identifying characteristics, such as physical descriptions, occupations, and places of residence.



ISBN 978-1-7366662-0-3 (print)
ISBN 978-1-7366662-1-0 (e-book)

Library of Congress Control Number 2021903531

The author can be reached at: jwriterp@gmail.com

*To my mother and father*

# Contents

## PART II: Appendices

# Preface: The American Dream

I was born in Lawrence, Kansas. Whenever people ask me where I was born, they inevitably do a double-take to my response. Or they raise an eyebrow. Most Korean-Americans of my generation (Gen X) were born on the coasts, specifically Los Angeles or New York City. Or they are Korean-born transplants who became permanent residents. I guess my curious questioners never suspected an ethnic Korean to come straight from America's heartland. But it's true, and I have my passport and birth certificate to prove it.

Dad was a professor at the University of Kansas, in the marketing department at the business school. To this day, I have never met anyone so wholeheartedly devoted to his career, nor one so single-mindedly self-managed. His successful professional life made my dad a strong provider and he also has been a loving father.

My mother was a fervent stay-at-home mom. She had received an excellent education in Korea at the top-ranked women's university, and was preternaturally bright. She could have had a career just as luminous and entrepreneurial as Dad's. But once my brother Gerry and I were born, she wholeheartedly concentrated on her two boys. Everything and everyone else came dead last to me and Gerry. Her hopes and dreams for us were boundless vistas of determined ambition.

Gerry was younger than me by eighteen months. Our different personalities were set from the beginning. He was the risk-hungry sort, whereas I was the more rule-abiding, risk-averse type. In our later years, Gerry entered the world of finance and successfully assumed a desk job, while I eschewed the security of office life to become a writer who set his own hours. And we never lost touch completely, though he and his wife raised a family, and solitude was the most fitting lifestyle for me.

* * *

Dad moved to the University of Pittsburgh in 1979, shortly after the National Football League Steelers had secured their fourth Super Bowl. "Welcome to the City of Champions!" his new colleagues boasted wildly. I started kindergarten at the Falk School, which admitted only the children of employees of "Pitt." Indeed, my parents were part of the city's educational elite because of their university membership based on my dad being a Pitt professor. Even Mom got into the act: she acquired an MBA from Pitt's Katz Graduate School of Business in 1983.

My dad would shuttle Gerry and me to school from the Pittsburgh suburb of Allison Park in the mornings, and then pick us up in the afternoons. The school student body, spanning from kindergarten kids to sixth graders, was extremely diverse. The inclusion of all sectors of society was part of its diversity initiative: race, religion, creed, class, economic status, country of origin, gender, and political affiliation. Over my seven years there, from kindergarten through sixth grade, I drilled down deep into the three Rs: reading, writing, and arithmetic. But I really flourished engaging in physical education, either on the concrete playground outside or on the wooden basketball court inside.

We eventually moved out of staunchly middle-class Allison Park to upper-middle-class Fox Chapel in 1986. Our family's life became much more comfortable. My parents took with them the upright piano I had tinkered with in Allison Park, which had come replete with lessons from the neighborhood teacher there. However, she approached my mother before the move: "Mrs. Park, I have taught everything I know to your son, and he needs more advanced instruction." I upgraded to Dr. Pamela Wilson, a piano professor at nearby Carlow College, and to a six-foot grand, a wood and cast-iron monster which reposed gracefully—or squatted balefully, if I did not practice on it—in the living room in the Fox Chapel house. For hours at a time: scales, arpeggios, velocity studies, études, coordination exercises, metronome beats... I became pretty good!

But Dr. Wilson could be extremely punitive, much more than my previous teacher had been. She would scream, "Jason, that was horrible! Didn't you practice?" Or she would shove my hands off the keyboard as I was playing a passage of Beethoven, and then show me how it's really supposed to be played. And then I had to show up for those horrid nerve-wracking recitals. Not to mention the competitions, which involved practicing six hours a day (three in the afternoon, three in the evening, and even more on the weekends), in order to win a strip of flimsy fabric or a plastic plaque. And yes, I did win at the competitions. And yes, I performed at famous concert halls... But while I could appreciate Dr. Wilson as a piano pedagogue, I learned, poisonously, to fear and hate her as a person.

* * *

After Falk School, my academic institution switched to Dorseyville Middle School upon the beginning of seventh grade. The two years there were extremely painful for me. The school—whose constituents were mostly rural, unlike Falk School's—had a student body much more homogeneously white than I had ever witnessed. I simply did not fit in, and the kids knew that. Bullying was a problem not just with a few kids (although they made the worst of it), but it seemed like it came from everybody. I couldn't fight the whole damn school. I was called viciously a "chink," "gook," or "jap" I don't know how many multiple times a day. Other students would make karate-chop sounds and emulate kung-fu gestures with their hands.

After two years of Dorseyville, Fox Chapel Area High School was relatively easier, and the kids had mostly outgrown their insecurities by then. And by high school, I decided to challenge myself on the three A's: (1) Academics, (2) Athletics, and (3) Arts. As for Academics, I took the gamut of Advanced Placement (AP) courses in English, Calculus AB, Calculus BC, Chemistry, Biology, and I always strove for all A's. As for the Arts, I continued the music lessons and the piano competitions and practiced multiple hours on the piano a day. And as for Athletics, I chose lacrosse, which emphasized finesse over force. It still was a contact sport, which allowed me to get my pent-up aggression out. Plus, as a midfielder, I got my exercise.

But in addition to the three A's, there was (4) Addiction. I felt a strong pull towards marijuana and alcohol. I started drinking from a bottle of Chivas Regal that had been stored in my parents' closet by them. The rotgut had always been there, but one day, as I was rummaging around for a screwdriver, the bottle seemed to generate a fascinating allure. I began to wonder what it would be like to try some of its contents. Despite the disgustingly awful taste, it generated a pleasant buzz inside of me. Marijuana was trickier. I had the courage to try it because "everyone else was doing it." I remember the first time being high, and feeling as if my head had inflated with a hollow space inside. It was a pleasant feeling, although I could see how some people wouldn't like that experience.

In high school, I began to suffer from "down" moods and depression. It was like Winston Churchill's self-referenced "black dogs"; it blanketed me all over so that I felt suffocated and could barely move. This happened more than once at school. I would just look down, open-mouthed, eyelids nearly shut, until I got called upon by the teacher, and I would often manage to answer the question right: "Jason, what is the chemical formula for sodium chloride?" "Uh, NaCl?" Of course, that only happened if I listened to the discussion when within concentrated earshot. When I could not do that, I was lost until "saved by the bell!" All four A's made their mark, and in the future I would go down the Road of the Unhealthy One, but I changed my mind towards the end in favor of the Road of the Healthy Ones.

* * *

Excelling in the "triple crown" of Academics, Athletics, and Art—and merely dabbling with Addiction—carried the day for me in my high school quest to get into Harvard. Getting in, however, was the easy part. Getting out of Harvard—well, now that was the hard part. One of the reasons was the absence of my parents from campus. Away from home, on the East Coast, there was no light of maternal love or paternal support to bask in, except for always one distance removed. To compensate, I got into Addiction (again). This time, at college, hard drugs became readily available. I loved XTC, a methamphetamine, consumed at underground rave parties. As a result, I became rail-thin, at 5' 9" and 150 pounds. I could be very manipulative and quite charming if I needed or wanted drugs.

My use of drugs—mostly alcohol, XTC, and pot—became more and more extreme as the first three years of college proceeded. I just couldn't think properly throughout the semesters, until I sobered up, just before final exam periods. And behaviorally, while I could become chatty during the highs, I would also retreat into my room when not on alcohol or drugs and isolate myself completely, simply because I felt sad and worried. I was self-medicating.

As a senior at Harvard, I had to choose between scraping by and partying to graduation, on one hand, or ending the hanky-panky once and for all. I chose the latter… and that made all the difference.

As the Addictions ended, so did the scene. Party friends no longer came wandering into my room, looking for fun times. I stared off at my computer monitor, focusing on notes and papers for classes which needed to be taken to graduate. To be honest, I don't know how I did it. I just knew that there was more to life than "sex, drugs, and rock n' roll," and that there was life after college, which I had to prepare for.

However, there was a price to be paid. The academic stress and partying to excess during four years of college had taken its toll. The candle that is burnt at both ends burns twice as brightly but only lasts half as long. And so there I was, on my twenty-second birthday, and I asked myself, "Now what?"

* * *

# PART I

# Bliss + Blues = Bipolar

CHAPTER 1

# L.A. Law

I had just graduated with honors from Harvard, and yet on the plane headed from the East Coast to the West, in June 1997, I felt horrible. I figured that burning out from studying and partying had something to do with it, but what exactly I didn't know. However, I was aware that whatever I was feeling internally was affecting my behavior externally.

You'd think that the plane ride would have been easy enough; after all, all I had to do was "have a seat." And for the most part, that's pretty much what I did. Throughout the five-hour flight, I would mostly just sit there, depressed and down, dejected and despondent, mired in the mud of my morbid moods. All the emotional lifeblood had been sucked out of me, leaving me a feeling-less robot. I feared asking even the simplest request: "Pardon me, I need to use the restroom." And it took the greatest effort to offer the simplest answer: "Yes, I'd like peanuts with my ginger ale."

But then there came a time to let my emotions run loose! Suddenly, out of the blue (as it were), as if in random happenstance, feelings of ecstasy and elation, excitement and exultation slipped their noose and bounded upward on a propellant rocket booster headed only one way: straight UP! And then there I was, in seconds, on Cloud 9, in a limitless vista of euphoric, sky-high bliss, as if the weight of the world had just been lifted from my shoulders. Free at last, free of whatever afflictions had hindered me and had weighed me down just moments previously.

At these high points, it was all I could do to sit in my seat. For I now desperately wanted to chat it up with the stewardess, or begin a hurried conversation with the portly gentleman sitting next to me. This was out of an overwhelming need to make up for the time I had lost just sitting there in my seat like a jackass. If I had been competing at a track and field meet, I would have churned out a 100-meter sprint in seconds flat. And yet at the same time, something inside me knew that the urge to reach out was abnormal. So by sheer force of will I barely resisted contact with others, for fear that I would draw undue attention.

But sometimes the sky-high moods during the plane ride were not characterized by blissed out happiness, but a blighted irritability. Then it would only be a matter of time before I was in danger of actually upsetting somebody. Despite my greatest striving, while in this mind-space it was impossible for me not to rub people the wrong way. And so I had this incredible urge to yell to the same stewardess on the plane, "I said I wanted peanuts with my ginger ale, Goddammit!" or to the passenger on my left I might see myself screaming out, "Move your damn arm, you jerk!" Or some other similar outburst which I could barely contain myself from actually engaging in. Whether it was irritability or ecstasy that characterized my elevated moods, it was not the right time for me to be close to anyone.

But then, a mere five minutes later, my super-inflated ego would collapse under its own weight into the deepest of deep blues, so that I couldn't even move a finger without monumental effort. It was frightening. As I sat there, motionless, my emotions whizzed back and forth, up and down, side to side, and I didn't know what to do with them, precisely because I couldn't control them. There was a screw loose, a gasket undone, a cog unmeshed, that no longer allowed emotional self-regulation. I didn't know who I was: the misery-prone Jason or the elated Jason or the irritable Jason—and the normal Jason was nowhere to be found. Sure, everybody has their ups and downs, of course, but my ups were REALLY up, and my downs were REALLY down, and there was no soothing equilibrium, as if my *emotional* personality had been split in two.

* * *

It was more of the same once I arrived in Los Angeles. My parents let me stay in one of the upper-floor bedrooms in their Bel Air home, so that I could ease into my job at the law firm in downtown Los Angeles. For hours at a time I would sit, inert and motionless, on the family room couch, unable to extricate myself from the stranglehold of my mysterious ailment. But that was only until I spotted the family pet sauntering past, and with a banshee-like scream, I upped and gave wild chase all over the house after the now-terrified beagle.

Mom and Dad must have suspected that something was amiss, while my brother Gerry, who was on summer break before his own senior year at Harvard, confided openly to them, "Wow, Harvard philosophy really screwed Jason up!" Indeed, I became known as the "Brooding Philosopher" in family circles.

One night, while my parents were sitting on the couch in the family room, watching a public TV program special rerun of *The Lawrence Welk Show*, I ran down the steps and stood before them, arms akimbo, feet spread, spitting to the side and then yelling: "You kiss ass, Dad! You kiss ass! You kiss ass at work!" And then in a huff, I ran back upstairs to my room. I thought I knew what I was doing, but then no more than five minutes later, I ran down the stairs, and stood in front of my parents again, asking them with a smile, "So, how are you doing? What are you watching?" I was counting on their good graces to excuse my previous outburst. But Dad scowled and shook his head, opining: "This is not normal, Jason. This is *definitely* not normal." Well put, I had to admit. Then Mom murmured her assent. I turned around and walked back up the stairs, remorseful and contrite.

My parents didn't care so much about the disciplinary problems as they did about my happiness. Out of a desire to cheer me up, and also to foster my autonomy, they bought me a silver Honda Civic coupe as a graduation present. In Los Angeles a car is a necessity; without one, you're pretty much a zero. But again, this time in the process of getting the car, I managed to have another outburst, this one with the car salesman. I screamed at him, "I'm not trying to give you crap, but you said the car would be delivered in a few hours' time and we're now over the limit and it's still not here yet!" My screaming got the attention of the senior management at Santa Monica Honda, who came to the rescue and tried to placate me as best they could. I calmed down then, knowing that I didn't want to get into a fistfight and into real trouble. So despite my childish temper tantrum, I got away with this behavior without serious consequences. In the end I got my shiny new toy with my parents' largesse and the dealership's restraint.

My parents were concerned, because they had never seen this type of behavior in me before. One day, when my Uncle Oh arrived from Korea to stay a couple of nights with us to visit the family and celebrate my college graduation, I walked right past him, completely refusing to acknowledge his presence. My dad, who was present at the scene, jumped from his sofa seat and angrily ordered me, "Jason! Say hi to your uncle!" I replied in a sideways manner, "I already did," although I hadn't. Dad couldn't believe it. What was his son thinking? How could he so disrespectfully treat his own close relative, who had come all the way from Korea to see us? My uncle started to pace around the backyard, trying to make sense of what had just happened. I skipped the subsequent family dinner, and didn't bother to acknowledge my uncle's departure.

I helplessly counted the days until after Independence Day, when I would have to leave the realm of family and assert my own professional independence, by starting my job as a litigation clerk in a high-powered corporate law firm. Was I ready for it? Well, I wouldn't know until I tried.

* * *

By July 1997, ready or not, I hit the mean streets of downtown Los Angeles, wearing a collared shirt and fashionable slacks for the office. But I dreaded meeting new people, for fear that I would turn into the "local asshole" in the entire organization... due to my verbal outbursts, you know? Well, apparently that fear became a self-fulfilling prophecy, for I immediately gained a reputation for tussling with people, especially those of higher rank.

Egotism wasn't befitting someone on the lowest rung of the organizational ladder. As a litigation clerk, I was paid the least, not even $20,000 annually, even though I processed the most paperwork—more even than the paralegals, the associates, and the partners (in that order). It was completely unfair, but that's how you paid your dues to the legal field, I guessed. I didn't mind it, at least initially. After all, it was the most money I'd been paid by any employer—including in part-time jobs in high school and in college. But after realizing the inordinate skew in paycheck versus paperwork, where partners made the most money and did the least paperwork, this observation began to consume me, to the point where I became insubordinate and quarrelsome.

There was one time when I was working for an associate named Larry who welcomed me cordially to his office. I replied sportingly and with a smile, "So should I call you Mr. Weiss?"

"No, Larry is fine!" *Seems like a really nice guy...*

Well, he had me fill up file folders with photocopies of the originals. I was having difficulty with the assignment because the original documents were not in order, so naturally the reproductions were out of order, too. It was OK that they were not in order, because Larry and I agreed that I would be given instructions to put them in order later. But for some reason I then assumed that someone had nefariously disordered them to frustrate me. It was completely irrational of me to make that mental jump. After all, why would someone do that? But I somehow harbored the suspicion that somebody was out to trick me. And what do you know, that someone would be...

I ran to Larry's office and banged on the door. Not waiting for him to answer it, I burst in and caught him typing away on the desktop.

"Larry, dammit, I'm the only one doing the copying and the files are not in order!" *Ah, I gotcha!*

"I'm sorry, Jason, what...?" Larry left off, open-mouthed.

"No, I'm just saying, something's not RIGHT here!" I rattled off. *C'mon, man, do I have to spell it out for you?*

After a brief pause to collect himself, Larry asked me, "OK, now tell me, what's going on?" He was composed, in command of the situation and had hands on hips as he straightened himself up in his chair.

I explained: "I just think SOMEONE'S GIVING ME THE RUNAROUND!"

Larry heaved a sigh, swiveled his chair around, his back to me, and replied in a measured, quiet tone: "Jason, no one is giving you the runaround."

Still angry but also feeling a bit sheepish, because Larry had been unfazed by my indirect accusations at him, I now closed the door to his office and returned to mine. There, within a couple of minutes, *a complete and utter 180-degree turnaround occurred in my perception and thinking.* It was wrong of me to have assumed the worst of somebody who I didn't even really know. It was illogical to assume that Larry had evil intentions. He had never tried to take advantage of me or fluster me. I had flown off the handle, and had potentially alienated an important ally and a benevolent supervisor. Just as distraught as before, but this time not with indignation but with panic, I went up the elevator as fast as possible and got out to run down the hall.

I ran to Larry's office, banged on the door, and again entered without waiting for him to answer.

This time Larry was ready for me. "OK, now Jason, I just checked with the mail room guys and they are positive the correct documents were..." Larry was all-business and now he sounded a bit cross, too.

But I cut him off. "No, Larry, look, I'm sorry, really," I pleaded with clasped hands and an honest smile. "I'm just very sorry for the way I barged in on you before. I just wanted to apologize for my behavior."

At that, something changed in Larry's face, from stern frown to caring countenance. I was trying to make things right, but didn't know if I could. It depended on the reception on Larry's part to my entreaty.

After a sigh, and a smile, Larry asked me, "Is everything all right, Jason?"

Oh, dear. I wasn't expecting that one. I had expected the worst. And, of course, nothing was all right. Everything was all wrong. But I didn't have the courage to admit that my world was crashing down around me. Nor was I willing to reveal a personal problem that was so huge in magnitude and extent that all the support and resources the organization could have brought to the table would not have been enough to resolve it.

I replied quietly, belying the great tension I felt inside, "Yes, Larry, everything is fine." And I smiled back. What else could I say or do? I simply refused to unload or "dump" on anybody. I just kept bottling it up inside.

Larry replied, "OK. Well, then, let's continue as before, and let's just forget this whole thing."

He stood up and closed the door to his office behind me as I walked out. Larry was a real class act, a stand-up supervisor, and here I was, the bad guy, the ignoble subordinate, for indirectly accusing him of malfeasance. And I didn't know what was wrong with me. I would ask myself that all the time: *Why, oh why, am I running, yelling, and screaming in anger, forcing my pompous personality on others, only to then later come back, completely apologetic?* The situation was grave and getting increasingly out of control.

* * *

I had expressed deep disillusionment on multiple occasions to whomever would listen about working at a law firm like the one I was at that was so prestigious but so "disappointing" to work in. This was irrational behavior on my part, because more complaints led to more difficult assignments, while rosy praise led to easier, more glamorous work assignments. You simply did not want to gripe, bitch, and moan because the management would throw you to the wolves. Well, somebody in authority to assign work details must have heard about this disenchantment of mine, because I was soon called out of the office to an individual matchup with the Devil himself.

At a long conference table sat Frank, a senior partner of the firm. He was wearing a Hawaiian shirt and possessed a lazy eye, but despite his relaxed appearance he was known for chewing out support staff and being extremely demanding. A real Dr. Jekyll and Mr. Hyde, apparently. I guess this was someone people thought could get a grip on my insubordination. Indeed, it was odd that only I was assigned to him; usually a bevy of clerks were needed to handle the paperwork. He took one look at me, winced, and hit himself on the head, muttering, "Why do they send me these stupid useless kids?" I sensed he was going to chew me up and spit me out.

Well, he seemed resigned to the fact that management had me in store for him. As soon as the door closed, Frank started to run down the list of deposition documents quickly while growling out the instructions, apparently not caring one bit about my level of comprehension. I sat there, outwardly expressionless, across the conference table from Frank, just taking it all in, but soon I began to object to his rhetoric. He began, "Now, I want you to list the articles in the following order: "A, B, C, D, E, F, G..." as in alphabetical order. Now I understood this. It made sense to me. There wasn't anything wrong necessarily about Frank's approach. It would have worked out between him and me. The only problem was, in my questionable state of mind, I wanted to do things more efficiently and more productively. But then again, would I dare to differ as a clerk with a partner?

To me, "G, F, E, D, C, B, A," was far better because this way had a definite ending with the last deposition article ending in "A," in order of increasing incrimination, rather than trailing off into "G," which lacked a more compelling internal logic. But Frank wanted to plod on with "business as usual." I couldn't tell you how much I was really chomping at the bit!

"But Frank," I implored in a tiny voice, "I don't think that's the best way to document the sequence."

"Just follow me," he insisted, in that frightfully boring way of his. Frank then again pursued his train of thought, obviously figuring he was doing me a favor by deflecting my complaint. "Again, Document A precedes Document B..."

"Yeah, but..." Again, I jumped ahead of him, more stridently this time, but still got cut off.

"No, no, no, that's not how you do it, kid—" he interrupted, hurried, not bothering about whether his way of doing things was the best..

So with my short fuse lit, and completely distraught because of Frank's poor-quality tutorial, I finally blew up in his face, screaming at the top of my lungs and pointing a finger a hair's breadth from his nose, "HEY LOOK, MAN, I'M NOT TRYING TO GIVE YOU CRAP!" I was panting and infuriated.

Frank's eyes, even the lazy one, popped wide open, his mouth dropped underneath his handlebar moustache, he clasped one hand in the other, and he glared at me in dark disapproval. Even his moustache looked as if it were frowning. He may have been afraid of me—after all, I was pretty afraid of myself, what with my threatening gestures—but at his 6' 2" and 210 pounds to my 5' 9" and 155 pounds, I think he had the better argument.

But before he could say anything, I got my two cents' worth in, enunciating clearly for him, "Frank, LOOK! All I'm saying is I believe that the sequence of deposition documents should be followed in a different, more efficient, and better manner than the one you have suggested."

At that, still unsure of what I was talking about, but now genuinely curious, Frank got up from his chair, shuffled around the long end of the conference table, and sat down next to me, this little peacock of a litigation clerk, to get a better view of the deposition documents from another angle. I showed Frank a still correct but what I considered to be a logically better sequence to place the documents in, to which he replied, "Oh, I see... yes, I see now!"

Pretty soon, after a few iterations, he said, "Oh, we're cookin' now! All right, kid, proceed as usual. Here..." he handed me his credit card. "Get whatever you'd like for dinner. And let's move on with this project until it's complete." So I guess he was happy just to get me out of his hair, to save himself from more work, and to avoid any more dire confrontations!

Frank went out the door and left me to my own devices, and this time I did what I wanted on the assignment.

I was surprised myself that I didn't order four double whiskies and three surf-and-turf dishes from the local steakhouse. But I didn't want to take advantage of Frank, even though his card probably had a million-dollar credit limit on it that I couldn't possibly max out. I got Chinese takeout instead with a couple regular sodas. Anyhow, that's how it started off between Frank and me.

Once this project was complete, I wanted more work, of higher legal complexity. I had thought to myself that I had the inside track with Frank. But he didn't seem to be forthcoming. So I reached out to Frank (in my own way, of course), picked up the phone, and bellowed into his voicemail, "Frank, this is Jason Park. I am anxiously waiting for more clerical work on any cases you're working on. I expect to be given every opportunity to prove myself. JUST GIVE ME A CHANCE, FRANK, DAMMIT, AND I'LL SHOW YOU WHAT I CAN DO!!!"

In response, his legal assistant called back and attempted to reassure me in an exasperated tone, "Jason, this is Kate, Frank's assistant. He has no work for you at this given time, and he will call you when he does." Click.

I fumed because Frank didn't have any more work for me. Well, take my lumps and move on, I guess.

* * *

About six months into the job, I was called into my administrator's office. And I knew why. For half a year, the entire organization had put up with my misbehavior and crazy antics.

Nancy, who had initially hired me, said I should take a seat. She had short blonde hair, was approaching middle-age, and displayed a poor sense of style. She wore a pressed smile on her face, a slightly welcome contrast to her unadorned office with its scattered white papers on her desk and yellow Post-its on the wall.

She began: "Jason, we want you to know that we've been in touch with some of your colleagues and co-workers and we just wanted to reach out to you."

"OK," I said quietly, hands clasped in my lap, not sure of what was next, and looking intently at her.

"Jason, you know, we have therapists and counselors you can talk to about any personal issues you may have, if that would help you and you're willing to try it."

After a brief pause, I realized I was off the hook for my behavior, and that the organization only wanted to help. But I didn't want the help, because if I accepted Nancy's offer, it would have been tantamount to admitting, to myself and to others, that I had a problem. I simply refused that verdict, even though I was erupting all over everybody around me. Again, no amount of persuading or convincing would have swayed me to give in, although this goes to show that admitting a problem is the first, most critical step towards recovery. So I elicited a final "No, I think I'll be fine," and again, as before, neglected myself.

I paid the price the next time, after about three more months full of antisocial and belligerent behavior, when in March 1998 Nancy gave me the pink slip and exit interview.

"Jason, you're fired," she said, steely-eyed and unsmiling now. "You may say to future employers, as to under what conditions you left the firm, that you were downsized."

"But why? In my defense, I did my job," I replied, my eyes starting to water as angry despair descended over me like a heavy fog. *No one understands me! Everybody only sees a part of me! People obviously don't see what a heavy payload I'm carrying on my back.*

"Yes, well, we can't have you sitting around listening to CDs all day long!" she criticized, apparently having found out about my fascination for jazz music played on a portable CD player in my office to soothe my labile moods.

"But the paperwork on that particular job is almost finished and isn't due for a year—!"

"And there are plenty of complaints coming from staff about your attitude and behavior towards them."

It was true, I had been abrasive to everybody, and more than a few individuals in the organization had gotten tired of forgiving me, despite the repeat apologizing.

"Well, I, uh—"

"Don't worry, Jason, learn to appreciate what you have. I didn't have any college degree, let alone one from Harvard, and growing up, I didn't even have a supportive family, which you have, and ultimately I still made out OK. You'll be fine after you get used to getting fired."

As it was clear what was about to happen, I got up to leave. Nancy followed me to the elevator and back to my office and then started giving me directions about clearing out my desk.

The commotion attracted the attention of one of my colleagues. "Wait, what's going on?" she asked out loud, while looking on, confused by the ruckus.

"Jason is no longer with us," Nancy replied hawkishly.

"What?!"

People started to gather near me, but I didn't want to stick around for the negative attention. I quickly left the building in downtown L.A. with my small set of belongings in tow: a lamp, my picture frames, the portable CD player, etc.

* * *

As I drove away from downtown L.A., I became sick to my stomach. So I dropped by a spot in Griffith Park and sat myself down on the lush, manicured green, with tears welling up in my eyes. I put my head in my hands and let the droplets flow. *What did I do to deserve this? Why am I back to worse off than before?* I couldn't put a bandage over that gaping wound of helplessness about my behavior, which seemed to be the cause of my black misery and blue despair.

I gathered myself up after fifteen minutes.

When I got back to my parents' place, I said to myself, "I'm gonna sit right down and write myself a letter" in the best impression of the jazz musician Fats Waller that I could manage. I seated myself in front of the family computer and typed:

Dear Ms. Pfendler,

Thank you for meeting with me today, March 12, 1998.

Our conversation became rather frank towards the end. You should know that my parents are the type who are more than willing to support, at least financially, whatever professional or educational initiatives I wish to pursue, if nothing else.

Let me also say that despite my college degree, I have met people in my lifetime who were of low educational achievement, who did not even have their G.E.D. diploma from high school, and yet who accepted me wholeheartedly and with open arms. It is their example I will continue to follow in life, not yours.

In the nine months that I have been at your organization, I have had the good fortune of encountering a couple of the firm's senior partners, a duo of the firm's associates, two of your paralegals and a pair of my fellow litigation clerks. They are all fine people. Your conduct is completely unbecoming what I believe befits the employees of an organization as committed to excellence as this firm is.

I will definitely forgive, but certainly not forget, this event. I remain,

Very truly yours,

Jason W. Park

I vacated my seat in front of the computer and walked downstairs to deposit the stamped envelope with the letter inside into the mailbox. Mom approached me. She looked depressed and disappointed—you would have thought she had just come from a state funeral. She had called the law firm to see how I was doing, and apparently Nancy had intercepted the call and told Mom what had happened. I understood Mom's reaction, but tried to see the bright side of things. *American kids move from job to job all the time before they land their dream job. Why couldn't I get fired once before I found mine?*

About a week later, a letter arrived in the mail from the firm—a short, perfunctory note from a high-level administrator:

> Dear Mr. Park,
> Thank you for your letter addressed to Nancy Pfendler dated March 12, 1998.
>
> While we appreciate your sentiments, please understand that the termination of employment decision was an organizational one.
>
> In closing, we wish you the very best of success in your future professional career.
>
> Sincerely,
> Emily Weaver
> Human Resources Administrator

Yeah, well, I could have seen that coming from a mile away, if my reality were not so skewed: an *organizational* decision. It wasn't just any one isolated individual that had fired me; it was the whole damn firm. And right along with and underneath my righteous indignation was the underlying suspicion: *Yeah, I deserved it.*

* * *

CHAPTER 2

# Time for a Therapist

My parents' bewilderment regarding my behavior now turned into alarm as the firing left me without any form of economic self-sufficiency. Their concern coincided with my upcoming twenty-third birthday in June 1998, and Dad—deciding that pulling me out of my funk required pulling out all the stops—declared one night over dinner with as much gusto as he could muster: "OK, Jason, let's celebrate your birthday!"

And the celebration was: an all-expenses paid vacation tour of the Grand Canyon, replete with dinghy rides on Lake Powell, views of the impressive Southern Rim, fine dining accommodations, sumptuous hotel stays, and the like. And the vacation was indeed marvelous. We had never seen the Grand Canyon before as a family (especially the eye-catching Southern Rim), or taken a dinghy ride down from Lake Powell to the Colorado River to see and feel the contrast between searing-hot rock and frigid cold water. The dining was completely world-class; I think I ate meat and potatoes every meal, which was my choice. And the hotel accommodations were second-to-none. A/C blasting, comfortable soft beds, plenty of space for the three of us, and a professional concierge staff to accommodate any need. I tried my best to have a good time.

But even the vacation trip didn't work. For most of the time, I just wanted to stay in my hotel room, roll up in a fetal position, and cry quietly to myself. It wasn't enough to send me out on a holiday, as if leaving the smog of Los Angeles would cure me of my affliction.

* * *

Upon our return to Los Angeles from the Grand Canyon, after dinner one evening, I disappeared into my room. There I sat, motionless on the side of my bed, all by my lonesome, totally despondent, engaged in vitriolic inner dialogue—*Why must I go on? Dammit, Jason, we ALL go on!*—when Mom and Dad, who usually left me alone, suddenly burst in through my bedroom door.

"Jason, what's wrong?" Mom started sniffling, pleading with me, sitting next to me on the bed, absorbing her tears into a tissue that she held in one hand and holding one of my hands in her other, as she watched, helpless to upturn my downcast countenance.

Parents don't always realize that their children's mental quirks can mask deeper, underlying symptoms. As a result, they'll say, "Snap out of it!" when a child is listless, or "What's wrong with you?" when they don't understand. But my parents were genuinely concerned by this point, because the symptoms of mania and depression were quite apparent by then.

"I'm fine," I growled irritably, more to myself than to my parents, to get them to leave me alone.

"Jason, I think if you saw a therapist for a while, to establish trust and talk about your issues, it would do you a lot of good," Dad said, a hint of calm desperation entering his voice, as if he were an admiral on the bridge going down with the sinking ship.

That's when Dad told me about Dr. Frances, a psychologist who had helped one of Dad's colleagues.

"OK, all right, I'll do it," I muttered, still irritated at my parents' bursting through the door. *At least now they'll just leave me alone,* I thought to myself. And at least now I would seek help.

* * *

At my parents' suggestion, I called Dr. Frances the next day, and immediately nickel-and-dimed a lower hourly rate, from $150 to $125, before scheduling an initial appointment. I headed downstairs and told my mom and dad.

"Hmmm," Dad considered out loud, "even doctors can be bargained with."

He returned to consuming the large soup bowl of ramen noodles and *kimchi* lovingly prepared by Mom.

Dad had sounded surprised about the price change. I wasn't sure why I felt the need to haggle, but in my then-*modus operandi,* I guess it was because I thought that I should be prudent about how I spent my parents' money (after all, Dad was paying for it, not me). Then again, I wasn't sure why Dad expressed wonderment at my lowballing Dr. Frances. I was sure that everybody pretty much did it when bargaining for something and when money was at stake. But then again, maybe my behavior belied a deeper problem, right?

Dr. Frances wore long black hair and had bright, chirpy eyes above sharp, narrow lips. She was in her early 50s, and cut a decent figure for her age. I picked up on her Eastern European accent. She had a home office in Costa Mesa, a neighborhood of large bungalows and tightly manicured lawns.

Dr. Frances wanted to see me for an hour and a half for the initial consultation meeting. I didn't mind this at all because I just wanted to lie on my side on that comfy yellow couch of hers, cradle my broken head in my hands, and try to rid myself of the horrible and unpredictable sensations inside my skull.

"So Jason," she started calmly, "please lie down." She motioned to her couch, and I acquiesced right away.

"Do you have any experience with street drugs?"

"Yes, everything but heroin."

"What is your sexual orientation?"

I shifted in my seat. "Heterosexual."

"What is your highest educational attainment?"

"Bachelor's."

"And what is your parents' educational achievement?"

"Dad has a Ph.D., Mom has a MBA."

"And your family structure?"

"My parents are still together, and it's always been a nuclear family."

"Any brothers or sisters?"

I moved a leg. "One brother."

"How many friends do you have?"

"Lots. They're back east. Mostly from college."

"And how many sexual partners have you had?"

I thought about this one. "About ten."

"Any history of mental illness in the family?"

"No, not that I'm aware of."

"Any suicide attempts?"

"One."

She asked these questions in a rather benevolent manner, so it didn't pain me at all to answer. I wasn't sure what she was driving at, especially since this was a "self-report" process, and I suppose I could have fabricated a big fat lie. She was relying on me to be honest, but my past wasn't necessarily highlighted in sharp relief for me either. I guess she had to make do with what information I provided.

We continued to chat quietly as I felt the pressure that filled my skull slowly lift. And that was what the illness *literally* felt like, when unmedicated and undiagnosed: a gaseous pressure inside my head that had to be released through talk therapy, to avoid either: (1) an explosive outburst or (2) an immobilizing depression. And those two radically different "exit-strategies," if you will, were the only ones that existed *outside* the therapist's office; I had to either explode or implode. But inside Dr. Frances's office, it was possible to avoid explosive outbursts and paralyzing despondence through talking.

"So now the time is over," she announced.

Dr. Frances moved to her desk and began to scrawl something on a notepad.

"Jason, this is the name and number of a noted psychiatrist, Dr. Diego. I want you to visit his office for a follow-up referral and consultation, OK?"

She extended her hand and we concluded the session with a handshake, and I admittedly felt a lot better coming out than going in.

"I want to schedule you twice weekly for now, on Mondays and Thursdays, because 'twice as often is more than twice as good.'"

"I couldn't agree with you more, Doc," I said, in tune with the lady's advice, as I began to lean on her heavily for support. As for Dr. Diego...

* * *

I remember that guy, Dr. Diego. His office was located in downtown Santa Monica, and I felt honored and privileged to meet with him. His receptionist noted my arrival, and in minutes, the door to the plain, fluorescent-lit waiting room opened to reveal a warmly sunlit hallway leading to a doorway at the end.

There Dr. Diego was, standing by the door. He was benevolent-looking, soft-spoken, with rather scraggly dark brown hair on top but with a scraped chin on the lower part of his face. He had a sense of intellectual curiosity about him. I felt comfortable, safe, and relaxed in his presence. Of course, I also felt psychologically exhausted, and had to let my guard down sooner or later.

Dr. Diego's armchair was oxblood red and grandly upholstered, and there was no doubt it was the king's seat in the court. My own place was with the commoners: three "paean" pillows on a three-seater, less ravishingly decorated. I sat down, and after pleasantries were exchanged, I asked a question that had been bothering me.

"Dr. Diego, can you tell me why am I seeing two doctors, you and Dr. Frances, concurrently?"

"Oh," Dr. Diego replied, "Dr. Frances is a psychologist, I am a psychiatrist. She treats you with talk therapy, while I prescribe you medication. For mental illnesses, a combination of talk therapy with psychotropic medication produces the best results."

I became nervous about his mentioning medication. Didn't only wackos take medication? But I decided to go with the flow as Dr. Diego began to ask me questions. Under the doctor's calm gaze, I capitulated to the physician's probing queries... Yes, yes, I had answered them a week ago in Dr. Frances's office.

"How many sexual partners..." "Sexual orientation..." "Highest educational attainment..." "Family structure..." "Any siblings..." so on and so forth. Finally, Dr. Diego's gaze fell downward, and he became quiet towards the end of the last question, as he scribbled some notes on a pad of paper. Then he looked up and dropped a bomb on me.

"Jason, I spoke beforehand to Dr. Frances, whom you saw a week ago," he began. "She made a diagnosis based on your visit with her, and I now concur with hers. Your diagnosis is bipolar disorder."

"Bipolar disorder," I repeated dumbly, utterly mystified. "What is it?"

"It's a mood disorder. It used to be called manic depression. In your case, episodes of deep sadness alternate with episodes of extreme irritability or euphoria. Dr. Frances and I are lucky to have corroborated each other's medical opinions so quickly."

I was dying to ask him, "Are you sure?" but couldn't think of what else it could be that I was suffering from. Verily, I could contradict one doctor's medical opinion, but two at the same time? No. So I accepted the diagnosis as fact and went from there.

"Did the drugs I take in college have anything to do with it?" I asked, grasping at straws.

"No, it didn't cause it, but it may have made it worse. There is a phenomenon called 'kindling,' where the constant repeated use of an illicit drug can eventually produce the onset of symptoms. There is also 'self-medication,' when you take illicit drugs in order to help yourself cope with the emerging symptoms of the mental illness you are starting to have."

Open-mouthed, in shock, I looked at Dr. Diego blankly. Then I recovered, and giving up to Fate, I asked, "So how is bipolar disorder treated? Can it be cured?"

"There is no cure, Jason," Dr. Diego said, "although recovery is possible and the condition can go into remission. It is best treated with a combination of therapy and medication. I'm going to start you out with Effexor and you should continue your visits with Dr. Frances."

He scribbled on a prescription pad of his and ripped off the script, starting to pass it on to me.

"Whoa whoa whoa whoa, hold on, Doc..." I said, stopping him, and he momentarily looked up, arm outstretched with the script, to meet my gaze. "You mean I have to take medication?"

"For now, Jason. It will help you feel better in the short run," Dr. Diego responded. Then he shifted in his seat. "Jason, you studied philosophy at Harvard, so this will make sense to you. Someone very famous said a long time ago that *the unexamined life is not worth living.* But I submit to you that the corollary of that is also true: *the unlived life is not worth examining.* Be well, young man."

With that I stumbled out of the doctor's office, stunned by the prognosis as I made my way towards the parking lot. *Do I have to accept the unacceptable? Mental illness? Will I be locked up in an asylum, in a cuckoo's nest? How long will recovery take, if at all? Can I treat and manage this challenge? Will I have to take medication forever? How do I explain this to my friends and family?*

As I strapped myself into my coupe and then rolled out of the Santa Monica parking lot onto Ocean Drive, I mulled over the philosophical truism Dr. Diego had provided me... *The unexamined life is not worth living... the unlived life is not worth examining.*

* * *

In the beginning, Dr. Frances and I first used broad descriptive brushstrokes to sketch out a rough portrait of my life. The little details were not worth paying attention to yet. She wanted to explore my life up to the present.

"So doctor I am an Ivy League graduate and I performed at Carnegie Hall a couple of times."

In fact, I almost *had* to mention these things; it was as if there was nothing else to talk about in my life, as if only the bright accomplishments defined me and made me who I was. Of course, the fact that I brought those academic and musical feats up implied much more: a strongly supportive family milieu and a focus on high achievement.

Dr. Frances led me to reconsider my relationship with my parents. Perhaps they had an agenda for me.

"Agenda," I intoned as I thought about how that sounded. It didn't sound good, as if I were not in control of my own destiny. *And there is something sinister about it, too,* I thought to myself. *My parents tried to control me as a child, and now as an adult I resent them.* Of course, it didn't register with me that maybe my parents were looking out for my own best interests, and that it was out of caring and concern that they felt such a need to be in command of my life.

And, yes, perhaps my parents had been somewhat overbearing. But did that justify blaming them for their type of love and support? It became clear to me at the time that whatever bad parenting my mom and dad were supposedly guilty of required equally "bad" behavior on my part as their child. Did that sort of "tit-for-tat" relationship make sense? No, it didn't make any sense whatsoever. It wasn't that way. But that is how I was starting to feel. A whole bunch of feelings starting emerging with the whole hot-button issue of parenting and expectations.

"And then," I also told Dr. Frances, "I face an intellectual crisis that was written up in my senior honors thesis at Harvard: *Virtue versus the Passions*. Another way of saying it is *Reason versus Emotion*."

"So what matters more, Jason, or which one takes precedence?"

"Well, that debate is as old as civilization itself, older than the Bible, older than Plato in the West and Confucius in the East."

"Jason, you are highly developed rationally. After all, a Harvard college degree, especially in philosophy, indicates rational achievement. But are you in touch with your feelings?"

"Well, a deficiency exists there," I admitted. "Either I put a very tight lid on my emotions, or I founder when they come completely unloosened."

I took a sip of my bottled water to give myself a moment to think. Then I pondered out loud, "Besides, another clue to the puzzle I'm facing is that bipolar disorder is a *mood* disorder, not a thought disorder like schizophrenia. This again suggests that while my Reason is OK, my Emotions are not."

Dr. Frances noted, "And yet the manic episodes of bipolar disorder typically reveal a psychosis, or a state out of touch with reality. So maybe your Reason needs major adjustment, too."

Dr. Frances suggested a book for me to read: *The Road Less Traveled*, by M. Scott Peck, M.D. I found it a page-turner, and I recommended it to my mom, too, who is an avid reader. But the part of the book that I remember most, that "many psychological disorders are due to bad parenting," left my mom clucking disapprovingly. Back then, having read the book for the first time, the idea had an unsettling effect on me: *Ah, I now renounce all responsibility over my mental illness and now I will blame my parents for everything...* This was completely unacceptable reasoning in hindsight, however understandable.

In my Abnormal Psychology class at Harvard, I had read about the Freudian psychodynamic theorists who argued that psychological disorders occur because of unresolved trauma occurring in childhood as a result of deficient parenting. But by the mid-1990s, it had been especially pointed out that bipolar disorder had clearly originated in *nature*, not nurture. Psychodynamic theories simply do not explain the underlying causes for bipolar disorder very well, which is pretty much a chemical imbalance in the brain brought about by genetic dispositions. And yet with Dr. Frances, I was looking at the psychodynamic explanation as much as anything else. Thus the anger inside of me came from looking at the childhood roots of the problem, not necessarily from the biochemical nature of the illness itself.

Throughout, Dr. Frances tapped into the suppressed rage I had held inside myself throughout my young adult life. She voiced it directly, implied its existence indirectly, or allowed me to infer its influence via subtle language. This rage of mine was directed primarily at my parents who, according to my damaged, deranged mind, had hindered my road to independence. In other words, I had been an emotional train-wreck that had never left the station. I had never confidently tackled uncharted vistas with me at the helm.

Everything that I had supposedly done for myself, even through college, was a justification of my parents' choices for me. For example, there was what academic major I chose, philosophy as a pre-law major, a very conservative choice of a bourgeois profession that would be appreciated in my parents' social circles. Or how about what athletic and artistic extracurriculars I engaged in? Lacrosse player and jazz DJ aficionado, both safe bets with a cachet of prestige that could be explored without being too risqué. So I had been pushed, and then I had learned to push myself, and supposedly everything I was doing was a result of my parents' overbearing nature. This was, in my injured mind, entirely self-serving on the part of my parents, that they had "molded" me, while I lacked autonomy and was enslaved to my family. I was the mascot of the family, carrying out every single initiative Mom and Dad had spearheaded, and now it was coming to a head. That was how I felt. There was only one problem with this assessment: it was not couched in reality, because my parents cared for and loved me.

* * *

After working with Dr. Frances continuously for a couple of months, I had had enough. I was going to act unilaterally and on my own, finally and for the first time in my life (supposedly). On a sweltering and sun-blasted Monday afternoon in August 1998, with no job or career to attend to and no attachments formed with anyone, I grabbed a forty-ounce bottle of *Colt 45* malt liquor from the local convenience store and drove back over to my parents' house. Once having parked myself in the patio in a lounge chair, I began chugging the harsh malt liquor, without nursing it. Of course, mixing meds with alcohol was a no-no, because then no one knew what affected the brain. This really was my first case of a "fuck-it," a deliberate attempt to renounce self-responsibility and to self-sabotage my own recovery. Most importantly, I was going to get back at Dad and Mom, and this time, they were going to pay.

Mom and Dad were upstairs at the time, both of them watching television. I wanted to lose all inhibitions and be menacing, like a lion. I spied the 5-iron that I'd picked up at a local sports shop days before, leaning against the outdoors refrigerator, and soon I felt its heft and weight in my hand. The perfect instrument, I thought to myself, for a *gentleman's* game, and I shrieked in drunken laughter.

Dad came down to hear what exactly the ruckus was about. He was wearing cargo shorts and a white T-shirt, exactly identical to what I was wearing. I had picked up that outfit combination in college as a rollerblader. *Ha-ha! See, he's copying me!* I was having fun whacking away at the roses in the topiary bordering the lawn when I heard Dad's voice: "Jason! What are you doing? Stop it now!"

And with that, the first manic episode of my life let loose. I had been hypomanic before, with elevated and hostile mood, but never wildly out of control. During those hypomanic times, whenever I could apply myself to constructive ends, I became productive and efficient. But now, in this unadulterated mania, I was not in control of my faculties. This was not a feeling of elevated excitement, like an XTC high, but an explosive outburst of temper.

What transpired next was a very disagreeable scene with plenty of bad language. I picked up my golf club and started taunting my dad.

"Come on, Dad, let's go RIGHT NOW!" I said as I brandished the club.

"Jason! I am your father! I am your father!" Dad admonished.

Not having expected an out-and-out fight, Dad started backing up, silent in astonishment at my stalking. He tripped over the floor mat and sat down hard on the stone flooring of the patio.

I menaced him: "I'm going to kick your ass, Dad!" and from my superior vantage point, I took a clumsy jab at his face with my club. I missed badly.

Time seemed to stand still, and I waved my club round and around in Dad's direction, yelling at him all sorts of expletives.

"Jason?" A voice had emerged from nowhere. I disengaged from my dad momentarily and wandered into the lawn. Dad disappeared into the house.

"Yeah!" I shouted in a moment of subdued clarity.

"Are you OK?" It was Anne, the next-door neighbor. "Just checking to make sure you're all right. It sounded like you were having some trouble."

"I'll be all right," I answered with renewed purpose.

"OK then, Jason," and Anne ended our conversation there.

Meanwhile, after going inside, Dad had locked the heavy wooden sliding doors to the lower level behind him. I couldn't get into the house.

* * *

The next thing I remember was the sound of police sirens approaching. Party time was over. I went out around the side of the house to the front lawn to meet them, as if to honorably admit guilt.

"It was me, officer, I did it," I claimed to the black officer.

"Oh you did, huh?" he said with a snide smile. "Well, let's see what these people say."

They had me sit on the curb, while they deliberated with my dad, who had entered the conversation as to what to do. He seemed to understand that I was drunk and deranged, and not in the right frame of mind because of medication issues. But whereas Dad didn't want to go along with their taking me in, the police certainly wanted to arrest me.

So outside, in front of the house, the black officer told me, "Jason, put your hands behind your back and lean over the hood of the car."

I was restrained with handcuffs and placed in the back of a squad car. Then the three of us, the two officers and I, sat in the parked police vehicle for a short time.

One of the two officers, a white guy, said to me, in a disgusted and angry tone: "So why you? You went to Harvard, didn't you?" He sneered at me unabashedly.

These guys thought they were about to do a number on a naïve college kid who had never been to jail before.

After a brief pause, I countered, "THE SYSTEM IS CORRUPT!" to which the second officer, the black guy, laughed and yelled, "OOOOOOH."

Meanwhile his white partner did a complete 180-degree and exclaimed desperately, "Tell me about it, man; I work every day in it!"

As the officers prepared to leave for the nearest station, my dad looked through the half-open car window and exclaimed stoutly: "Jason! I will protect you!" And I remember Mom's crying face and comment, "Oh, Jason!"

By now, half the neighborhood seemed to have spilled onto the street to see what was going on. There was Anne and her stepchildren, all three of them; the troubled skateboarder from across the street and his family; the Raymonds, who owned a major newspaper in Los Angeles, and then there was Zachary, the producer of the TV show *Desperate Housefolk*. But there was no time for good-byes. The squad car slowly rumbled off and soon I was gone.

* * *

CHAPTER 3

# Go Directly to Jail

**Day 1 in jail:** I had last taken Effexor on a Monday morning at 9 AM, and here it was, Tuesday 3 PM, as I waited to get checked into jail in downtown L.A., thirty hours after the last administration of medication. The officers guided me into the intake process at the station, where I announced to everyone there, "Good afternoon, ladies and gentlemen!" as if to mock Lady Justice herself. The officers seated at the intake cubicles momentarily looked up, only to disregard me. But one of them, who had to take my picture, encouraged me to think about what I had done back at my parents' house. He encouraged me, with a kind smile: "The key is to understand what you did," to which I replied jovially, back at the camera lens: "Well, it was wrong, but I don't regret it!" *Wow. It is wrong but I don't regret it?* The officer lowered his smiling gaze and chuckled. "OK, young man. Good for you."

Another officer, a Hispanic fellow, said, "Well, I guess you're in here for the experience, huh?"

The issue then at hand was whether or not I deserved to get *out* of jail. Was I capable and deserving of reform? The criminal justice system in the United States has little understanding of mental illness, although things are getting better. One thing that it clearly didn't understand in my situation was my regimen of talk therapy and medication. If these were working well and in tandem, then I could modify my behavior appropriately and live a lawful life. The fact that medication is not prescribed to jail inmates is a telling indicator that jail is not the place to be for the mentally ill.

After the initial part of the intake, an officer sat me down on a bench with the cuffs behind my back. I couldn't tell what time it was, but I later learned I stayed there for several hours. It seemed as if the sun had set, based on how much time I had spent doing nothing. Then I was hoisted up by a couple of officers, un-cuffed, and sent away to another room for a body cavity search. How humiliating, to take off all my clothes and spread my butt cheeks so an officer could see if I was hiding anything in my ass. I couldn't help but think that this was some sort of sick joke. I paraded around in front of him, buck naked, as if to intimidate and entice the officer with my body. Another fellow intake, a Hispanic fellow, was having trouble following orders. He kept facing off with an officer, who was telling him in Spanish to undress, but the guy wasn't having any of it. I guess the officer is still waiting to this day for the guy to drop his drawers. Toward nighttime, I felt my drunken buzz disappear and I was left with only a hollowed out portion of my head left. At least for now, nothing was happening with my lack of medication.

**Night 1 in jail: Tuesday 9 PM**, thirty-six hours since the last administration of medication, and I was placed in a holding cell containing two bunk beds and a hole in the ground to defecate and urinate in, with a roll of toilet paper next to the hole, placed almost as an afterthought. *Goddamn, I can't believe this...* I commandeered the top bunk on one side, because some strange fear of mine at the time was that anybody else other than me on the top bunk would urinate in his sleep onto me. The cops kept their distance on the other side of the bars. My bunkmates, who I ignored, kept to themselves in turn, but it was still an unpleasant place to be in: no privacy, pungent body odor, stale sweat and close proximity to urine and feces. I unabashedly took a couple of dumps in the toilet myself, even though that meant I was exposed to my cellmates.

I managed to sleep a little bit that night, but only fitfully. The noises of yelling inmates, cell intakes, and pacing officers were a lot to handle. But it wouldn't be long before someone yelled, "Jason Park!" and the cell grating swung opened and I was led out by an officer. The officer said, "Jason Park, we're going to take you out to different quarters," to which I replied, "Well, I guess somebody likes me!" The officer nodded, almost in disbelief.

**Day 2: Wednesday 9 AM**, and now I was off medication for forty-eight hours. I started to feel strange sensations in my head. A little bit of lightning bolts bursting between my ears. My vision was obstructed. It was strange!

I was put in a holding cell—with about thirty blacks, Hispanics, and whites altogether. I was the only Asian in there. It was definitely less crowded than a cell for four bunkmates, but it was still a tense situation. When the others all saw me, they shouted out, "Yo, Bruce Lee!!!" I couldn't help but laugh out loud at this good-natured ignorance. It felt like a badge of honor to be associated with these thugs and hooligans who had rebelled at an unjust society. We just sat around, doing nothing, some talking, others sleeping. I isolated myself because I didn't feel as if I could relate to anybody there.

I lay for hours on a bench counter that extended from the wall, waiting for things to happen. My calm resting and measured breathing continued peacefully when all of a sudden, WHAM! my lower body jumped up, flew off the bench, and crumpled onto the ground, nearly carrying my whole body off with it. I recovered quickly, and saw the cause of the commotion: a skinny twenty-something Hispanic kid with a shaved head, baggy jeans, and T-shirt had angrily kicked my feet off the bench and sat himself down in the space vacated by them. I was initially too taken aback to get upset; plus, I wasn't sure whether the culprit had acted alone or at the behest of a fellow co-conspirator. I thought it was also important to remember that we inmates were all in it together, that the common foe was society, not any one of us, and that the last thing we needed was more chaos and disorder in the cooler.

A hushed silence fell on the room and everybody watched in anticipation to see what would happen next. I supposed that everybody expected a fight to break out, right then and there. But I didn't retaliate. Instead, I got into a sitting position, rested my elbows on my bent knees, and started asking the young man questions.

Not knowing Spanish, I simply asked in English, "Hey, how old are you, man? What are you in here for? What's your name?" I tried my best not to hate nor get stirred up by what was probably just a big misunderstanding. The kid didn't seem to comprehend my questions. Perhaps he didn't understand English, or maybe he was simply being uncommunicative.

I was still trying to get information when, just then, an older Latino prisoner, perhaps in his upper-30s, slender, also with a shaved head, came over and started talking to this youngster in rapid-fire Spanish. What exactly he said, to this day I don't know, but I suspected it may have been to tell Youngblood to chill out and relax. The older Latino went over some points in Spanish, which were elaborated with body language.

Then the older guy turned to me and asked, "So, hey buddy, what're you in here for?"

"I hit somebody," I replied despondently.

"Yeah? Hey, I'm here because I hit my girlfriend."

I inwardly winced to hear this, but internally processed two truths: (1) the guy was taking me in confidence and (2) I didn't have all the facts of this fellow's situation either. So I tempered my reaction; I just nodded and pressed my lips to show appreciation for the guy's sharing.

Another Latino guy, maybe upper-40s, a mean-looking heavyset hombre with a considerable amount of stubble on his face, asked gruffly, "Yo, Chino, whatsa matter? Why you in here? Don't your people got money to get you out?" He said it really mean and nasty.

"They're working on it," I replied weakly, not really sure about what I had just said.

"What was that, Chino?"

Somebody answered for me to this Latino guy, "They're working on it, man, that's what he said!"

With this, I got up from the bench and went to lie down on another one, facing away from everybody and towards the wall. I tried to sleep but only managed fitful bouts. And now the lack of sleep along with the lack of medication began taking its toll on me.

Wednesday night passed, during which I woke up now and then from a light sleep. I knew that losing sleep was not good for my mental health, but I just could not relax in jail.

**Day 3: Thursday 9 AM.** Seventy-two hours off medication, and at about this point, I began to experience even more strange sensations inside my head—flashes of light and electric shocks that went off, bang! like fireworks at a July 4th parade. I didn't even bother asking for my medication, thinking: *Asking for psychotropic medication would just fall on deaf ears.*

Seeing that my cohort of prisoners was still there, I asked more than a few of them about what their issues were. It was any number of things: public intoxication, petty theft, disorderly conduct, trespass, vandalism, reckless driving... you name it, they had done it. But it wasn't long before we were all corralled into a smaller room, where a beefy white bald police officer dressed in navy blue uniform addressed us as we all sat, willy-nilly, on the floor. It must have been morning, because court was about to be held in session, and the floor was cold.

"All right, you guys, it's your turn to head to court," he told us. "You're not the convicted felons in here for the serious shit, you're just the bullshit misdemeanors. So there's time for you to reform if you show good behavior in the courtroom in front of the judge."

With a wave of a baton, he concluded, "Let's go."

Here was a good example of the police clumping everyone together to deliver a little pep talk, as if it had any effect. But I was glad to get moving. I had been sitting around all day and all night, waiting for something to happen. We were corralled into another room just outside of the courtroom, opposite to the bailiff's station. The courtroom was visible from my vantage point, even though the door was only slightly open.

"Jason Park!" called out someone in a position of authority. It was another police officer. I followed him into the courtroom to the visitor's terminal, where I sat down. I could see my mother and father sitting in the plaintiff's section of the courtroom, where a white gentleman in a double-breasted glen plaid suit, white shirt and nondescript greyish patterned tie was talking to them. Apparently it was my attorney.

Toward my seat in the visitor's terminal, the judge addressed me with some legal rigmarole: "Do you know the charges against you? Have you been offered a public defender? Are you aware that you may use one if you choose to do so?" And so on and so forth, against the quiet din of the courtroom in session.

I was led back to the holding pen that I had been in a few minutes earlier, and then someone in a position of authority called out, "Jason Park!" This was met by one expression in the peanut gallery, "What, man? Jason Park? Again?" So I strolled right out of holding pen and back into the courtroom's visitor terminal.

This time the man who had been with my parents approached me from the other side of a Plexiglas wall and extended his hand through the opening.

"Mr. Park, it's nice to meet you, I'm Mr. Walker, your lawyer, and I have been appointed by your parents—"

I glared at him. "Look, man, I'm just trying to get out of here, I'm not here to be made into some local joke—"

Mr. Walker waved me off. "I'll see you tomorrow and we'll hear your case in court."

See how silly that was of me? Here was this man, an attorney of high caliber, approaching me in a civil manner, hired by my parents to get me out of an exceedingly difficult legal predicament, and yet I refused even to shake his hand. Unbelievable of me... how shameful! I was led away to the back room, out of the courtroom.

**Day 4: Friday 9 AM,** and now approximately ninety-six hours without medication, and counting. I was back in the courtroom for more legal antics. I remember sitting there in the courtroom, watching a video about the criminal justice system and what my legal options were. Despite its boring nature, the video caught my attention, since I was no longer inebriated or enraged, and there was nothing else to do in that freezing, wood-paneled courtroom, while I wore shorts and a white, stained T-shirt. Still, the video quite cynically advertised, rather than seriously pursued, the issue of justice for its constituents.

Then the judge, a white man with a ruddy face and rimless eyeglasses complimenting his black robe, entered the room, while the bailiff declared, "All rise!" The judge called the court to order. Mr. Walker appeared by my side. Apparently the man had forgotten or at least disregarded the verbal barb I had spit at him the previous day. He and I stood there together in the court in a show of mock solidarity. I argued with him quietly but venomously that I wanted to say something to the judge. Mr. Walker tried to calm me down, but I really did want to say something.

Finally, the judge asked, "Counsel, does your client need to say anything?"

To which, my lawyer resigned himself to having me embarrass him by responding, "Yes, he does."

"Mr. Park?"

"Your Honor, I'd like to exercise my right to a court-appointed attorney!"

There was a long pause, as the judge looked down at his paperwork. Then he told me, "That depends. Are you unemployed?"

"I am, Your Honor," I replied.

And then Mr. Walker whispered in my ear, "Don't worry, they'll take care of you." But that was the end of him.

So by Day 4's end, after working with three public defenders, the charge was not "assault with a deadly weapon," which was what everyone involved in my case was concerned about, but rather "simple assault." So this misdemeanor was a relative slap on the wrist, unlike a felony, which would have had serious consequences to my future job and career plans. With my silly, unnecessary brinksmanship, which had strained relations among me, my parents, my lawyer, the judge, and the public defenders, I had gotten away with a flesh wound: simple assault and three years' probation. The probation would require meeting with a judge every six months for thirty-six months and informing the judge of my attempts at re-entering into society, such as productive work employment, a clean bill of legal health, with no more crimes committed above a moving violation, and the like.

**Night 4: Friday 9 PM.** As nine o'clock approached, and after I had clocked over 100 consecutive hours without medication, the Court ended my stay in the criminal justice system. I was still aggravated but also exhausted, and when the Twin Towers in downtown L.A. discharged me on my own recognizance, I grabbed a taxi with the $27.56 I still had and asked the driver to take me to Bel Air. There, I knocked on my parents' front door, and Mom let me in.

I had nowhere else to go, and besides, even if I did, I would have had to pick up my belongings first. I went upstairs and took a shower. I knew that Dr. Frances and I would have a lot to talk about, and Dr. Diego would have to switch my meds drastically. That damned legal system: absolutely no understanding of mental illness. Well, by now I had been off medication over four days and three nights in jail.

* * *

CHAPTER 4

# Down (But Not Out) in L.A.

In time, I began taking my medication again and renewed my visits with Drs. Frances and Diego. The medication regimen, once resumed, seemed to calm me down, at least to the point where I wasn't violently psychotic. And I stayed away from alcohol for a while. In the meantime, my parents were furious at Dr. Frances for not having told them that I might fly off the handle. Dr. Frances explained to my parents that she had not expected me to do something like that. She also explained to me that she had been in jail herself back in Israel for chasing after her boyfriend who had been inducted into the army, so being arrested was nothing too out of the ordinary for her, I suppose. Still, at every session from that point forward, she held an emergency line button that she could press in case I were to become violent in her presence at her home office. That got me to thinking: *Wow, people are actually scared of me!* In fact, Dr.

Frances described what I had gone through as a grown-up temper tantrum. Yes, I certainly did have a violent temper.

Dr. Diego immediately had me take a mood stabilizer in addition to the anti-depressant Effexor; it was called Depakote. He informed me that there was a specific protocol for mentally ill lawbreakers in California: the "5150" (an involuntary psychiatric hold). Specifically, the police should have been called to a "5150," in order to confine me to a psychiatric hospital for up to seventy-two hours, to determine whether or not I was a threat to myself (suicidal), or to others (homicidal), or I was "gravely disabled." Obviously, there was nothing Dr. Diego or anyone else could do now about the assault charge or the resultant probationary period, but the information about 5150s would come in handy on future occasions. Strangely, at the time I didn't feel much upset with either Dr. Frances or Dr. Diego, although I would soon leave that treatment team in no uncertain terms for other uncharted vistas. I was still just getting my feet wet, you could say, in terms of my treatment.

While the Effexor lifted the depression somewhat, I had become quite irritable, a well-known side effect of Effexor—and perhaps this anti-depressant had sent me into a manic rage. Dr. Diego elevated the dosage from 75 mg to 150 mg, which I faithfully persisted in taking for a couple of months, from September to December 1998.

But by New Year's Day 1999, I started taking the situation into my own hands. I switched treatment teams, from Dr. Frances to Dr. Vicky and from Dr. Diego to Dr. Iovina. I had met them through a group therapy professional that Dr. Frances had recommended. With my parents' support, I met with Dr. Vicky for talk therapy three times per week, forty-five minutes per session, in her Huntington Beach office. And I met with Dr. Iovina once a month at her Seal Beach office. But things headed south right away. Dr. Iovina placed me on an anti-psychotic, which lifted the skew in my perception of reality, a characteristic feature of bipolar patients with psychotic features. But there was a pretty lousy side effect of weight gain of thirty pounds. I went from 170 pounds to 200 pounds, and on a 5' 9" frame, I didn't look good and I didn't feel good. Furthermore, the therapy sessions with Dr. Vicky would go absolutely nowhere at times.

"So, Jason, what did you have to go through since our last meeting?"

"Well, Doc, I'm trying to lose the weight I've put on from taking the anti-psychotic Dr. Iovina prescribed me."

"So, Jason, how does that make you feel?"

Gosh, how I HATED that question. Irritably I would reply, "Well, what do you mean, Doctor, how does that make me feel? It makes me feel like crap, of course."

"And so how does feeling like crap make you feel?"

And thus we talked about nothing.

At the time, Dr. Vicky and Dr. Iovina did not see it, but the reason for the bipolar symptoms was that the explosive manias served a "defensive" purpose, in that they were meant to prevent depressive episodes from spreading and taking over. Over time, a number of interactions with others that made me feel depressed about myself would accumulate, until a "defensive" mania would emerge to make me feel grandiose about myself, as a compensation. Thus, the real strategy should have been not to allow these emotionally negative events to accumulate over time.

I also hated filling out Dr. Vicky's insurance paperwork and transferring the insurance reimbursement checks to my parents. I wasn't an accountant! And it made the whole business of caring just that: a business. Everyone else benefited but me, although perhaps that was not necessarily true: I benefited marginally from therapy. But I didn't like being the go-between and messenger boy, because I felt used.

When I met with Dr. Iovina once a month, these meetings consisted of my sitting in a loveseat in her home office, while she would just fill the air with her obsessive prattle, talking, talking, talking, for a full hour, while I could barely get a word in edgewise. I would come out of those sessions feeling tired and exhausted by the need to keep quiet, even though I wanted to speak up. It is true that she provided an excellent anti-psychotic to calm the psychotic features of my explosive anger. In any case, she expected an expression of desire for treatment from the patient before she would do any work. That is perhaps how she operated as a physician: talk, talk, and talk until the patient interjected his or her own agenda. But I still believe the physician has to reach out to the patient just as much as the patient reaches out to the physician. And another thing: Dr. Iovina was always an organized one for billing my parents for her services, which is the hallmark of a great businessperson but not necessarily the best physician.

It soon became the turn of the century, and I didn't know how I had become lost engaging in lackluster talk-therapy and taking medication with huge side-effects. All I knew was that I was trying to escape from my life-situation, and I wanted a talk-therapy that would lift me up entirely, and I wanted a medication that would work like a magic pill, and I wanted a life with an unconditionally supportive family and super-easy expectations. But you have to take control of your own situation, and your mental health has to be *your* number one priority, not somebody else's. I was the boxer, and the physicians, family, and friends were in my corner, not the other way around. I had to be willing to enter the ring and box against my mental illness.

But perhaps you also have to be ready for recovery, like what they say about quitting smoking: *When you're ready to quit, you will.* Maybe that's what the doctors had secretly been attempting to do: to hurl as much stuff at the wall until something stuck, until the light bulb went on inside my head.

* * *

I could only do odd jobs now, since the downfall from the law firm and a brief respite from work to focus on my recovery. My parents were willing to pay for obtaining an apartment and the rent, but I still needed to work to afford something to eat and pay the bills. So the first thing I did post-law firm was to respond to a classified ad for telemarketers. Wow, was I in for a treat. In early 1999, for a few months, I did nothing but "cold call" people. Sometimes a Chinese person would pick up the phone and answer in sing-song Mandarin. Of course, there was no way to figure that out, so I would just say, "OK, good-bye!" and hang up. At other times, people would be really rude and say, "How did you get my number? Don't you ever call me again. Damn you!" and hang up, and I would get the short end of the stick. And so it went on like this for three months, where I had to kiss ass to each called recipient, young or old, male or female, professional or working-class, rich or poor... humiliating but at times hilarious.

When that ended, in 2000 I secured entry into a top-notch consulting firm through my dad's connections. There was a Harvard Business School professor named Oscar there, working in the academic branch of the consulting gig, and there was Silas, a subordinate of Oscar's. I impressed both Oscar and Silas with my Harvard liberal education, but it wasn't enough for me to stay in a business-minded organization. I was nearly manic when I attended a nationwide conference at the home office in Cambridge, Massachusetts.

At one point the conference broke up into groups to discuss the presentation of the CEO of a large-size online recruiting firm earlier that day. My group decided, with much lobbying on my part, that the CEO was guilty of hubris—overweening pride—and so therefore ought to be fired immediately! The de facto leader of my group announced our decision to the assembled conference afterward, which was in an uproar upon hearing of our bombastic plans. The CEO left right away from the premises upon hearing the news. I guess he wasn't too happy about the feedback.

Realizing that I'd made quite the commotion, after the conference I quit voluntarily after talking to Silas.

"Don't I get, like, two weeks' compensation for quitting my employment?"

"No, Jason, I can't do that, that's not what employment law states."

"Then why can't you just fire me, and then I can take the early termination compensation, which is longer anyhow?"

"No, Jason, I can't do that to you."

"All right, then, I just quit."

"That's fine, Jason, I will accept your voluntary resignation. By the way, I like you." Silas ended the conversation with a bemused smile.

A couple of days later I engaged in a virulent, completely nonsensical shouting match on the phone with Silas's voicemail: "You have no right to treat me this way! YOU HAVE NO DAMN RIGHT TO TREAT ME THIS WAY! Who do you think you are? WHO THE HELL DO YOU THINK YOU ARE? Man, Silas, you've really gotten to me this time! YOU'VE REALLY GOTTEN TO ME THIS TIME!" I felt that I had contributed already so much to the firm that I didn't deserve to go out unrecognized or uncompensated. Since I had already left the organization, located in a short black building in downtown Santa Monica on Arizona Boulevard, I felt safe yelling remotely into the mouthpiece of a cell phone.

It was odd how, days later, after my temper had dissolved, I could look back on that screaming match with an answering machine and not believe that it was me who had engaged in that. It was almost as if my emotions changed me into another person, someone who had the same name and body and looked like Jason Park, but was not really me, like a demon cooped up in me that threatened to run amok upon the slightest provocation.

Afterwards, Dad told me that Silas had wondered if he should call the police after the phone tirade. Dad was infuriated by my conduct. But it was over, no more future in consulting. And now I was frightened at how I felt, as if I had no control over this "dark side" that strained to cut loose. A real-time strange case of Dr. Jekyll and Mr. Hyde, for sure.

* * *

Starting in 2001 and for a couple of years, I became a car messenger. Let's just say that all I knew at this lost time in my life was I needed to make money, and I had a car, and I could meet the demand (for money) with my supply (of a car) by driving around Los Angeles all day long, delivering packages and getting paid to do it. At the very least it didn't require any job skills or certification, and no one cared about any criminal record. For two years, I rode like the wind as far north as Santa Barbara, as far east as San Bernardino, and as far south as San Diego, and along the Pacific Ocean coastline, and everything within this geographical triangle. I knew all the freeways: the 405, 101, 10, 710, 605, 110, 5, 91, 60, 57, 105, and 805.

The company I worked for had two major stations: one in Studio City, which housed a dispatcher, and the other in Santa Monica, which was a drop-off and entry point for a major entertainment company, which I will call Music Corporation A. Most of my time was spent on the road, but briefly I was promoted to operations manager in the studio mailroom, where I had to manage three unruly teenage Latinos, all by myself.

One time the dispatcher in Studio City took me into confidence and said that a middle-aged Hispanic driver named Santiago had called me a "chino" behind my back. I made a mental note of it. Later, when I saw Santiago outside Music Corporation A, I told him to go fuck himself. Santiago, undoubtedly surprised by this affront to his dignity, replied, "Hey, punk, you better watch who you're talking to. I don't see a good future for you, man, that's totally wrong on your part." I took it all in stride, ready to explode in Santiago's face. It made sense that this was happening that day, because another driver had noted it was the full moon that evening, the time for lunacy. Santiago and I squared off at each other, engaging in verbal sparring, which drew the attention of the security guard standing nearby at the entrance to the building.

Santiago finally told me to go to hell, which set me off: "OH YEAH? WELL, DON'T CALL ME CHINO! I HATE THAT WORD! THAT'S A CRAPPY WORD! AND WHAT YOU SAID, THAT'S A FEDERAL OFFENSE!" I was referring obliquely to hate-speech and discriminatory language.

Santiago responded, "OK, OK..." backing off.

In any case, the security guard said, "Understood, I'll take your side, young man; just relax and go back indoors."

Pretty soon after that, Santiago left the firm, and I, feeling sick to my stomach, went my separate way, too.

It was very frustrating, working while disabled. I couldn't hold down a job for long. And most of these jobs were thankless, to begin with. But I managed, despite the fact that I was known for having a rather violent temper at times, primarily out of discontent. That was the only way I could actually justify my behavior to others, or even to myself. Still, the split emotional personality that I felt, like a "Good versus Evil," haunted me and gave me no peace.

* * *

Finally, three years of probation were over, and it was January 2001, after all the bizarre interactions with people from all walks of life in all those odd jobs. I appeared before the judge with my parents seated in the back of the courtroom. Mom teared up quietly in a dark understated dress while Dad looked formal and stern in a somber navy suit with dark navy necktie and stiff white shirt. The brown wood paneling of the courtroom and the fluorescent lighting from the ceiling, along with the black robe of the judge and the tan and green uniform of the bailiff, would put anybody in a somber mood, but I was *elated* at seeing the light at the end of the tunnel.

My lawyer read off the script: "Your Honor, I would like to enter a motion to expunge the misdemeanor assault charge from my client's record, concurrent with the successful completion of the three-year probationary period."

The judge, an Asian woman, insisted that my lawyer (a white guy) read through all the details, even though clearly he would rather just gloss over the factual niceties.

"Read it through," she stated.

"Uh, Your Honor, I have already—" he demurred.

"Read it through again, I said," she repeated, cross with him now.

I stood there, feeling vulnerable and helpless, feeling naked in public. I knew that whatever the judge and the lawyer were going over was completely out of my hands and over my head. I just hoped the lawyer wouldn't bungle the job, and the judge would tolerate him.

There were a couple of long silences as the bailiff came over to me and my attorney to take whatever paperwork over to the judge. It was all procedural stuff, you could tell, but it had to be done and couldn't be rushed. Finally...

"Motion to expunge the misdemeanor assault charge is hereby accepted," the judge confirmed. She then turned to face and address me. "Mr. Park!"

"Yes, Your Honor." I was speaking up, loud and clear, in charge of my faculties.

"Do you understand that your record will no longer contain mention of the misdemeanor assault charge, and that your probationary period is now over?"

"I do, Your Honor," I responded clearly, making sure she heard me the first time.

"OK. You are on your own recognizance, Mr. Park. Bailiff, please escort Mr. Park outside the courtroom."

And that was it, and I was reunited, albeit temporarily, with my parents, who had just come out from the back of the courtroom where the benches were. Once they joined me outside in the sunny Southern California air, I embraced Mom, who was still upset by the labyrinthine legal process of getting me permanently out of the system. Dad kept up his stone-faced Korean father "façade," but I knew inside he was gratified. I myself was utterly and completely relieved, no longer weighed down, but wanting to jump up and down.

* * *

CHAPTER 5

# Back to School

It was now 2002, and I was twenty-seven and growing tired of Los Angeles. The scene had become so "plastic." The vibrancy, dynamism, and energy that had hit me like a tidal wave from the city was now lost on me. But the problem wasn't L.A.; it was me. I was doing nothing with my life. I needed a vector. As the big 3-0 approached, having done nothing since college rang hollow in my ears. Even my fellow car messenger drivers, who were not exactly high-achievers, had asked me: "Seriously, Jason, what have you done with your life up to this point?"

So I asked Dad for career advice. It was a strange turn of events, given that I had never asked him for career advice earlier. But I knew that my dad, more than anybody else, had my best interests at heart. My request would come at Dr. Vicky's office one day.

During a special family therapy session there, Dad started crying and said, "Jason, you have so much potential, and you're wasting it."

So I asked him, in the presence of Mom and my brother Gerry: "So Dad, what career do you think I should pursue?"

To which Dad replied, "Jason... follow your heart. Do what you want."

By then, after the various altercations I had been involved with, Dad had seen enough to relinquish control over his son.

But I replied, completely unexpectedly: "OK, Dad, I want to be a professor—like you," which astonished Dr. Vicky, who pointed out to Dad the clear and unswerving 180-degree turn in my thinking.

"Did you see that, Dr. Park?" Dr. Vicky exclaimed. "Your son wants to be like you!" and then "How does that make you feel?"

Oh, boy, here we go again.

But Dad cut Dr. Vicky off, apparently relieved that I had put myself back in a conventional career game, and intervened, saying, "OK, then let's start the process of getting you into grad school" as he wiped away his tears.

Of course, little did I know what I was up against. Then again, if I had known, I would never have even tried.

* * *

*I remember... it was October 2003*, and I was practicing the General Management Admissions Test (GMAT) at a standardized test consulting firm. This was my first test of getting back into the academy. The Harvard degree was considered "ahead of the curve" to most admissions representatives, but a high standardized test score paired with the 3.25 GPA from Harvard would make my application so much more competitive. Although the test was no more difficult than tenth-grade math, the test's questions evoked confusion. Still, there was a way to crack the GMAT, and my initial 600 out of 800 was a sign that I had a learnable exam on my hands.

*I remember... it was November 2003*, and I received the test results for my first formal stab at the GMAT, registering the score 720. Mom yelled joyously, while slapping me on the thigh, "See? You are my son! You are my son!" She was overjoyed to have me back, after all those lost years frittering my talent away. The 720 score was automatically sent by the GMAT admissions committee to my set of preferred schools.

*I remember... it was December 2003*, and I was finally buckling down mentally and physically, by sitting still at a desk without fidgeting, and concentrating my cognitions on just one type of question across all the grad school applications, and writing down practice answers onto paper: "So, why Pitt?" "So, why University of Iowa at Bloomfield?" "So, why Stanford?" "So, why Michigan?" "So, why NYU?" And "So, why UCLA?"

*I remember... it was January 2004*, and I was writing the personal statement to the University of Pittsburgh, where the application asked, "So why Pitt?" My answer: "My dad was a Professor at Pitt for almost twenty years, in fact, and he would tell me that the University of Pittsburgh's Katz School of Business took research very seriously..."

*I remember... it was February 2004*. This being the age before electronic applications, I was submitting paper applications through the mail. All six of them, unwieldy and heavy, with the concomitant need to include a sealed recommendation letter, one for each school application, with the seal of Harvard University stamped, and centered across the top and bottom cross-flaps of the back of the envelopes.

*I remember... it was late March 2004*, and I was reading the Offer of Admission into the University of Pittsburgh's Katz Graduate School of Business's Ph.D. program in Organizational

Behavior/Human Resources (OB/HR): "We would like to offer you a fast-track admissions decision, if you answer within the next two weeks."

*I remember... it was early April 2004.* At the time, Dean Wade of University of Iowa at Bloomfield, who had been a colleague of Dad's, told me that he was planning to offer a positive admissions decision to me. But I informed Dean Wade of Pitt's offer to move more quickly on my application, and that I would have to take it since, as the Dean explained to me, Iowa couldn't move faster than two weeks on its own initiative. It was a classic case of a bird in hand versus two in the bush. Dean Wade expressed upset at Pitt's "ungentlemanly" and "dishonorable" tactic. But no other college or university would take me so soon.

*I remember... it was May 2004.* I had committed to Pitt's offer, yet was feeling ambivalent about getting into the University of Pittsburgh. Here I was, a graduate of Harvard, and I had not received any official offers from any school other than only one—Pittsburgh. So yes, I was pleased that I had gotten into at least one school—all you need is one—but I felt less than, as if I only had gotten into a backup school, a far cry from when, as a high school senior, I treated Harvard as my backup.

*I remember... it was June 2004,* and I was hanging out with my buddies and discussing the acceptance letter with them. All of them concluded that the Ph.D. program, even one not necessarily at a higher ranked research institution than Pitt, was a tremendous opportunity that should not be wasted. And so, feeling vindicated, I began to focus on the future, and forget about the past.

* * *

The day came in August 2004 when I had to leave Los Angeles for Pittsburgh. The chosen vehicle was my parents' black Honda Accord, aging but serviceable. With Mom and Dad's help, I loaded the trunk, back and passenger seats with clothes, laundry baskets filled with more clothes, suitcases filled with even more clothes, desk lamps, research articles and printer paper, Dad's laptop, some foodstuffs, and some blankets for the sure-to-come Pittsburgh winters.

In the kitchen, before my final send-off, Mom presented me with plenty of American Express traveler's checks.

"Try to keep your expenses under this amount, Jason, OK?" Shortly thereafter, we said our good-byes quickly, and without much fanfare. I went towards Dad for a hug, as he stood stone-faced and expressionless. "See you, Dad. I'll call along the way, at nighttime, when I pull over for the evenings."

"OK, Jason. Take care."

Mom wept, her arms at her sides, for joy or out of sadness, perhaps both. "Bye, Mom."

"OK, Jason. See you."

For me, it was a bittersweet occasion. I was elated, because I was ending my sojourn of aimless wandering, and engaging in a significance-laden journey. But I felt depressed too, because it was a long-distance, no-reversal parting, and an end to being in close physical proximity to the people in my life.

With a plan to drive daytime and stop over by night, I road-tripped outside California on the I-10 into Arizona. Just outside the L.A. city limits, I slowly chugged along in the enveloping darkness and then continued on until I got to Phoenix. There I pulled over into a Motel 6 lot for the night.

The motels were "bare-bones," for the most part. No princely accommodations like those found in Los Angeles. But they provided the necessary creature comforts: a bed, air-conditioning, lights, a TV with basic cable, a bathroom with shower, sink and toilet, a mini-kitchen replete with stove, fan, fridge, sink and faucet, and some basic furniture. Oh, and a place to put my backpack with my most important belongings: wallet, keys, cell phone, traveler's checks, digital camera, and finally a slim laptop.

Toward the end of my trip, I drove on Route 376 through the Fort Pitt tunnel, headed for the city, and emerged into a view of downtown Pittsburgh. In the late August of 2004, the sunshine bathed the city in a healthy summer glow, while the air above blued the downtown skyline. The Fort Pitt Bridge was painted a bright happy yellow, as in a smiley-face sticker, and the pointy Pittsburgh Plate Glass Towers gleamed shiny grey in the bright summer sun. The University of Pittsburgh Medical Center building towered along with the rest of the skyline, a concrete and glass rainbow of varying shades of geometrically gridded green, brown, blue, ivory, and amber. The naturally sculpted and curvy shaped oaks and maples rustled in the torrid summer wind and framed, with green leaves and ash trunks, the concrete and metal skyscrapers.

I could see the flat and sparkling, dark blue and muddy brown Monongahela, Ohio, and Allegheny Rivers meet down at the Point, where a gigantic water fountain spritzed and spouted at their confluence. Speedboats whooshed by, trailing white wakes in the water, while the Gateway Clipper, Pittsburgh's signature riverboat, lay moored next to land.

As I slowed down to coast slowly with the road traffic, I looked left over to the North Shore to catch a glimpse of PNC Park and Heinz Field, home of the Major League Baseball Pirates and National Football League Steelers, respectively. I made careful note of the bright green road signs posted on the Fort Pitt Bridge overhang, from left to right: "279 North/North

Shore (EXIT ONLY)." Then "Ft. Duquesne Blvd/Convention Ctr/Strip District (EXIT ONLY)." Then "Blvd of Allies/Liberty Ave." Then "376E/Monroeville." This last one, the one most to the right, was my exit!

I methodically signaled my lane shift and turned into the rightmost line, Interstate 376 East towards Monroeville, and took the parkway along the north side of the "Mon." I cruised a mile or so past the downtown skyline on the left, and noting the aged and rusted highway sign up ahead, elevated to Forbes Avenue over the Boulevard of the Allies.

As I made the winding counterclockwise turn to head to the University of Pittsburgh campus, to my wondrous astonishment, I saw the Cathedral of Learning, the quintessential symbol of Pitt, all 535 feet and 42 stories of it, towering in the near-distance, like a sacred, holy monument. I cruised up Forbes Avenue past Bigelow Boulevard, with "Cathy" on my left. The hairs on my back stood on end upon this return to my home away from home; it had been over seven very long and momentous years since I had last seen the neighborhood.

Bubbling over with joy, I felt as if I could coast, like the traffic, through the rest of my sunny summer life, now that I was there in Steel City. Yet little did I know that I would be faced with educational challenges and personal struggles, the likes of which I had never experienced before.

* * *

It was late August, days before the first semester of the Ph.D. program at the University of Pittsburgh, Katz Graduate School of Business, Department of Organizational Behavior and Human Resources. I took a break to contact Will, my old buddy from the working-class neighborhood of Troy Hill, someone I had kept up with since my college years. He was now living a few blocks downhill from his dad's, and somehow Will had achieved "work-life balance" to a certainly interesting degree. Even after a grueling ten hours of commercial painting, he would invite the whole neighborhood into his backyard, where to the back wall of his Victorian row house he would hammer down a white cloth tarp as a projection screen and shoot up rays of Steelers football games from a video projector. Along with plenty of Italian sausage and bread, chips and soda and bottled beer, every Monday night football game in Troy Hill was memorable.

I hung out on breaks at Will's home from the week or so of that sultry summer before school started, and on through the winter of 2004. I did it to escape the tense pressure-cooker atmosphere of Mervis Hall, which housed Pittsburgh's Katz Graduate School of Business. Mervis Hall was a modern-styled building with a tinted glass exterior façade, so it was mirrored and opaque from the outside, although from the inside offices you could see clearly outside to Posvar Hall across the other side of Roberto Clemente Drive. The modern architectural style of Mervis Hall fondly reminded me of the times that my dad was a professor in the same building, yet I found its inhabitants conservative, pretentious, and boring. Little did it occur to me at the time that some of them were actually very progressive, high-minded, and interesting. I just wrote everybody off indiscriminately, that's all.

Nevertheless, initially I abhorred the professors who would "tear me a new one" whenever I didn't rigorously analyze an article. I detested seminars, which numbered a few classmates, leaving me with nowhere to hide, unlike undergraduate classes featuring hundreds of students. I avoided my classmates, who were from other parts of the world. And I hated the anxiety of getting good grades. All of these aversions produced tremendous discomfort: I felt like doing drugs, drinking a fifth of Scotch, leaving the room, cursing the professor, jumping up and down like a chimpanzee. While at the university, I felt like doing all these things, and all of them simultaneously.

But back to Troy Hill for a second. Not just Will, but his family, too, was chock-full of personalities. One time, "for shits and giggles," Will and I, thoroughly blitzed on beer, paid his dad a visit. The man lived up the hill in another set of rowhouses, a mere stone's throw away from Will's.

"Mr. Fitzsimmons," I bellowed, raising a silly drunken question, "who's more powerful, the Pope or the President?"

After some thought, Mr. Fitzsimmons yelled out the only possible answer: "The Pope! He tells the Italians, 'Move it, all you DAGOS, out of my way, or I'll run you over with my Pope mobile!'"

Will's kids—Tina, Grace, and Tom, with a fourth on the way—brought good cheer, making the chaos in the household all worthwhile. I remember a comment Will's wife Olivia once made about having kids: "One is a piece of cake, two is a walk in the park, but three is completely unmanageable!" But Olivia was an excellent manager: she tripled as loyal wife (doting on Will), loving mom (sharing child-rearing duties), and teammate breadwinner (school teaching in the Bethel Park District of Pittsburgh).

* * *

I established relationships with a therapist and a psychiatrist within a month after the start of the academic semester. To do that, I consulted a VIP at Mervis Hall, indeed the most important person in the doctoral program.

Abigail was the Assistant Doctoral Program Director, only second in the chain of command to the Director. I still remember that sunny fall afternoon, when I threw myself at her feet: "Abigail, I need to see a psychiatrist and a psychologist NOW!"

Her smile froze, her eyes glazed over, her long-nailed fingers paused in their constant drumming and typing... she didn't know what to make of my pleading. But right away, she directed me to University of Pittsburgh's Western Psychiatric Institute and Clinic. And I badly needed the help, because I was engaging in a familiar pattern from my Harvard days: work hard at Mervis (school), party hard in Troy Hill (personal time).

I was assigned to Paul, a Licensed Clinical Social Worker (LCSW). He was a thin gentleman with a receding hairline and prominent horn-rimmed glasses. He liked to stomp around in running shoes. In the beginning, to me, Paul didn't seem like a good guy or a bad guy, just neutral. In fact, I couldn't get a read on him the first dozen times I met with him. Indeed, I managed not to have a single coherent conversation with Paul for a while. He and I just kept going round and round in circles.

"Can I trust you?" I'd ask, to which Paul replied, over and over again, for the whole first semester, "Yes, you can trust me," untiringly.

"But then you might take advantage of me, Paul, right?"

"No, Jason, I am bound by confidentiality laws not to disclose any part of our conversations to third parties."

"So then, can I trust you?" Over and over again, *ad infinitum*.

As you can tell, I was skeptical of Paul's ability to counsel me wisely. But then again, the inability to trust is a symptom in and of itself of poor mental health.

In addition to Paul, I was assigned to Dr. Baereyan, Associate Clinical Professor of Psychiatry. He was responsible for my medication, and I had been told that his patients didn't leave him. He was an Egyptian gentleman who had continued his education and training in the U.S. But the relationship between Dr. Baereyan and me didn't go anywhere either. It stagnated in the same sense that my clinical relationship with Paul didn't go anywhere, either: just round and round in circles and for one very long semester.

At first Dr. Baereyan was generous, offering free drug samples of the medications I was taking, and donating a gigantic month-long pill tray, separated by days and weeks, to help me organize my medications. But unfortunately I senselessly annoyed and alienated him. I called him derisively "the Egyptian Magician" after a practical joke I had heard featuring somebody with that title. Dr. Baereyan would reply somberly, "No, Jason, there's no magic here." It wasn't by any stretch of the imagination a funny joke. It was demeaning and degrading to offer a tasteless pun of that ethnic profile, to somebody of that ethnic profile, when you yourself are not a member of that ethnic profile, especially to somebody who prescribes you psychotropic medication. In fact I should have befriended him. It was only funny to me because of my own crooked sense of humor, a sign that I was not in my right mind. Dr. Baereyan gave up on me early, and stopped helping. So I saw him for fifteen minutes, once every eight weeks—given my lack of enthusiasm in taking charge of my own mental health.

* * *

CHAPTER 6

# Getting Off on the Wrong Foot

I was initially all gung-ho about doing well in class, but in hindsight I see that I wasn't ready for Ph.D. work. It wasn't about cramming only some of the weekly readings right before class. No, you had to do *all* the readings, *all well in advance*. I wasn't yet a serious graduate school student, despite my college *cum laude* degree. And I kept deluding myself that Ph.D. work was like an undergraduate program.

There were two seminars that first semester: Pitt Professor Deborah's "Foundations of Organizational Behavior," which was co-taught with Professor Harry from Carnegie-Mellon University, and then next, Pitt Professor Xavier's "Behavioral Systems and Management Thought." But in both classes there was cause for concern about the very remedial nature of the questions I asked and the issues I raised. In addition, I was drawing Professor Harry's ire with my slightly inappropriate verbal poking and prodding.

One time, I remarked how the French were notoriously xenophobic, to which he replied, "Well, *I* was received *very* well on numerous occasions by the French when I visited their country..." And when the topic of discussion was organizational culture, I quipped, "Well, one thing we do know is that animals do not have a culture," to which Professor Harry replied haughtily, "Well, *yes*, young man, that is true, animals do not have a culture, and that is a very interesting point, but it doesn't get us anywhere on our main topic..." I also mentioned, in a politically incorrect tone in the presence of an Indian classmate, that there is no typical McDonald's in India because there the cow is sacred. Professor Harry noticed her discomfort and tried to smooth things over with some diplomatic language, which he did in disapproval of me.

I made a point of talking with Professor Deborah after class about halfway through the semester. To Deborah I admitted, "Professor, I am dealing with a psychiatric illness..."

Her brow began to furrow.

"...it's called bipolar disorder, have you ever heard of it?"

"I have, and now I know what I can do to help you."

She planned to prevent Professor Harry of CMU from grading my term paper, and to grade the paper herself.

It was a real gift she was giving me. She was very nurturing and very benevolent, too.

However, Pitt Professor Xavier had the "stick" approach to teaching. I didn't ask to see him; he called me into his office around the same time I had talked to Professor Deborah, after Xavier had witnessed a couple months of my stutter-stepping in his seminar. In class, I had mused excessively about the love life of sociologist Chester Bernard, made small talk of the French engineer-executive Henri Fayol, exhibited an incapacity to appreciate Frederick Winslow Taylor's "Principles of Scientific

Management," and had laughed out loud at Elton Mayo's famous and important Hawthorne Studies, dismissing them as simpleton work.

Xavier stated: "Jason, let me be very frank with you. You are not performing in class at a level that is adequate to a passing grade, and now over half of the semester is already over." So whereas Deborah provided me with more support if necessary, Xavier gave me a choice: shape up or ship out.

Afterwards, I explained to Xavier in an email in vague terms that I had a mood disorder. The self-disclosure was a dangerous situation I put myself into, of being "outed," just as I had taken a risk telling Professor Deborah of my condition. But my state of mind then was to self-disclose to my professional relations, because I was really rather trusting, perhaps characteristic of someone with low self-esteem and negative self-image. And recall that with the therapist Paul and psychiatrist Baereyan, I wasn't disclosing anything at all. But it was with them that I should have been unloading!

In any case, I couldn't find a compelling reason to shape up *or* ship out. I felt stuck between: (1) excelling in school and (2) dropping out completely. Why was I stuck? It was the aversion to pain. Both options required painfully overcoming resistance, and I didn't have that facility yet. A stern warning was appropriate, and essentially compelled me to push forward for the duration of the first semester.

I received Bs for the two seminars: just barely passing for graduate school. In other words, I had "scraped by," not a very sporting approach to serious academia. To Professor Deborah's point, I needed academic help, and she provided it. But would fixing my grades this way solve the problem? I couldn't rely on her to keep my grades afloat; I wouldn't be taking courses with her all the time. Besides, the help I really needed—(1) talk therapy and (2) medication compliance—did not register with me back then, because they depended on my own efforts. And those efforts were not forthcoming.

* * *

In January 2005, I tried to right the listing ship after having returned from a winter-break family visit to Los Angeles. First of all, I had to deal with an East Coast winter for the first time in seven years, and I didn't like being stuffed in sweaters and a parka up top and heavy jeans and thick boots down below. I hadn't seen snow in all those years either, but the novelty wore off quickly. It was still all-important for me to have mobility, but driving was now hazardous. Getting to Troy Hill to my buddy Will's place was no longer a short jaunt for my sedan, which now had to chug up the hills of Pittsburgh without snow chains or snow tires. And it was a prime time to get sick—the worst of wintertime. I once caught something that was either a dull throbbing flu or a nasty vicious cold, with aches, pains, chills, fever, and vomiting, and it packed a vicious punch, making me lie down for over a week. Its only saving grace was as a half-reason to skip class, along with the other half-reason to drink.

My spring semester included one more seminar in OB/HR, "Topics of Organizational Behavior," taught by Professor Fabiola, a skinny elderly lady with a short brunette coif. She would always start off the seminar with some homemade bromide such as "Remember, it always starts with the dependent variable," which she must have picked up from somewhere. A lot of the Ph.D. students seemed to kiss up to her, as if she were the Dean herself: "So, Professor Fabiola, how do you feel about the state of research and where it's going in the field of organizational behavior?"

"Well, it will definitely head away from focus on the dependent variable..." and there she would go. Go where? Do what with the dependent variable? I had no clue what she was talking about, despite her pointed mannerisms. I just wasn't convinced of anything she said.

Well, I felt lost, intellectually and emotionally. I couldn't follow the lines of the argument that Fabiola and my classmates were carrying on with, although I knew enough that it was total balderdash. But I myself would just sit there in my seat, like a jackass, pretending to take notes, nodding my head, parroting the other Ph.D. students. The sense of being intellectually lost made me feel that I wasn't smart enough to handle the mental load.

"You with me, Jason?" Fabiola would say, calling me out, and I would nod my head and reply, beginning with: "Yes, the dependent variable plays a huge part of importance in OB/HR research..." In answering, I would mimic her pompous self-importance.

And emotionally, being lost led to depression in class, which I masked with a bright, anxiety-ridden, and Marilyn Monroe-type grin. Even Professor Fabiola noticed it.

"Yo, Jason, you've got that smile on your face again!" she would say and grin, as if it were something comical. But not to me.

Thus, I was living a lie. What I had on my plate was overwhelming, for even the stoutest of souls. Somehow I got an A in Professor Fabiola's course. I checked with my classmates; she was an easy grader. But things in truth were getting worse.

* * *

Spring arrived, haltingly and with the occasional snowstorm in April 2005, but definitively. That was Pittsburgh weather; if you didn't like it, just wait!

Towards the end of spring, I remember spying through the window of a conference room on the third floor of Mervis Hall, the OB/HR faculty members sitting around the table: Fabiola, Deborah, and Xavier. They were going at it in conversation; one of my cohorts spied in, too, and quipped good-naturedly, "They're talking about us!" although I felt paranoia. I could only suspect that they were discussing my poor performance in class.

And then my biggest fear came true. I knew I was underachieving, and that there was going to be hell to pay for the one-two punch of wasting time off-campus and underperforming on-campus. Professor Xavier, who was the Chair of the Department of Organizational Behavior and Human Resources, called me into his office one April day, just as he had done when he reprimanded me for the poor performance I had exhibited the preceding fall.

The sun was setting outside his office, which was walled with windows that faced westward, overlooking the cobblestone road, Joncaire Street. Xavier's desk was strewn with papers and a laptop, while the other wall had apparently been constructed by a book worm: there were a couple dozen bookshelves, from all the way up to all the way down, from all the way to the right to all the way to the left, with all sorts of books and journals lined up in rows. I recognized a few journals here and there, from their colors: *Strategic Management Journal* was a notable pink. A big potted palm stood, out of the way of foot traffic. I remembered reading from Xavier's website that he was into gardening.

"Jason, have a seat."

I willingly complied, and added, "Yes, sir," being my most decorous.

Xavier started by clearing his throat... "Ahem. Mr. Park, the Committee of Organizational Behavior and Human Resources here at Katz has come to an agreement regarding your performance in this first qualifying year of coursework. Rest assured that the decision has been made with the consultation of all faculty members of the department.

"As far as your performance goes thus far, in the first or fall semester, you received a B in Professor Deborah's seminar 'Foundations of Organizational Behavior,' a B in my concurrently held seminar 'Behavioral Systems and Management Thought,' and an A this semester in Professor Fabiola's spring 2005 seminar 'Topics of Organizational Behavior.'

"As Chair of the Department of Organizational Behavior and Human Resources, I must state unequivocally that your performance to date is not up to par with departmental standards. Your record of lackluster achievement—the two Bs and an A—is evidence of that fact. And mind you, Jason—I could have easily given you a C or a D rather than a B.

"To conclude, the committee does not recommend that you continue to stay in the program from this point forward. Our honest and frank advice is for you to pursue other career alternatives at this time. That is the recommendation of the committee. Thank you for your time, Jason; you're excused now."

With that, a whirlwind of emotions rose up inside myself—moral outrage, shell shock, grim despondence—as I shook Xavier's hand *pro forma* and headed out to the hall, head spinning and face contorted in a weak, shaky smile. I felt rage for having tried the best despite my condition, only to find out that it wasn't enough. The shell shock came from what I knew was inevitable, being held accountable for my actions. And the grim despondence was from being handed defeat at the hands of a mighty opponent. A triple-whammy!

* * *

As the dour feelings began to wear off, I started to rebound. But how and with whom? Since I was already in the building, I stopped by Professor Deborah's office on the third floor. She always seemed to be the most receptive to my entreaties.

I remember her office well: two desks, one rectangular and on top of which was perched a white desktop computer with stacks of research articles everywhere, and on the wall on the tack-board, pictures of her son and husband. The opposite wall stood behind a circular desk for mini-conferences or one-on-one meetings, and there was every sort of journal, textbook, book, and monograph you could imagine on the shelves.

"Professor Deborah?" I sneak-peeked timidly into her office, her back to me, her head positioned straight toward the monitor. I could sense the energy in the room, a level of energy which I didn't seem to possess. I was afraid of bothering her.

"Oh, yes, Jason, come in, have a seat," she said, friendly enough, but somewhat brusquely. She recognized my voice, but did not immediately turn to register my presence.

"Professor Deborah, Professor Xavier said that I should seek other career alternatives..." I trailed, despondent.

"Yes, I know, Jason. That was the decision of the committee as a whole, although my personal opinion was different." Deborah led off with this, as she finally swiveled in her seat, her attention squarely on me.

"How so, Professor?"

"Well, to me, it's obvious you can do the work. The question is: is this what you want to do for the rest of your life?"

"Well, of course it is..." I responded with wavering uncertainty in my voice.

"No, Jason. You really have to ask yourself," Deborah continued, "because, right now, you're not heading in the right trajectory, OK? You're going in the wrong direction."

"I think I can do it, you know."

"Yes again, I'm sure you can, Jason. You may be able to do it, but we're all limited in some way or another. Neither one of us will ever be world-class athletes, right? If I have a psychiatric disorder, it's not a good idea for me to do academic work, because I'm limited. Look, Jason, you have been very personal with me, and now I will be with you in turn. My son..." she waved to a picture pinned up to her wall, "...has Attention Deficit Disorder. That means that certain activities are off-limits to him. Like someone who has a wooden leg and wants to play professional soccer."

"Well, I see your point..."

"Besides, that was a little 'gift' I gave you, that B in my seminar. If I hadn't intervened, you would have gotten a much lower grade from Professor Harry of Carnegie Mellon. You can't count on those for the rest of the program from other professors.

"And remember, you're supposed to provide your own motivation while I and my colleagues place what you need to do in front of you, so that you can take over at a high level of autonomy. At this Ph.D. level, everyone is smart and everyone works hard. The question is, how badly do you want it? Are you willing to go the extra mile? You have to ask yourself that."

"OK, Deborah, thank you. Thank you very much for talking to me. It was reassuring."

"OK, you're welcome, Jason," she ended with a dry chuckle and wry smile.

Stunned, I headed out, suffering another blow to my self-esteem. Damn, I said to myself, cursing my luck. No one is in my corner now. Even Deborah was pulling up the drawbridge, withdrawing support and no longer offering safe haven. You can imagine the discomfort at this point.

The only other person I could think of turning to was Dad. After exiting Deborah's office and finding a quiet patch in Mervis Hall's basement loading docks, I called Dad on the cell, to inform him of the goings-on of the day.

"Dad, Professor Xavier and the rest of the faculty in OB/HR suggested that I leave the program. Xavier said I should pursue other career alternatives and that my performance fell short of passing standards."

"They WHAT?!" Dad exclaimed, trying to make sense of it all.

"Yeah, they're trying to kick me out," I babbled resignedly.

"Look, Jason, this is no time for giving up. I still don't see why they would say that to you, a Harvard grad. Tell them you can do it and that you will put in a heroic effort, because you have that in you! Indeed, I think the best thing you should do is write to and meet with the faculty members, Xavier, Deborah, and Fabiola. Tell them that you really want to be there and you will work very hard for them. Tell them to give you another chance."

"OK, Dad, sure," I said, knowing that the end was near. What could I do? Just listen and take instruction. I clicked "END" on my phone and walked to my desk in Room 247, to type away some much-needed emails and arrange for some appointments.

* * *

I made a call to Will, shortly after the last nail in the coffin of the Ph.D. program was seemingly secured. I didn't want to go to Troy Hill anymore. Now I had my back to the wall and all the partying done there, which had distracted me from school and had affected my performance as a student, was clear to see in high relief. From Day 1, Will had always listened closely to my litany of problems, but admittedly after a while it must have been like listening to a broken record for him. I kept complaining to him about the same old things—professors and classes and students and grades—and all without a resolution. Will humored me in the end. After all, I could probably have opted out of the Ph.D. program and done something else... who knows, I was still under thirty. There were possibilities, right?

But Will was dealing with some real-world problems to which, and truth be told, mine paled in comparison: (1) being a loving dad to four young children, (2) paying the mortgage and the bills, (3) providing for his wife to make ends meet, (4) dealing with difficult neighbors, (5) distributing babysitting duties among various relatives, and (6) holding down a job with barely a high school education. I really should not have belabored Will with my problems.

By this time, Will had had enough, and he was prepared with some readymade stock responses to answer my questions. After that, it was as if he were going through a laundry list of items:

"Hey, Jason, just relax and forget about school."

"Hey, Jason, you need a girlfriend, all right?"

"Hey, Jason, just have a beer, OK?"

Will was trying to help me in the way he knew. But the life that was for him, and that suited him, wasn't for me. I needed to get serious. To be more specific: (1) I didn't need to be drunk,

(2) I needed to get all A's, (3) I needed emotional independence, not sexual relief.

The whole shebang culminated in an argumentative back and forth:

"Dammit, Will, why don't you call me sometime? Why do I always have to call you?"

"Oh, yeah, right, Jason, it's always you, isn't it? It always has to be about you."

"What is it man, are you avoiding me or something?"

"Jason, I'm NOT avoiding you, man, just take it easy."

"Dude, Will, it's like you always talk down to me, you know that?"

"Oh yeah? Well, then, what am I supposed to do, talk up to you?"

"Well, don't you want to change for the better? To better yourself?"

"Jason, I'm not here to change for you! I'm not going to change for you! Look, the only reason why I'm talking to you right now is because I care about you. So that's all I'm going to say, if you want to play ball, go ahead, if not, fine."

"All right, Will, I guess you spoke your peace. I'm going to take off." I hung up.

And here's exactly what happened next: my performance in school began to take off.

* * *

CHAPTER 7

# The Comeback Kid

In the end, the committee of the OB/HR department went on its "crippled" way, and relented to me. I had followed my father's advice to write a letter to Paul, Fabiola, and Deborah, and at my insistence, they decided I could stay on for another semester. Of course, it was true that they had lost confidence in me, and they really didn't see the point of having me on board for any longer. But I was ready for the ultimate comeback. Maybe I didn't know how, but I would do it. For me, where there's a will there's a way.

Responding to the "seek other alternatives" message from Professor Xavier, as the summer semester approached, I began sustained effort on my recovery, using therapy and medication. I told my licensed clinical social worker Paul, "OK, I'm ready to work with you, and all the other nonsense we've been talking about, about trusting, and confidentiality issues, and being taken advantage of, is all basically poppycock. So let's get to work."

"OK, then," Paul agreed.

That was when I became aware that Paul was remarkably well-read outside of the strict confines of psychology. Paul was raised Catholic, but had sworn off Catholicism in his adult life. He focused his training on death and dying, so the two of us relayed our sometimes differing, and sometimes coinciding opinions and convictions about God and the afterlife. Paul talked about all these things, as well as current events, the politics for him of working at the University of Pittsburgh's Medical Center, and the nature of my bipolar disorder.

Most important, Paul helped me manage the Ph.D. program, which we talked about the most. The effectiveness of my treatment would rest on the zest with which I now approached the degree program. And that's where Paul's help came in. There were many times, when I would come back from a seminar, and throw myself at Paul's feet, telling him: "Paul, I don't think I can handle this! I can't take it anymore. I can't do this! I just can't!"

But with a few choicely placed words and a "laying on of hands," Paul would get me to turn myself around. It wasn't so much the advice that he would give, but rather the *insight* into my problems that Paul provided for me that let me make choices about what next steps to take. I was very lucky to have him in my corner. Indeed, it went to show that it wasn't so much the letters after your name—e.g., LCSW, MSW, MFT, PsyD, PhD—as it was the skillfulness of your practice. I immediately responded well to Paul once *I* took *him* seriously.

The issues weren't financial. The university provided "tuition remission," which was essentially free school, for the first four years. For salary, I carried out research duties part-time at twenty hours per week which gave me a stipend and health insurance. The $1,200 monthly stipend wasn't enough for me to live on, so I took out educational loans of $18,000 per school year through the local bank. The health insurance let me meet with Paul and Dr. Baereyan for a co-pay of $5 a visit: almost nothing.

* * *

By the time I was given notice that I was about to get the boot from the OB/HR department, I ran to my psychiatrist Dr. Baereyan and implored him to do something.

"What do you want me to do?" was his tired reply. He had kept me on the medication that I'd already been prescribed by Dr. Iovina. Dr. Baereyan hadn't put in any effort to take control of the situation for me, nor had he stepped in to offer me something different. But I hadn't given him a pretext to, and instead had insulted him numerous times.

"Doctor, I want you to do much more for me as far as prescribing me medications that you feel would be better for my mental health than the ones I'm currently on."

"So you're in trouble, aren't you, Jason?" he stridently replied. I had told him earlier on in the meeting that I might be leaving the program.

"Well, if you and I work together earnestly, that possibility might be averted," I told him.

"Jason, look, if I have a mental illness, it's probably not a good idea to go into academia, just as if I were four feet tall and wanted to play basketball, or I couldn't bench press 100 pounds and wanted to play football." This was starting to sound eerily like the conversation I had had with Professor Deborah.

"Look, I know I can do it, Doctor," I said over and over again, maintaining this line of argument against every counter Dr. Baereyan could throw at me. This was reaching a crisis stage. I must have sounded like a broken record, sort of like how

I had been with Will, with the same repetitiveness except the opposite message: an "I can do it" with Dr. Baereyan rather than a "I can't do it" with Will.

In the end, after a meeting that lasted over an hour, with the next patient having waited 45 minutes for her own appointment, Dr. Baereyan relented. I had persisted for so long that the outcome was a good one. The good doctor gave me the scripts for four medications for me to fill at the local pharmacy: (1) Prozac 40 mg daily, (2) Cytomel 5 mcg daily, (3) Depakote 750 mg daily, and (4) Risperdal 4 mg daily.

Prozac was an anti-depressant to be taken in the morning, Cytomel was a synthetic hormone for energy to be taken in the morning, Depakote was a mood stabilizer to be taken at night, and Risperdal was an anti-psychotic to be taken at night.

* * *

As the summer semester approached in May 2005, it was clear that I would have to make my stand. To me, nothing less than all-A's would suffice to prove to the OB/HR committee that I could hang in there. The licking of my wounds metamorphosed into counterattacking at my assailants. *How dare you attack me? How dare you trample all over me? How dare you not show me respect?* I would wrest respect from those who had dared to disrespect me, and battle against those who had attacked me without fear of retaliation. *Vengeance is mine, I will repay...*

The course most relevant that summer semester was Professor Sean's "Strategic Planning Systems." Professor Sean was in the Strategy group, not OB/HR. But no matter, I would still need to prove myself to him because the other two summer courses I would take were in statistics, which was auxiliary to the management focus. I went through the readings in earnest.

And all earnestness was necessary, because I was under the gun with rigid and unforgiving scrutiny.

The readings were God-awful. The writing style in which many of these research articles were churned out was cramped. Oftentimes even the most interesting concepts in strategic management were made dry, boring, and uninteresting by the poorest and dullest of styles of written expression. Some articles seemed "sexy," but the author wrote in tedious prose. So it was hard to determine what material was important and what was superfluous, a distinction important to note because I could not distribute all my time and energy evenly on every single part of every article. I needed to boil down a lot of complex information into a few simple propositions. Initially this was difficult.

Another constant problem that had emerged even in the first year was that these research authors already assumed a certain remedial level of knowledge of strategic management principles on the part of the reader. The result of all this was that I would begin burrowing into the work steadfastly and purposefully, only to find that by the fifth page of a thirty-page article, I was *completely* lost. I had no idea what the authors were talking about. This was infuriating and demoralizing. Google made some information about the topic available to me, but still it was hard to pin down exactly the answer I was looking for. Ultimately, I had to read the article from the start all over again as I extrapolated what would have been the prior knowledge needed to understand the work as a whole.

Another problem was that after a while, I got stuck, uncomprehending, on certain parts of the articles. They were written in a specific sequence: (1) Introduction, (2) Theory, (3) Hypotheses, (4) Methodology, (5) Results, and (6) Conclusion. I would say to myself, "OK, let's begin... introduction, easy enough, right? Then the theory... OK, so far so good, then the development of the hypotheses... continue onward... statistical methodology—*what the...?!*"

It was always the methodology section that would bring me to my knees. I just didn't have the same facility with numbers as with words. Statistics always made me yell "Uncle!" Sure, I could follow basic issues, such as p-values, statistical significance, numerical proxies, etc. But I had real difficulty seeing the forest for the trees. I got so lost in the intricacies of the statistical details that I couldn't quite see the "big picture." And the authors expected the reader to follow their argument from beginning to end. So I would just helplessly scan through the numbers, completely lost, until I regained my footing in the Results section. So I was on very shaky ground by the time I got to the Discussion section. And the Conclusion was usually tacked on as an afterthought, although the really good article-writers didn't B.S. that job either.

And never mind the sheer number of articles we were required to read between meetings. While one professor would give me no more than five article readings a week, another professor required me to read ten. That was enormously upsetting. I used to schedule my readings for three articles a day for six days: from 10 AM-1 PM, then lunch, then 2-5 PM, then dinner, and then 7-10 PM. Rarely did I ever achieve this; it was just an approximation, to be sure. But I made it a guiding principle not to show up unprepared for class ever again.

* * *

But hard work pays off! It was fitting that the summer semester of 2005 was a watershed in my development as a Ph.D. student. My grade report was two A+'s and an A, and one of those A+'s were awarded by Professor Sean. Much, much better! I was ecstatic, and so was Dad—"I'm so proud of you, Jason!"—when we met in Manhattan Beach, California, hugging each other ecstatically.

Before I left Pittsburgh for the remainder of the summer, I had come up with a "strategy" all of my own to combat "seeking alternative career paths," as Dr. Xavier had suggested. I approached Professor Sean shortly after he concluded our seminar. It was late July 2005. He was always dressed in a somber dark suit, stiff-collared white shirt and silk tie, gold rings on his fingers, greying hair, and round glasses that suited his angular face. He always commanded authority with his sartorial splendor and gracefully aging good looks.

"Professor Sean," I asked politely, "could I have a minute?"

He was standing in his office, reaching up for a book on one of his voluminous bookshelves when he turned around to me, a warm smile on his face.

"Yes, Jason, how can I help you?"

Sean had known my dad well. In fact, his office used to be my dad's corner office on the third floor of Mervis. Sean turned back to the bookshelf and found his book. After settling down in his desk chair, he focused his full attention on me, one hand on the book, as I stood in the doorway.

"Yes, well, how would you feel if I wanted to leave the Organizational Behavior and Human Resources Department, which I am currently a member of, and transition into the Strategy Department?" I upturned the question with a bit of helpless pleading. A lot was riding on this conversation turning out the right way.

"Yes!" came the immediate reply.

Yes what? I looked at him quizzically, with a "deer in the headlights" gaze. My mouth hung open.

He continued. “Yes, I think you would make an excellent contribution to the Strategy Department, and you have my support and vote.”

With my head bowing slightly, I asked, “You really mean that? I mean, you’re not just saying that, are you?”

To which Professor Sean replied, “I knew your dad well, Jason. His son must be brilliant, too!” Sean smiled.

“Thank you, Professor” I had added the “Professor” salutation as an expression of respect, admiration, and appreciation.

“Look, you went to Harvard, Jason, so to me that’s the ‘Good Housekeeping Seal of Approval,’” Sean stated. He himself had gone to Harvard Business School. “I think you’ll do wonderfully and make a great contribution to the department. So go see Professor Kabelo and talk to the other members of the department, including Ian and Hannah. You will want to get to know them better.”

I held my breath while I offered my ending salutation, “Yes, sir, I will, and thanks again!”

I took Shawn’s hand in a sweaty embrace, slick with sweat from anxiety. Shawn quickly removed his hand.

I walked out of his office, breathing a deep sigh of relief. Thank God that worked out!

Well, assuming the other strategy faculty had no complaints, I could follow the advice that Xavier had recommended: PURSUE OTHER CAREER PATHS? Sure, Xavier! Whatever you say!

* * *

In the second year of the Ph.D. program, which was my first year as a Strategy Ph.D. student, I continued to rack up knowledge on strategy research and OB/HR (OB/HR was now my minor and strategy was my major). Statistics courses began to pile on their burdensome workloads, and yet I managed to get by somehow.

The three other individuals that comprised the core of the Strategy faculty included—besides Sean—Hannah, Ian, and Kabelo. Hannah had short brown hair and was in her late 30s. She had accomplished quite a bit in her short lifetime: written at least six A-level journal articles, garnered tenure, and had her first child, all at about the same time!

Kabelo was Chair of the Strategy Department. He had a dark-haired moustache and glasses and looked quite distinguished in an aristocratic, New England sort of way. He preferred sweaters in the winter over suits and ties, and inclined towards shorts in the summer rather than linen pants and rayon/polyester slacks. He taught me concepts about strategy that I only thought of in an inchoate manner previously, such as the three strategic paradigms—(1) psychology, (2) economics, and (3) sociology—and the three different units of analysis—(1) manager, (2) firm, and (3) industry, respectively. That totally blew me away. Up to that point, I was clueless as to what was going on theoretically in strategy, but after that, I got it.

The last person was Ian. You could identify him as the person with a dour smile on his face, as if he had eaten something that tasted bad. Ian had a slight build, and he appeared to those who didn't know him as retiring, but anybody who got to know him beyond surface appearances knew that he had a razor-sharp edge. He wasn't a pushover by any stretch of the imagination.

The second year of course-taking included one with Hannah in Fall 2005, two (one a semester) with Kabelo in Spring and Summer 2006, and two courses (one a semester) with Ian in Fall 2006 and Spring 2007. But of course I didn't just take one course a semester. I also had to keep up with taking statistics courses, and I still needed seventy-two credits of coursework to graduate. That's when Abigail, the Assistant Doctoral Program Director, stepped in and allowed me to take short, six-week "mini-courses" over at nearby Carnegie Mellon University.

CMU was a whole other ballgame. Pitt was known as a generally friendly place, a little bit watered down in terms of competitiveness. But Carnegie Mellon had just recently received a $60 million grant from a rich and generous benefactor, and the previously known Department of Industrial Administration was now the Tepper School of Business.

So I got my fair share of classes in, and the 2005-2006 academic year was spent doing coursework over at CMU, strategy courses, statistics classes and the like. And you could say that was a "ditto" for the 2006-2007 school year, too. By the third year, the course schedule was getting old, but I had promised myself a while ago that there would be no turning back!

* * *

At the end of my third year of coursework, I was ready to segue from the first half of the Ph.D. program to the second half. Now it was summer 2007, and the transition to fall 2007 was big, because that meant that I could teach undergraduates—if I showed that I knew my stuff! And that transition was symbolized by the comprehensive examinations, or "comps," which tested my knowledge of strategy concepts. There were two parts to the exam, which occurred after the coursework and before the dissertation research: (1) written and (2) oral.

The two parts were over before I knew it. The written portion was actually quite enjoyable, because I knew the literature well enough that I could answer in terms of the breadth and depth of the question. That required reading the articles, of course, but it also required making enough connections between enough articles. There was something that Ian had taught me to aid in my study of the readings: each article is a branch, and each week's worth of readings is a tree (with branches), and each semester's worth of readings is a forest, and a different faculty member's seminar is a different forest. When he described it to me that way, and I began to apply those metaphors in intellectual practice, everything started to make sense, and began to fall into place. It was very helpful to me to use those metaphors. The point was to connect every article's thesis, as much as possible, to every other article's. That was the idea of it being called a "comprehensive examination." Every concept deserved to be "microscopically" analyzed, but also "holistically" examined.

The oral defense was not what I had expected. In fact, I didn't know what to expect, although based on my honors thesis defense at Harvard, I hoped that it would be relatively painless. In fact, it was sort of fun, an enjoyable process, and a badge of honor, not a spooky initiation. All four members of the committee were in attendance.

Ian, who had led the discussion, concluded, "Jason, the committee feels that you answered the questions all in an excellent manner, garnering and deserving passing with distinction. Congratulations!"

The crowd of four applauded vigorously.

"Thank you, everyone, it's a great feeling!"

"We, however, have a question that we would like to ask you in the interests of the time remaining."

"OK," I replied, smiling now and genuinely happy. And curious. And smug.

Hannah started. "Jason, where do you think the future of strategic management will be, or what direction, in other words, will it be taking, in terms of theories, methodologies, and data streams?"

Wow, was that from left field! I was stumped. And I hadn't spent any time thinking about the "state of the field," which was why it was a damn good question!

I didn't know how I got into this, but I answered that a meta-theory may be at hand, one that integrates many dissimilar theories into one theoretical umbrella. I used the description of the schools of abnormal psychology that I knew from back in my Harvard days in the mid-1990s. The reason why I had studied these schools of abnormal psychology was to get a handle on psychology as a discipline, and to understand myself and my own pathologies better.

"Well, there's the biological model, then there's the Freudian psychodynamic model, then there's the cognitive-behavioral model, then there's the humanistic-existential model, then there's the socio-cultural model..."

What I was suggesting by extension was that there might be a theoretical model for psychological disorders that assimilated all of the five preceding theoretical models. That would make a big contribution, one which would provide great intellectual advancement to the field. I also thought that would allow more data driven (i.e. inductive) theorizing, more qualitative (i.e., words-based) data, and more small-N (i.e., few data points) studies. Interestingly, this was the direction I would be headed in for my dissertation in strategy, to seek an "overall" or "covering" theory to supplant all the previous theories on a phenomenon. But that was to be in the future.

"You didn't really answer the question," Hannah quipped.

Really? I thought I had said something on the mark.

But they let me go after that, and since the questioning was merely an add-on to my passing with distinction, my social status within the Katz School organization bumped up a notch and was elevated to ABD—"All But Dissertation"—not just a lowly Ph.D. candidate anymore! Business cards were cut for me to distribute to other school representatives at job markets and at international conferences. It was a great feeling, and I was on my way to bigger and better things.

* * *

Shortly before the comprehensive exams, I met Priscilla. We initially connected on a dating site. My profile was replete with a picture and some introductory information. She had taken a sneak-peek, so I reached out her, offering her a coffee date. She replied, "Well, this is normally not what I do to meet people, but I am willing to give it a shot!" So our paths crossed at the Coffee Bean Roasters on Acorn Street in the South Side section of town. Right away I knew she was unique, because Priscilla was the real thing: a beautiful brunette, brown-eyed lady, model tall, athletically built, and fetching in the face, too. But what was her personality like?

After a friendly handshake, we sat down.

"So where do you work?" I queried.

"Oh, at American Clothing, as a marketing analyst. You know the one?" She smiled straight at me.

"Sure I do!" *Wow, a Fortune 500 firm. And she's good at numbers, too.*

"What about you?" Priscilla asked, as she sipped her coffee.

"At Pitt, in the business school, as a Ph.D. student." *So I'm all business, she's all business. This is getting good!*

We continued to engage in casual banter, until we went to go our separate ways, she to her Chevy Trailblazer, I to my Honda Accord.

It quickly became an important pastime to hang out with her, as a counterpoint to school. I guess that was why we met, because we were both in a similar vein to meet others different from ourselves. Corporate America is probably the last place where you would find me working. I just wouldn't be able to handle the work stress or take orders from an insensitive boss. Priscilla managed to do both, and that's why I found her fascinating. She could do things from a professional standpoint that I simply could not or would not do, even though I very much wanted to have those qualities. As for me, Priscilla liked the fact that as an academic I had a quirky personality, unique in many respects, and that I was atypical in my thinking and acting. So we both reached out to each other, and that's what made it work, at least in the beginning.

Priscilla also had a real "salt of the earth" Pittsburgh personality. Pittsburghers are extremely decent people with very good instincts. And although they may lack the sophistication you would find in a New Yorker or an Angeleno, Pittsburghers more than made up for it in honest-to-goodness friendliness and helpfulness. I think one of the reasons for this is that Pittsburghers do not leave the city, and many stay roughly within a fifty-mile radius of their home. Priscilla, for example, had many dozens of family members living around Grove City, just north of Pittsburgh. In fact one time as proof she showed me pictures of her annual family reunions, populated literally by hundreds of relatives!

The rest of the summer was spent with us going out on dinner dates typically, either in Oakland where the University of Pittsburgh's main campus was, or in the South Side, across the Hot Metal Bridge, where she lived and worked. We also spent time relaxing in the local Schenley Park in the mercurial Pittsburgh weather of summertime, uncomfortably hot and humid at times, but also pleasantly warm and dry at other times. One mild summer day, we drove to nearby Beaver State Park, and for the occasion, she packed cubes of fruit—watermelon, cantaloupe, and honeydew—sliced perfectly. Another time, for my birthday, in June 2007, she baked an enormous triple-layer cake, and although the sweetness of the icing made my teeth shiver, I ate nearly three-quarters of this pastry monster myself.

* * *

Professor Kabelo had season tickets to the Steelers games, which he gave on a couple of occasions to me and Priscilla to enjoy ourselves at Heinz Field. One game in particular sticks out in memory, which we attended on a terrifically stormy night. We left from Oakland in the late afternoon under dry, grey skies that Sunday, when she picked me up in her Trailblazer and headed to the North Shore. But then sheets of rain spattered down all over the stadium just minutes prior to kickoff. The walk from the parking lot to the stadium felt like a cold bathroom shower.

Priscilla looked at me with a wan smile, just as we were walking through the lobby, and said, "I have to sit down."

I looked at her quizzically. "Yeah?" I smiled. "Yeah, me too, haha!" I giggled.

"No, Jason, I don't feel well."

My laughter evaporated into a concerned gaze.

"OK," I said, still not sure what she was getting at. So I found an empty one-seated couch nearby in the lobby, and I guided her to it.

"Thanks, Jace."

"Is everything all right? What can I do to help?" I asked her.

A cloud of grey had come over her smile.

"Can you get me a cup of hot water?"

I bee-lined straight for the concession stand, and brought the scalding hot water back to her, gently putting the Styrofoam cup in her hands.

By this point I couldn't have cared less about the game. Clearly something was up. And that's when she told me: ovarian cysts. One of them had ruptured, just as we were headed to our seats. Apparently a rupture was very painful. So I stayed by her side, until she felt comfortable enough to stand and move slowly outside to the seating.

We didn't miss much of the game. The final score was 3-0 in favor of the Steelers over the Dolphins. The field was so muddy by game time that fourth-down punts ended with the football stuck halfway down in the boggy mess. Even a field-goal try, which turned out to be the winner, was a dangerous undertaking in the muck. Priscilla and I left the game, completely soaked and shivering (like everybody else), but elated and upbeat about the game's ultimate outcome.

It was around this time in our relationship that I had "the talk" with Priscilla. Over dinner at Primanti Bros. restaurant, I told her: "Priscilla, there's something about me you should know. It needs the level of self-disclosure similar to how you told mc about your cysts."

"Go ahead, Jason!" she beamed at me. She always got me with that smile.

"It's called bipolar disorder. Have you heard of it?"

"No, what is it?"

"Well, it used to be called manic depression. You know when a person is abnormally depressed and then abnormally irritable or euphoric?"

"Well, I don't know anybody like that, but what do you do about it?"

"You see, you do talk therapy and take medication for it, and that's how you handle it."

"Well, you seem to handle it really well!"

And that's how the walls came down. Both of us had something that we didn't want to admit, or disclose for that matter. But it came up in passing, and our relationship gradually became closer and closer over time.

Of course, she probably did know someone with a mental health diagnosis, if not necessarily bipolar disorder, but that someone did not choose to reveal it to her. Besides, when she was introduced to my circle of friends and acquaintances, she would say, "You academics are all the same. You're all just a little bit off!" to which I had to laugh good-naturedly. Well, after a while, hearing that soured on me a little bit, but I never expressed the worst of my downside to her until much later.

* * *

CHAPTER 8

# On the Rebound

The second half of the Ph.D. program was broken up into three year-long stages: (1) proposal, (2) overview, (3) defense. It was nice that for each of the next three years, in the dissertation stage, that there were such comforting checkpoints.

In short, the proposal was simply a thirty-page or longer literature review, to identify any gaps in the existing research that inadequately covered the phenomenon in question. The proposal also stated the research question.

The committee met in one of the atrium conference rooms of Katz for the proposal in the spring of 2008: Kabelo, Hannah, Jacques (who was a Carnegie-Mellon University professor), Ian, and Quincy (a scholar in Pitt's Psychology in Education Department), and a sixth member of the committee, a finance scholar at Pitt, Professor Remington. Remington, realizing that my committee did not consist of lightweights, agreed to join. If nothing else, he was an excellent Devil's advocate for conventional economic thinking.

I was in the room ahead of time, hooking up the projector, assembling my notes, and all around being busy and attentive to the task at hand. Then the committee members arrived. When they were all there, Ian asked me, "Jason, could you give us a moment?" and then he motioned me out of the room.

"Sure," I complied gracefully.

It took about five excruciatingly long minutes alone in the atrium of Katz when Ian opened the door and motioned me back in, with a smile!

As he sat back down in his chair, among the other committee members, he began: "Jason, the committee members all think that you have a promising dissertation proposal and we will give you an unconditional pass!"

"Thank you, Ian, thank you to you all," I replied happily.

Afterwards, Professor Jacques and I met constantly to discuss our theories.

* * *

Along came obtaining the data, which, fortunately, had been published on the Internet for free! So no exorbitant fees or charges for expensive data sets. And with Professor Quincy's statistical powers, updating the data set with new information was a cinch.

By the time of the overview, the literature review was coupled with initial data testing for a dissertation having reached half-completion. By fall 2009, the committee convened for the overview. This was the hard one. The proposal before was a cinch, because it was merely introductory in tone and taste. And the defense afterward would be relatively easy because the "powers that be" simply wanted to send you off. But the overview would test my mettle. The committee expected a level of excellence to be met on my part.

Kabelo, Quincy, Remington, Hannah, Ian, and Jacques sat around the conference table, as I set up my PowerPoint slides. I began with Slide 1 and was going to turn to Slide Two when Kabelo interjected: "But how do you make the assertion that it is a power law distribution in the first place?"

I felt cut off, but tried not to take it personally. I answered, "Because there are various line-fitting programs that I used to test the accuracy of the curve to meet the power law distribution in the tail."

Before I got on Slide 4, Hannah raised another doozy of a question: "What is your justification for claiming that the Gaussian statistics could not handle the empirical distribution, while the Pareto statistics can now handle it better?"

Feeling under duress, I stated quietly, "Because what I know without question is that all scientific explanations are ultimately provisional."

Jacques immediately straightened up in his chair, and exclaimed, "Yes! In physics there is always one truth, and then there is another truth after that, and then yet another truth after that! Yes, I totally agree!"

I found a friend in Jacques, from that point forward in the dissertation process.

Remington later expressed skepticism with the Complex Adaptive Systems Theory, saying, "I just really don't know how you can say that Self-Organized Criticality could serve as a mechanism for your theory."

To this I replied angrily, feeling my top go off in steam, "Well, it's in my dissertation. Didn't you read it?!"

At this, Ian reached out a hand to Remington, to placate him from reacting to my outburst. But Remington didn't seem to be angry.

Quincy was also helpful, like Jacques. I guessed that Quincy, a statistician, was just as neutral as anybody else in the room at that time, and the process was less adversarial with him than with anybody else. With Remington, I had to win his favor, whereas with Quincy he was already leaning to my side.

In any case, towards the end of an hour's worth of grilling, I was sent out of the room, to let the committee decide on my fate. I nervously bounced a knee up and down while I sat in the cushioned navy and beige University-colored chairs in the Atrium of Mervis Hall. Then Ian came out of the room and motioned me inside. I followed him into the conference room and had a seat. With Ian now seated, I listened anxiously.

Ian began. "Jason, the committee would like to offer you a pass on your Dissertation Overview. Congratulations and thanks for your presentation."

With that, I replied, "Thank you, thank you," somewhat over-profusely, a bit too peasant-like in greeting. The committee filed out.

* * *

After the scene calmed with the overview's passing, Ian, Jacques, and I planned to submit to a journal the first part of my dissertation. It was titled "Surf's Up! Distributional Properties of M&A Waves" in order to borrow surfer parlance, and to describe the defining features of mergers and acquisition waves as a whole. We submitted the first draft around the late fall of 2009, and waited for a response from the academic journal, *Academy of Management Journal,* a top A-level management journal. Ian calmed my anxiety by letting me know that longer wait-times were better; it meant that the committee of reviewers and editors were taking the work seriously, whereas shorter wait-times meant that a dismissive "desk-reject" was most likely forthcoming.

Amazingly, in early January of 2010, an email entered my inbox from *Academy of Management Journal*. Our article had received a "Revise & Resubmit" decision from the journal's two anonymous reviewers and the associate editor Dr. Skylar! This was spectacular news. It was exceedingly difficult to get an R&R from a top A-level journal, while "Reject" decisions were a dime a dozen; even top professors received desk-rejects all the time. So I was ecstatic.

To my way of thinking, the "R&R" decision from *Academy of Management Journal* confirmed my ability to (1) do research, (2) conclude the Ph.D. program, and (3) get a job. I experienced huge sighs of relief from February 2010 onward. I finally felt that I had "arrived," that I knew what I was doing, that I was an Old Master in my own way, and that now I was a real Ph.D. I felt as if I had accomplished a lot.

* * *

As far as my mental state, i.e., stability and health, I felt that it was taken care of and that it would be another "more of the same" from here on in. I continued to take the anti-depressant Prozac, the mood stabilizer Depakote, the thyroid hormone Cytomel, and the anti-psychotic Risperdal. I also saw Dr. Baereyan for thirty minutes, once a month. Sometimes we would change the medication dosages, such as 40 mg Prozac to 30 mg, to get me on less medication. But people around me, such as my dad during my summer break, noticed that I was quieter than usual. So I asked Dr. Baereyan to up the dosage back to 40 mg. I also played around with the Risperdal anti-psychotic, going from 4 mg down to 2 mg occasionally.

At one point Dr. Baereyan commented, "Jason, you know, that's almost like taking nothing."

"OK, then let's bump it up back to four milligrams right away," which the good doctor did without hesitation. So I would go back up to 4 mg, especially if I started smoking a lot more. Apparently, those with thought disorders, such as schizophrenics, smoke a lot because it helps calm down their thought processes. Not that I was a schizophrenic, but I was taking the Risperdal anti-psychotic for a reason, so if I needed the Risperdal I ought to take it, right? Right!

I continued my visits with my clinical social worker Paul, generally speaking once a week. I tried to time it between seminars or maybe after seminars, when the pressure to relieve stress was the greatest. I couldn't show up, however, in the morning, and I let him know that, too.

Paul was in demand as a therapist. Occasionally, he would beseech me outside his office to cancel the meeting, for some crazy crisis situation that he had on his hands. I would oblige willingly, knowing that others were in a worse state, and that Paul's request was genuine. And then we would continue on as before, the next week. It was a lesson in distress tolerance.

I really didn't know what was going on with me, and again, how damaging and destructive six years of stress could be, if only kept at bay, but not resolved. Indeed, I had been *hypomanic* most of my six years in the program. After all, how else would I have been able to manage the workload and be so productive? I could be quite loquacious in class, and I might have ruffled some feathers for being so verbose. But I didn't mind... I had to focus on myself and not anyone else, and not care about what others thought of me.

* * *

The job search began in earnest once I received the email in January 2010 of the Revise & Resubmit decision. I emailed out to the universities throughout the United States and to those in the rest of the world of my situation. I got three expressions of interest in Hong Kong, SAR (Special Administrative Region) China alone. I traveled back and forth twice to deliver my job talk presentation three times. While my presentation was met with bewilderment by a couple universities, City University of Hong Kong decided to extend me an offer. And considering that all I needed was one job offer, I took it.

The defense document was a completed project with literature review, hypothesis development, methodology and data, support from the empirical testing of hypotheses, results and conclusion. Up till late April 2010, I fine-tuned the entire dissertation document until it was razor-sharp. There would be no obstacles in my quest to achieve total victory! And the committee pretty much knew it. Although there were some weaker points in the theoretical argument, as well as in the methods in sourcing the data and also the empirical support for the theory, the committee members knew that no dissertation was perfect. Indeed, if anything, any dissertation given a so-called 100% would be suspect in the eyes of most scholars. Yet, in the back of my mind, I worried that someone on the committee would feel buyer's remorse after the Dissertation Overview, and would not sign off on the document. But the actual defense meeting went along without much of a hitch. It was a formality, and the committee gave its rubber stamp of approval without resistance.

* * *

CHAPTER 9

# A Final Hurdle

There was one final hurdle, a speed bump, to cross before I left Pittsburgh.

In July 2010, two weeks before the graduation ceremony, Ian and I disagreed on how to end the article for the journal. Ian insisted that something be kept sparingly to a footnote, whereas I wanted to spend a page or two on it. I lost my temper; my anger rose out of my heart and through my mouth like a garden hose turned on all the way up, vitriol spouting all over the place.

"Jason," Ian stated matter-of-factly, "I'm just trying to help you..."

"DAMMIT, IAN, WHEN HAVE YOU EVER HELPED ME?!"

I wasn't just angry at Ian about this issue, but about *everything* Ian supposedly hadn't done for me as my professor and chair: not assisting me enough with getting in touch with prospective school-hiring officials, not helping me enough with writing the dissertation, and not providing enough support in class and seminars with the readings. The accumulated stress made me fume, and it all came to a head in Ian's office.

"OK, Jason, we're going to keep this strictly professional from now on," Ian stated, very calmly, as if my outburst meant nothing, as he turned back to his typing. His pulse couldn't have been over sixty the whole time. But his cool reaction was even more infuriating. I almost wanted him to be upset, as much as I was, because then that would mean that I had gotten under his skin. I was in danger of spiraling out of complete emotional control.

I just sat there behind Ian, at his round desk, coming to the realization that I had just alienated my dissertation chair. So after the engines had died down, I spent a few seconds cooling off, and reversed myself in a matter of seconds.

"OK, Ian, I apologize, I'm sorry," I admitted. "I'm just stressed out, that's all."

That seemed to do the trick, because he stopped typing, and turned around again. "All right, Jason, let's keep the idea to a footnote in the text."

"OK," I said, with a sheepish half-smile.

I got out of his office, completely relieved that the meeting was over. I wasn't sure if I had been angry or symptomatic. There was obviously a difference. Being angry is, well, being angry, but being symptomatic is abnormal. Bipolar individuals tend to feel emotions a lot more intensely than most people do. And I decided that the symptoms were starting to manifest themselves in my rage. I felt that something was going on and that this was not the normal Jason I knew myself to be. Instead, I was leading toward a self-destructive impulse.

I nearly ran to the Doctoral Office and told Abigail I needed to go to the emergency room at Western Psychiatric Institute and Clinic (WPIC) because I felt like hurting myself. Abigail was on the phone at the time but I went ahead to WPIC and she met me there afterward to confirm my check-in. Through the window in the double doors, I gave Abigail the "thumbs up" before she left me on my own recognizance.

* * *

Upon intake, my clothes were checked for weapons, and I wrote my personal information on a clipboard. It was strangely quiet in the waiting room, while I talked in a low murmur to the attending nurses and physicians. A middle-aged man, soft-spoken and benevolent, with a lanyard around his neck with his ID card clipped to it, asked me whether I was aware of the wait-times and the procedure of checking into an emergency room for psychiatric illnesses.

"Yes, I do," I told him.

The neat thing was that they fed me: turkey and cheese sandwiches with packets of mayonnaise, as well as those small juice cartons that required drinking half a dozen to quench one's thirst. Hospital food... delicious and nutritious!

But then they moved me into an interior waiting room, not just for intake, but this time as a real holding pen for the serious and mild cases together. It was terrifying. One big beefy guy, with a scruffy beard and dirty flannel shirt, baggy jeans, and a wild glint in his eye, kept interrupting the attending doctor on call from seeing the patients in the order in which they were taken in. I thought the guy was going to explode at any minute, the only thing preventing him from doing so being the lack of a weapon. As for me, I just sat there in one of the durable "carpet wool" upholstered chairs, trying to stay away from the big beefy guy, who would on occasion obtrusively come over to check on me, to make sure I didn't get ahead of him in line. The fear must have shown in my darting eyes, furrowed brow, glum frown, constant sniffling, and head held in my hands. Whenever the big beefy guy came by, I shuffled in a barely controlled anxious gait away to the other side of the room.

For some reason, at the time I chose not to go to my girlfriend Priscilla for council or for help. Today, I don't doubt why I didn't go to her for support first. I knew that she hadn't seen that part of me and moreover she wouldn't know what to do with me if she had. And I didn't want to reveal that lousy part of my life to anyone that I cared about, as if Priscilla deserved no memory of it. She knew only half of me, even though I had been upfront with disclosing information about my bipolar disorder to her a few months into the relationship, when I felt the timing was right. And she didn't reject me for that, to her credit. But I didn't trust her to be my partner, in case the going got rough. Indeed, there had been times in our relationship when I felt as if I were *her* therapist. So when I had to practice self-care, I didn't trust her to help me do it and I wanted to do it alone, to have control over myself, even when I was not necessarily the best executor of my own estate.

The doctor finally saw me after what seemed like days. I relaxed in relief that the wait was finally over. I knew from a window in the upper part of one of the walls that the sun was high in the sky when I first checked in, and it was starting to set by the time I met with the doctor (this was late July, the height of summer, with long days). The doctor led me into yet another waiting room, this time with nobody in it, sparsely furnished with a couch and a few chairs, and absolutely quiet, thank God. The first name on the physician's lanyard ID was Ron. In any case, without obfuscation, I explained that I had gotten into an argument with my dissertation chair and this had unnerved me.

At first the doctor seemed a bit skeptical as to the severity of my illness and the urgency of my situation.

But then I went on. "My dissertation chair's name is Ian Taft..." I told him, with all the internal calm and inner restraint I could muster. And articulateness, too.

And then the look on the doctor's face changed. "Oh, Ian!" he remarked with gusto. "I hope he's doing well." Yes, Ian was a big name at the business school, and well-known on campus. Then there was a sea change in the doctor's visage. "OK, Jason, do you feel like you need the help or not? Just to let you know, because it's up to you, I will make the resources available, if you want," he told me with concern.

"Would I still be able to go to my graduation ceremony on August 9, two weeks away?"

"Chances are you wouldn't, Jason," the doctor said with a wry, sad smile. "We'd probably have to keep you longer than two weeks."

That was the real deal-breaker for me: receive vital medical support but miss graduation? On the one hand, I didn't want to take chances with my mental health. All too many times terrible things had happened if I were overly stressed or under too much duress. Things such as getting into fights with my dad or with the committee members, for example, or sexual liaisons with fast women, spending too much money, dabbling in drugs and alcohol. I wanted to avoid diving into those behaviors. But everybody was coming to the awards ceremony, and I thought I wouldn't be awarded my degree if I missed it. Mom and Dad would soon arrive from Los Angeles, Gerry from Philadelphia, and Priscilla planned to take time out of her busy schedule from her corporate job in Pittsburgh—everybody was counting on me to show up at the final awards ceremony and receive my degree.

The doctor rose to leave and then told me that I would be meeting with a couple other staff members. The next person was a medical intern who was two months away from obtaining her M.D., as she told me. Her name was Diane, and I remember her slim frame nicely embellished by her ID card and lanyard. I complimented her on her achievement of becoming a doctor, although she laughed out loud good-naturedly and put the brakes on that with: "Well, I'm not a doctor yet, you know!"

Then we got down to business. I told her I didn't know what I wanted to do, as the doctor before her had presented me with a choice between two different tradeoffs: commit myself and forget about the degree program for now, or go back to the degree program and take a chance with my mental health.

She said, "It's up to you, Jason. As the doctor said, you have a choice here."

I told her, "Well, one thing's for sure, Doctor, I feel safe, in here, with you," referring to our room, "but I do NOT feel safe out there, in that waiting room!" Yeah, the one waiting room with the big beefy guy stalking everybody in sight.

"Yes, it is pretty scary out there sometimes," she murmured in agreement.

She departed, and then the third and final staff member came to see me. He was a heavyset man with a moustache, also soft-spoken like the gentleman at initial intake, but this fellow was a Licensed Clinical Social Worker like Paul.

"Hi Jason, I'm Pete, one of the Licensed Clinical Social Workers here at Western Psychiatric Institute and Clinic," he said, introducing himself and shaking my hand. The man had a firm grip. "How are you this evening?" he asked me in a caring tone.

"I'm fine, Pete, I'm fine, just hanging in there," I answered, as I struggled for the right words.

"So, Jason, I understand your situation, and there is an alternative. On Penn Avenue, adjacent to Oakland, we have a clinic that allows you to spend time there, where you can check in as a WPIC patient and live for a few weeks if you need to, with all the amenities, take showers, they'll feed you, you'll have separate beds, that sort of thing, and if you'd like I can take your name down."

Looking back on this offer, I should have probably taken it, even though I hadn't taken the more involved option of committing myself into a locked facility, offered by the first doctor. But what did I know? I thought and felt that I was too good for it, that to embark on my professional career meant that nothing was going to get in the way of it now. It was also a potential dent to my pride. I had been progressing steadily for four years straight in my recovery while achieving academic milestone after academic milestone. It seemed as if that should continue, regardless!

"No, Pete, no, I think I'll be OK, but thanks for the offer, though," I replied in a shaky stutter, none too sure of myself.

And with that, discharge was in a matter of minutes (rather than hours for intake). I just wasn't going to take a hit to my career to attend to my mental health. And yes, I guessed I could put it on the backburner for a while. But there would be far-reaching consequences.

* * *

The award ceremony was held in Alumni Hall, which housed the Connolly Ballroom, large and classy enough to hold the reception afterward. The diploma I held was of more interest to me than the award ceremony. I opened up the paper packet:

The University of Pittsburgh
JOSEPH M. KATZ GRADUATE SCHOOL OF BUSINESS
UPON RECOMMENDATION OF THE FACULTY,
AND BY AUTHORITY OF THE BOARD OF TRUSTEES,
CONFERS UPON

JASON W. PARK
THE DEGREE OF
DOCTOR OF PHILOSOPHY

WITH ALL THE RIGHTS, PRIVILEGES AND
RESPONSIBILITIES PERTAINING THERETO. IN WITNESS
THEREOF, THE SEAL OF THE UNIVERSITY AND THE
SIGNATURES OF THE AUTHORIZED OFFICERS ARE
AFFIXED AT PITTBSURGH, PENNSYLVANIA.
AUGUST 9, 2010

Tristan Twitch, CHAIRMAN, BOARD OF TRUSTEES
Stephen Berg, PROVOST
Mark Nordenberg, CHANCELLOR
Thomas Delaney, DEAN,
THE JOSEPH M. KATZ SCHOOL OF BUSINESS

The Connolly Ballroom was high-ceilinged, wooden-floored, spacious, ornate, reminiscent of "Gilded Age" brassiness but also slightly art-deco-like with its statuesque, clean architectural lines shooting up from the floor. It could have held five hundred people, and it had to, because it wasn't just the Ph.D. graduates and faculty and staff, but MBA graduates as well, not to mention *everyone's* friends and family: spouses, children, parents, grandparents even, and many members of the extended family traveling across the oceans, Pacific and Atlantic, from Australasia, Africa, and Europe, as well as upland from the southern hemisphere in Central and Southern America.

Well, my parents and brother showed up, and so did Priscilla, looking all sleek and shiny in her silver dress. She towered at 5'10" in flat heels over the crowd, and attracted a lot of male and jealous female attention, what with her long brown hair and sun-kissed skin. I thought to myself, *Ha, others may be professors or own a brownstone in New York, but no girl of theirs will ever match her!*

So I paraded around with Priscilla, my parents and my brother Gerry in close proximity, while we made the rounds. Ian was an obvious person to approach. Ian mentioned to Mom that he had done "very little work" on my dissertation and that I had done most of the heavy lifting. This was meant as a compliment, but it did come across as a snide repartee for the tussles he and I had gotten into recently. And I had told nobody about the trip to the emergency room at WPIC; the only person who knew was Abigail, the Assistant Doctoral Program Director.

I was happy, but not blissed out... happy of course that the current adversity had been overcome, but not overly so because I felt as if I were on a treadmill, exhausted. Professor Kabelo had put it in perspective shortly before my job offer: "Jason, listen, it doesn't let up, ever, you know. First you have to get a job, then you have to make tenure, then you have to make full professor, then you have to make chaired professor... it just doesn't let up." I thought of those remarks and teethed on those words.

Yet I do remember feeling *relieved* about a huge number of things, all at the same time... that I didn't have a relapse... that I had gotten a job... that my family had supported me unconditionally... that I had made my parents proud... that in my life was a woman I cared about. For that combination of achievements altogether to bring utter relief, I couldn't put a price on, truly. It was unbelievably gratifying to feel that way.

* * *

The plane was leaving from Pittsburgh International Airport on August 16, 2010, and my passport was stamped with a temporary visa allowing me to enter Hong Kong for up to two weeks after the date. Priscilla cried quietly; I held her hand, trying to console her. She was the last one to see me off; my family had to head back home, either to Los Angeles for my parents, or Philadelphia for my brother Gerry, mostly to work shortly after the awards ceremony. My luggage at least had been taken care of: eight suitcases full of clothes had been sent in advance to my serviced apartment in Hung Hom, on the Kowloon peninsula of Hong Kong, overlooking the Hong Kong Island.

Priscilla admonished me mock-petulantly for leaving her as she sniffled: "It's going to be lonely for me."

I said, in all earnestness, "It's not over, hon. I'll be back for you."

"Do you mean it? Will you come back for me?"

She looked into my eyes, and I looked at hers, all bright and shiny from a film of tears.

I said, "Sure! You're a great catch, remember?"

She chortled, and then gathered herself.

The loudspeaker was announcing my flight departure for Hong Kong by way of Los Angeles. I gathered my carry-on and turned to give Priscilla a farewell hug and a kiss. For some reason, while she cried, her cheeks had flushed as if she'd just run a couple of miles. She looked very pretty, very healthy, and also very tall, like a runway model. Well, *every sailor has his sweetheart*, I thought to myself.

I got in line, looking back every now and then towards Priscilla, giving her a flash of a winning smile and waving to her. She looked so alone there, amid that crowd of all those strangers sitting and standing around, anonymous and faceless, wearing somber blue and black and grey, while Priscilla wore red and yellow and green, raiment consonant with the colors of a shining rainbow.

Then after walking through the gateway and inside the plane, I sought to take my seat. It was American Airlines I was flying. Getting to Los Angeles was a cinch, in fact. It was only five hours at a time and I could sit there and read magazines and listen to music and stare at my laptop spreadsheets.

The stewardess asked, "Would you like anything to drink, sir?"

"Oh, some ginger ale would be fine. I've got a weak stomach."

"Of course."

*Glug, glug, glug, hmmm, yum, yummy in my tummy...*

* * *

Off the plane at LAX, then to the international area of the airport: Bradley Terminal. Things got rougher with this route. I was taking Cathay Pacific, a top-notch airline, straight to Hong Kong, but it would still be fifteen hours non-stop from Los Angeles. I waited an interminable amount of time by the gate to get on board, in an area chock-full of crying babies and lines of pushy people; getting seated seemed like a strategic game of chess. It was logical enough: just get in line whenever your section was called. But, inside the plane, sections spilled into other sections when certain people had trouble stowing their carry-on baggage. So then the staff would have to attend to them, and this slowed up boarding, and messed up the intendedly rational order of things.

Finally, after what seemed like a couple of very long hours, everybody was seated and headed on to bigger and better things. I smelled different body odors and perfume scents coming from people, a lot of it foreign and unaccounted for. The stewardesses were nice enough but because they were Singaporean, I was unsure what their cultural customs and mores were compared to my own. I heard languages on the loudspeakers voicing instructions in foreign tongues. The service was good, but the food was different: Asian, but definitely not Korean. There were more babies crying on the plane than at the gate, and the incessant fussing started to grate on my ears, even though I tried to hide my thoughts in the loud music of my iPod. The person seated next to me continuously elbowed me in the ribs with the rhythm of the turbulence. I found it rude, but this fellow passenger didn't seem to notice, or mind.

By the time the flight was over, I was tired and exhausted, flustered and harried... and I hadn't even moved a bit. *So this is what it's going to be like,* I remarked grimly to myself. *Jesus... that wasn't at all like the flight for the interview. Until Priscilla and I get married and move to Hong Kong, I'm gonna be scooting back and forth across the Pacific for the foreseeable future. I guess I should have been prepared for this. I hope it's not like this all the time. Maybe it'll be better next time...*

* * *

CHAPTER 10

# On a Slow Boat to China

In the fall of 2010, during my first semester in Hong Kong as a newly minted Assistant Professor, my treatment team was decided by the university's medical staff, which I called out of the blue one late afternoon. I felt, all of a sudden, an impending sense of doom, as if the sky were going to fall on me, or as if I could predict that an earthquake would upend Hong Kong in the next hour. I don't know why I felt it, but something that Priscilla had mentioned a few days before in October by Skype had me unwound. It was "Jason, remember, you have me now, so you don't need a therapist anymore."

I couldn't process that, and I couldn't protest that I did in fact need therapy, even if she was in my life.

I later talked to my brother Gerry about it, and he stated as a fact of life, "Jason, that sounds so blatantly wrong, that you don't need a therapist. It shows me that Priscilla doesn't understand that you do need therapy, and that she doesn't understand your condition."

So that statement of hers threw me for a loop, unfortunately. In fact, I was stunned. I had hung in there for about eight weeks in Hong Kong, without therapy, just simply relying on the medication that Dr. Baereyan in Pittsburgh had prescribed me, with no changes.

I called the operator on the medical school hotline and explained politely but still in a rush that I needed to see a psychologist and psychiatrist as soon as possible. She suggested that I meet with Dr. Xi, a psychiatrist, and Ms. Tsing, a therapist. The operator was very nice and kind enough to give me freely the numbers and addresses of their respective medical practice clinics.

Both individuals were in fact in the same office tower just four levels apart, 15 and 11. Their office building was in the crowded and bustling part of town called Tsim Tsa Tsui. It would be a very convenient arrangement as far as commuting from the Kowloon Tong subway station on the light-blue colored-coded line, a mere twenty-five minutes ride by subway. As it turned out, I preferred to take a taxi there, actually, when I wasn't over my HK$800 (about US$100) limit in daily spending. Taxis were a lot less stressful, and I could avoid standing on the subway station platforms and having to share a public space. However, since it would cost HK$100 roundtrip, it wasn't in my financial interest to call a cab every time.

I first met my therapist Ms. Tsing during fall 2010. She had kind Chinese features, wore large eyeglasses with gold frames, and dressed in an understated fashion. She wore a red sweater and black slacks that day, and she described her training with a sort of lullaby lilt to her voice.

"So Jason, I am practiced in Cognitive Behavioral Therapy or CBT, and I received my training in Australia, New South Wales."

I tried to be open-minded about it, but deep inside I was skeptical. I had studied Dialectical Behavioral Therapy (DBT), not CBT, at Pitt with Paul, so I wasn't familiar with her training, which was not obtained in the United States. Of course, I later found out that CBT was widely practiced in the States. The only issue was that DBT was a later modification of CBT because Buddhist monk Thich Nhat Hanh's version of unconditional regard for the patient in DBT replaced the "Rogerian" one found in CBT. However, there was indeed overlap.

But I was still justly worried: CBT may not be a good fit between me and my therapist. Nevertheless, I persisted and worked with her until other events persuaded me to try someone—or something—else.

Now with Dr. Xi, the psychiatrist, there was a similar issue. I remember my first meeting with him. He was wearing a conservatively colored navy three-piece suit—all at the height of a sultry Hong Kong summer (ninety degrees Fahrenheit, ninety percent humidity!). He asked me to talk about myself. So I began speaking, while he watched me closely and examined every twitch of my torso, every turn of my wrist, roll of my eyes, for clues as to dysfunction or symptoms. Going into this exercise, I knew, as Gerry and I had once talked about, that I had a habit of fooling or outsmarting my psychiatrists to think that I was all right. It wasn't a good characteristic of mine. The number one point about working with a psychiatrist: be brutally honest about how you feel! Unload on the psychiatrist! Their job is to listen to you!

"So, I graduated with a Ph.D. in strategic management from the University of Pittsburgh in Pittsburgh, Pennsylvania, the United States," I started with a turn of my wrists.

Dr. Xi's eyes immediately darted to the motion.

"I have a Bachelor's in Philosophy from Harvard University," I continued, with a twitch of my torso, which again Dr. Xi seemed to duly note. "And I am a professor in the Department of Management and Organization in the College of Business at City University of Hong Kong." I ended with a sigh, rolling my eyeballs round and round. Once more, Dr. Xi picked up on that.

We went through the hour and a half that Dr. Xi had allotted for me as he asked more questions about my personal life: sexual orientation, childhood traumas, relation to family, any personal network in Hong Kong, meetings with a therapist or psychologist, workload and stress at the job, any relationship I was in, and so on.

Dr. Xi also asked me if I had any questions, which I did: *Where did Dr. Xi get his training? (Australia) What medications did he think were good for me? Did I need a change in my "med dosages" or "med types?" Did he practice a particular style of psychiatry?* I exhausted a good part of the hour and a half myself, by asking these sorts of questions.

Toward the end of the session, I became concerned about the thoroughness and effectiveness of his training, but he was an M.D. and I wasn't about to challenge his expertise. I wanted to go into it with an open mind and try the best I could to do well by my treatment team.

In any case, after the consultation he decided to keep me on the medication regimen determined by Dr. Baereyan. He gave me a prescription for the synthetic hormone Cytomel, to get outside his own lab, since his did not have it, and besides I only had a week's supply left. He also decided to raise the Prozac to 60 mg from 40 mg, even though I hadn't let him know that I was feeling a bit down.

That's how we worked out the patient-client relationship, by my talking to him and his sleuthing about what I needed, medication-wise. Other than that, though, the cocktail I had been on at Pittsburgh was left untouched. It would change, in the future, however.

* * *

Priscilla visited me in Hong Kong a couple times. It was just a couple, because that was all she could tolerate. I first flew back during the winter of 2010 to secure the engagement ring from Mom, this particular ring being my grandmother's. Priscilla, whom I gave it to, wore it with pride wherever she went. I could tell Priscilla liked it, by the way she kept showing it off to me. I thought to myself, *There's nothing else she could possibly want other than such a beautiful ring. She's a keeper!*

I decided to set up her first trip to Hong Kong on my own dime, and I was glad for the opportunity to splurge on her. I wanted her to see my new digs and what the city had to offer. Priscilla did not like flying or getting into airplanes, she had told me, but did so willingly to see me. Her visit was approximately during U.S. Spring Break of 2011, although in Hong Kong there was no matching Spring Break on the exact same days.

We had just finished horseplaying with wild shrieks and splashing of water at the outdoor pool of the serviced apartment on her first full day. But after what seemed like hilarious laughter and fun pandemonium, the visit then took a bad turn in my room when she began sniffling and lay prone on my bed.

"Priss, what's wrong?"

"Oh, I just thought I could come here and not worry about my condition."

"What condition?"

"You know, Jace, down there," as she pointed to her abdomen.

"Oh, you mean the cysts?"

"Yeah, you know..."

Yeah, I knew. I had heard that scraping them off was one way to remedy the situation, but Priscilla seemed frightened of the thought of that, and conversation died whenever the topic came up. Again, it was one of those talks that we never had, at least to the point of resolving the issue. All couples, whether married or otherwise, need to sit down and have a chat now and then. I can't emphasize to you enough about the lack of conversation between us on most topics, whether about having children, how we would raise them, who would work and who wouldn't, how we would negotiate the long distance between Pittsburgh and Hong Kong... whatever.

Anyhow, it was clear in that moment what had to be done. "Priss, I'm going to make a call to the university health clinic. They should be able to get you in because of my connection."

She nodded and I made the call.

Then I held her hand gingerly as we got to the ground floor lobby of the apartment.

"Taxi!" I called out toward a red-colored cab, which would take us to City University of Hong Kong.

We got in the cab. Priscilla started crying.

"Dammit, Jason, I thought I could handle this myself."

"It's OK, dear. I'm with you now."

I wanted to yell at her to calm down. But I was in caregiver mode, as I had often been with her, and I refused to utter a single unkind word. At least we didn't have to get up or move around in the cab, and the cabbie let us off at the campus center circle, a short walk from the health clinic.

"Hi, Miss," I said to the clerk with my winningest smile, "I am Jason Park with my fiancée to see Dr. Lam."

The forty Hong-Kong dollar co-pay swiftly changed hands, and after we sat down in the waiting room for five minutes, our number was called.

Dr. Lam was a middle-aged lady with short hair who wore a white doctor's coat. We all shook hands (although this was not generally accepted practice in Hong Kong, for fear of contagion).

She asked, "So I understand this is an emergency. How can I help you?"

"Doctor, my fiancée Priscilla is here visiting me for a few days and she has some pain. I will let her explain what it is."

So Priscilla took the lead. "Doctor, I have cysts in my ovaries."

"I see. Can you lie down up here on the bed?"

"OK." Priscilla climbed up on top of it.

"So if I tap your abdomen and it does not pop back up, it might be something else." The test proved negative. "So it must have ruptured."

"Doctor," I gently interrupted, "is it possible that you could write a prescription for painkillers, so that Priscilla can do well enough for the rest of the vacation until she gets back to the U.S.?"

"Sure!" she smiled.

The doctor at my urging wrote a script for some strong painkillers, and off we went to the next-door dispensary to pick them up.

"For Jason Park," the pharmacist replied in no nonsense English, as we were dwarfed by the wall-to-wall shelves containing various chemical solid-state potions and elixirs.

* * *

Undeterred by this tough state of affairs, I made dinner reservations on a midweek night at the Steakhouse, a wonderfully upscale restaurant serving, of course, steak, in the sea-level basement of the luxurious Intercontinental Hotel overlooking Hong Kong Island from the Kowloon Peninsula. The restaurant was known for its open-hearth wood-charcoal grill, the only one of its kind in the city. The sauces and condiments, as well as the service and attentiveness, not to mention the main course, were all top-class.

"Here you go, Priscilla," I said as I urged her to sit down gingerly on the booth side, and then I took the chair side.

The waiter came by quickly and asked, "Your drink order, miss."

To this, Priscilla replied with a quiet smile: "House merlot, please."

The waiter turned to me, and I said, "Diet Coke," feeling sheepish. I almost sensed that he shrugged his shoulders, somewhat perplexed that I wasn't drinking. But no matter. Maybe I was just imagining things.

After the orders for drinks, which showed up quickly, we selected the main course, which of course was steak. When it arrived, we had as normal a meal as possible, what with her pain, and what with my helpless and unreasonable anger at her for screwing up the trip.

"Nice view, isn't it?" I chatted as we were seated just a few feet above sea level with an expansive view of the Hong Kong island.

She nodded.

"How's your steak?"

"Good."

I looked down at my food.

I tried to enjoy myself thoroughly, but there was a voice inside my head declaring, *Jason, you can't have fun if others around you aren't having fun.*

So it was just a blah, OK night.

* * *

The next day, I showed Priscilla my office and had her meet Beverly, the General Office Director for the Management and Organization Department.

"Hi Priscilla! I'm have been looking forward to meeting you."

Apparently the painkillers were working, because the three of us went out to lunch at the most popular restaurant, Chez Melange, in the adjacent mall next to campus, and the two ladies were exceedingly effusive in each other's company.

Priscilla whispered immediately, after the lunch, to me in confidence, "I could see myself spending more time with Beverly, for sure!"

I was very relieved to hear something positive, since I wondered if Priscilla might keel over and pass out at that moment.

I saw her off at the airport the next afternoon. It had been a stressful vacation, and I felt that she had put me in a lot of worrisome situations. She wasn't crying, and I asked her if I had treated her all right.

She said, "Yes, you took care of me, Jason."

But it took all my self-control to give her a loving send-off and kind well-wishes back to the States, instead of dropping her bags at the gate, turning around, and running like hell for the airport exit.

* * *

At the end of the spring 2011 semester, I had half-promised Priscilla that I could get back to the States in a few years' time, and that until then she could move to Hong Kong and not have to work. She was somewhat impressed by that offer, and agreed to it in principle.

But the second time she stopped by in Hong Kong, in the winter of 2011, things took a turn for the worse. The first thing I remember that afternoon of her sojourn was seeing her come out of the gate, crying, with a weak smile on her face. The flight had been bad; Priscilla was smiling only because she had gotten off the plane.

She told me, as I got her bags, "Jason, the flight made me sick. I was stuck, and I just couldn't get out of there."

Her fear of flying had gotten hold of her. Now what? I didn't know what to do to make it better.

She asked, "Jason, can we get some ginger ale and saltine crackers?"

But there were no stores, like the 7-11, at the exit of the Hong Kong airport, only at the entry.

So I said, "Priscilla, can we just wait until we get to my apartment? I'll take care of you."

After I struggled with her heavy baggage, I found that at least the taxi offered some relief for us. We rolled down the windows and took in the sooty Hong Kong air.

* * *

That evening, we wandered down to the waterfront, and although it was smelly and polluted, it offered some amusement with its statue of Bruce Lee in a martial arts pose along the walkway. We took pictures, of course.

But what would lead to trouble later was an email string I'd written to a young lady I knew in grad school, who commented on the picture of my niece Sarah that I had posted.

*Oh my God, Jason, is that your daughter? She's so cute!*

*No, that's my niece, but she's awesome, isn't she? Love, Jason*

I was woken up in the middle of the night by Priscilla, who demanded I get up and look at my computer screen, where the offending text was. This started a maelstrom of crying and screaming and throwing pillows.

"Jason! You're supposed to be in love with only one woman, me!"

*Oh, my God, what the hell is going on?* I just sat there on the couch in the living room, taking it all in. Priscilla was bawling now, in her shorts and sweatshirt, sitting on the ledge next to the window with her feet tucked up under herself. As I looked out the window from the couch, the lights outside appeared serene, so uninvolved with the tense situation inside.

*What should I do? Scream back? Reassure her? Hit her? No...* I just got up, left the room and went back to sleep. That was all I could do to defuse the situation, exit it.

The next morning, I found that Priscilla had locked herself in the other bedroom. I cajoled her to let me in with "Priscilla... I think I'll try to go for the empty post of Assistant Dean of the Department of Management and Organization."

Lisa opened the door. She had apparently been sniffling, and I felt bad about the situation, but I was rocked by it. *What had just happened? Is the relationship salvageable? Can we make it through this difficult situation?*

A few days later, I said good-bye to Priscilla at the airport... a brief farewell. Things seemed to be salvaged, although one couldn't tell for certain. My moods had been ripped apart by her ranting and raving. I still felt in shock, as if more was to come from me. I didn't feel that she deserved to get away with what she had done to me. I was angry, hurt, and confused, under the surface, even though the send-off at the airport was civil enough. But perhaps that was it: it was rudely polite.

* * *

From Day 1 in Hong Kong, I had been feverishly working every day on my first dissertation essay. My co-authors—Ian of Pitt and Jacques of Carnegie Mellon—were faraway in Pittsburgh, while I slaved on the paper's revisions. True, they had helped, but I was the first author and so I needed to carry the lion's share of the work. I constantly changed a paragraph here, a paragraph there, wording here, wording there, the list of references here, the list of references there, the statistical evidence here, the statistical evidence there, the figures here, the diagrams there. It was rough, time-consuming, and tedious, although I admit that once you "got the taste" for research, it became extremely engrossing.

But I was also struggling with teaching, which added even more stress. Dealing with undergraduate students who were more interested in taking bathroom breaks and cafeteria runs than learning something was one thing. And working with graduate students for the first time, who cared more about their grades than (again) learning something could be a real pain in the butt, and distracted me from doing research. Indeed, with teaching, I could "turn it on" and "turn it off," in the sense that I could shift into "entertainer mode" and clown around in front of my students, and then "downshift" back into researcher mode once I left the classroom. Then I would close the door to my office, sit in front of the computer monitor, and be left alone to play with data on a statistical software package or write my latest article on M&A Waves. I think that's what I really wanted at the time, to be left alone in my office to just do my own thing.

Well, in any case, I really enjoyed what I was doing, what with M&A Waves, power law distributions, and complexity theory. And I had done it for two years in Hong Kong. But then a professional bomb was dropped. In spring 2012, the head editor of *Academy of Management Journal*, emailed me a formal decision letter:

> Dear Dr. Park:
>
> I am sorry to be the bearer of bad news. I wish the situation could be more optimistic at this time. Upon the recommendation of the associate editors, I have decided that there is not enough support for your paper titled, "Riding the Wave: Distributional Properties of Mergers and Acquisitions Waves."
>
> The editors felt that the statistical evidence for your paper was still too weak for there to be empirical support for the theory you presented. Specifically, the second addition of a larger set of M&A waves, N=42, gave the impression that the data set was largely subjective and not impartial enough to provide solid support.
>
> I regret to tell you that your paper has been rejected at this time, and no further revisions may be made to it from this point forward. I wish you all success and achievements in your future endeavors.

I was crushed. How could this happen? I had put so much effort into the paper, especially with the last revision, that this decision was the least expected outcome. Jacques and Ian both agreed it was quite a pickle we were in.

At a meeting of my colleagues from the eight government-funded research universities in Hong Kong, I told them of the third round rejection of my paper. One fellow at Hong Kong University of Science and Technology told me, "Jason, listen, you have got to allow yourself no more than two weeks to be depressed about this, and then you have to move on. No more! Just two weeks. I'm sorry to hear about that."

We were all in the same boat. Hong Kong was far from the U.S., which was where all the academic action was. North America was the center of the dominant management research paradigm, as well as for most other academic disciplines. It was very frustrating to feel as if I were outside the general parameters, and not inside the constraints.

Hell, maybe I should have stuck up a middle finger and screamed out a general "Fuck You" to the editors who were not on my side, and then just let it go. But instead I emailed back:

> Dear Dr. Skylar,
>
> Many thanks for your decision. I and my co-authors are naturally disappointed that you did not view our work in a more positive light. The limitations of the empirical support which you pointed out are merely part and parcel of this type of research done in complexity theory. It is not a drawback that the data can be seen from more than one empirical perspective. However, we accept your opinion as final and appreciate all your efforts on our behalf.

I just couldn't get over it. I had made a serious commitment to make this article work, from the first essay, spending three years during grad school on it. After putting all my research eggs in one theoretical basket, I was back to square one, with an untested pipeline of similar manuscripts, and no others. Now I was eating the words of the scholar who once said, "Have a range of manuscripts, from those low-risk and high-acceptance, to those high-risk and low-acceptance, as well as those in-between. You need both types to get yourself through with a career."

At least, now I understood.

* * *

CHAPTER 11

# The Big Break

Personally speaking... well, that was the other type of bomb that fell on my life. The break-up of my engagement occurred in May 2012, soon after the academic year had ended. When Priscilla left for Pittsburgh after her second visit, I wrote an abusive, abrasive email attacking her personal character, accusing her of sabotaging our relationship, and wishing her ill in her professional life. I guess I felt that she deserved to be browbeaten for putting me through that hellish visit because of a misunderstanding over an email. She obviously had no remorse for putting me through the financial and emotional tolls I went through just to please her. For example, I had bought her the plane ticket, and had her holed up in my apartment, and had bought her dinner more than once at a fancy restaurant. The more I thought of it, the more I couldn't stand our relationship. It just didn't seem fair or equitable (assuming you considered relationships as tit-for-tat agreements).

After Priscilla had read my email, there was a teary-eyed farewell.

"Why, Priscilla? Why do you want me to call it off?" I asked gruffly. But I already knew the answer.

"Jason, I guess I'm just not the one who makes you happy... let's call it off, OK?" she begged me.

With that, I felt the weight of Fate press on my shoulders. There was nothing I could do to change her mind, I suppose.

"All right, then, fine." I said roughly, in a matter-of-fact tone of voice, as if it didn't bother me one damn bit, and as if I were genuinely cross with Priscilla.

"Oh, God!" Priscilla cried out in pain and anguish.

This had been coming for five years, essentially, since 2007, when we first met. Of course, it did bother me like hell, so the next day I called her cell phone so that we could talk on Skype. It was the middle of the workday on Wednesday in Pittsburgh. I had no sense about me. I just frantically wanted to see her and talk to her.

"Priscilla... marry me, please!" I hollered out loud as I broke down crying in front of the computer screen, blubber and snot clogging up my passageways. It was a strange feeling, as if I were forcing myself to make a show of it all, as if I didn't trust myself to just break up as Priscilla and I had done the night before. It was as if I had to make a big deal of the whole break-up.

Priscilla was teary-eyed again herself, and she said to me, "OK, Jason, I understand how you feel. Honestly, I do. Please try to calm down, and know that we will always love each other, OK? That's the important thing about our break-up. All right? We will always love each other."

This time it was my turn to sniffle. "Hmm, OK, I get it. We will always love each other," I phrased out loud.

It was a heartbreak, for sure. While other people go through break-ups, this was a five-year-long relationship and it broke down during the engagement phase, after I had given her my grandmother's two-carat ring, one that had been appraised at US$70,000 and the solitaire diamond was of the highest color, clarity, and cut, on a platinum band, six pronged.

Whereas before, in the first break-up conversation with her, I was angry, this last time I was hurt. A gamut of emotions ran inside of me: pain that we had said, "Till death do us part," but not genuinely so, jealousy that someone else might get her attention after our relationship, and shame that I had spent so much effort on the relationship to make it work, and now everybody around me was going to be gossiping about my failure as a potential mate.

That's how it ended, as a long-distance relationship. Perhaps I should have ended it when I left for Hong Kong. After all, I was a great catch to a lot of women in Hong Kong, and I should have taken the advice that other individuals who had been in long-distance relationships gave me, that they don't end well. I knew that Mom and Dad had thought I needed a companion, and they viewed Priscilla as a good woman. But I guess she wasn't the one.

I can be quite the jerk when I'm inadequately medicated and manic. And now I can tell that at that time I was inadequately medicated, because I *was* taking medication but it just wasn't working for me. I also upset my brother Gerry and my dad around this same time, with abrasive emails, Skype phone calls, and other forms of communication.

As I look back at the break-up, I realize there was nothing that I alone could have done to resolve the situation. I could not have willed the situation into a better one. Once the medication and (adjunctive) therapy regimen fails to treat my bipolar disorder, which is essentially a chemical imbalance, it becomes extremely difficult to reason with me to get on a medication regimen that would work. I essentially have to be captured and subdued, before I will return to baseline. It is not a good condition to be in or around.

* * *

As fall of 2012 approached, I decided to explore other treatments. I first cut ties with my therapist, Ms. Tsing, who had managed to catch my ire. She had once described how a former client of hers killed herself and blamed it on Ms. Tsing in a suicide note. So as I sat there, despondent with my bad luck with Priscilla and the way my career was heading, I quietly uttered to Ms. Tsing, in a monotone: "Hi Ms. Tsing. Your dead client's inside, here with me. Would you like to leave a message? I'll make sure she gets it."

Ms. Tsing herself quietly implored, "Oh, Jason, I'm so sorry you feel so angry with me."

But that was the last dialogue I would ever have with her.

With Dr. Xi, in our last meeting in his office, I cried out loudly, so that there was no chance he couldn't hear, "Please help me, Doctor! Won't you help me, please?! I am falling apart!"

But when it came to Dr. Xi, it was of course too little, too late. He wanted to put me on Effexor again! I had already taken Effexor with Dr. Diego, and it had made me nothing but extremely irritable.

My professional and personal lives were starting to crater, and I needed my therapist and psychiatrist to do more for me. So over the course of that summer of 2012, as I looked for a new treatment team, I switched between three or four different psychiatrists. Again, the lack of a strict regimen of talk therapy and medication compliance with committed health care providers was detrimental to my care. As a full month went by without my committing to any one particular psychiatrist, I became exasperated with the situation, and I was breaking down mentally. I finally decided on Dr. Fung, in the dead heat and soaking humidity of early August, a month before school was scheduled to begin.

During the first time I called the main office line for all physicians including Dr. Fung, I asked the operator aggressively: "So how much does Dr. Fung charge for his session?"

The lady replied in a brilliantly refined British accent, "One thousand dollars."

To this I screamed a litany of foul language. "One thousand dollars? Are you serious, one thousand friggin' dollars? You got to be crazy, lady! You're all a bunch of jerks..."

To which the operator yelled back at me, still in refined British English, "Sir, if you don't calm down, there's nothing we can do for you. I do not appreciate being called a jerk. Just stop it, right away."

At that point, I calmed down, realizing that the receptionist had power over me, and that I had just crossed a line. After all, I understood that secretaries and administrative assistants are very powerful in organizations.

I got the appointment with Dr. Fung, dressed up like a professional, wearing an ivory linen suit, a black belt around my waist to match my black boots, a white dress shirt, and an ivory Panama hat with black headband on top of my head.

And so I waited in the waiting room. And I waited. And I waited. Then one of the operators told me to go one floor down and wait there. So I did. And still, I waited and waited and waited. A few people passed by in the hall, but no one came towards me. Another hour went by. I felt like bursting at the seams, but another part of me just wanted to wait some more, since I had nothing else to do that day, and I was afraid of what kind of outburst I might deliver to the operator and other innocent victims around me. And then I told the operator I was going home and that was that.

I got back to my apartment on the twenty-second floor of Harbourfront Horizon, depressed and disillusioned. I had gone all the way to Central Station on Hong Kong Island, from Kowloon Peninsula, all profusely sweaty and borderline smelly, only to wait for three hours, and for nothing? What kind of nonsense was that? I too was upset even to be upset.

Well, the next time, which was a few days later, I spoke to Dr. Fung by phone and explained my situation. Apparently word of my tiff with the operator with the British accent had gotten around the office. I had made an enemy of the wrong person, and now Dr. Fung had to calm the situation down in order to get me an appointment with himself. Apparently, it was a lot more effort than it would have been if the tiff had never happened. Oh, well.

I made an appointment with Dr. Fung for the next week, resulting now in a seven-day wait which seemed to last longer than I could ever possibly have imagined. My anxiety grew and grew to a fever pitch in anticipation of the meeting, and yet at the same time, I couldn't have been more death-struck from the boredom I felt during that week. Finally I took a cab there. There was no way I would have survived a subway trip to the Island from Kowloon.

When we finally did meet, I was beset by an aging, white-haired Chinese gentleman with friendly eyes and a sense of joy about him. I wish I felt the way he looked. I myself was dressed again in the linen ivory suit, replete with Panama hat and black boots to contrast with the ivory tone. But while I looked like a million bucks, I felt short-changed in the feeling category.

He told me that he had heard about my conflict with the secretarial assistant. I apologized, I told him, but I was severely under duress. He understood, he said, and asked me for my diagnosis. I was ready for him, with my leather attaché case. I pulled out a sheet of paper, which contained the diagnosis from all the way back to Western Psychiatric Institute and Clinic. I handed it to him, and said as I began to cry, "Everywhere in the world there is pain, and the only option for me is to go to North Korea now," as I made no sense whatsoever.

Dr. Fung asked me to lie down, and he massaged my shoulders and back. "Now Jason, tell me, what medications are you taking?" I let him know.

"You know, Jason, I'm not a big fan of polypharmacy. You know, taking lots of different medications at the same time? Let's try to get you down on a cocktail of less dosage and less medications."

He had me try Saphris, which was speedy and made me feel woozy. I soon told Dr. Fung I wanted to try something else. He suggested another mood stabilizer. Upon starting the regimen I felt better, indeed less speedy of course, but I still felt psychologically fragile and weak. I was getting worried because we didn't have much time to experiment with different medications anymore, since the summer was closing and the fall of 2012 was about to start with the new academic semester. So I leaned hard on just that one medication.

"Pretty good, eh?" Fung remarked offhand. "I bet you haven't been on just one medication before, right?"

He smiled at me. I smiled back, but inside of me, I was so concerned. Again, I had fooled a psychiatrist from understanding the realities of my mood disorder.

* * *

As fall 2012 approached I was struggling with my mental health condition since I couldn't find a particular psychologist. That was until Dr. Fung recommended Dr. Ryker at the Central Station subway stop on the red line on the Island, the same area where Dr. Fung's office was located. It was a claustrophobically crowded area of town, where you would go for drama and action, but the kind of place you would run away from if you disliked close quarters.

I climbed up a steep hill and up the steps to Dr. Ryker's office building, just catty-corner from a semi-outdoors flower shop that I was told to look out for. As I pulled one of the glass doors to his office building open, I felt the blaring chill of processed air-conditioning, and proceeded into the metal-framed and wood-paneled elevator which *whooshed* me up.

I waited amongst the greenery of the plants in the waiting room for Dr. Ryker. His secretary kindly registered my presence in the office.

"Hello, young man! And who are you here to see?"

"Oh, I'm here to see Dr. Ryker at 2 PM."

"I see. Well, you're early, which is good. I'll let him know that his two o'clock is here," she said in a singsong Chinese-British accent.

And fortunately for my lucky stars, I didn't flip out on her.

"Hi Jason, it's good to see you!" greeted Dr. Ryker as he came out of his office.

He gave a firm handshake.

"How are you, doctor?" I said tiredly, trying hard to make eye contact.

With concern, Dr. Ryker responded as he led me toward his office, "Come right this way."

Soon I plunked myself onto his black leather couch, while he paced in his black double-breasted jacket and blue jeans and black oxfords.

"So why don't you tell me about yourself for a minute."

Now this was all fine, in the same manner I had done with Dr. Frances and Dr. Diego. But the problem was, school was two weeks away, and I couldn't achieve any meaningful progress in that time.

In other words, it was too little, too late from Dr. Ryker too, who kept talking, without allowing me many words in edgewise. Sure, he did ask me to talk about myself. But I was too weak to take control of my talk-therapy, and he triggered unhealthy emotions when he pontificated on subjects I would bring up—whether talking about controversial Chinese-Korean-Japanese relations, or mentioning the news that a boat had capsized with all passengers aboard, and that Dr. Ryker himself was one of the civilians who had helped lead survivors to shore. It seemed as if, in Dr. Ryker's eyes, "All Roads Led to America," and that was where I would be taking his stories. My mania was starting to punch upwards through my medication baseline. Once these "breakthrough symptoms" were no longer contained, I would be floating uncontrolled and ungrounded into manic territory.

* * *

I had just started teaching again that September of 2012. But I was abusing my power as a teacher. Instead of being a benevolent scholar, I began chasing students out of the classroom and yelling and hollering at those who were not part of my class but were using the computers in the lab. I was also castigating colleagues by email, sending pompous, asinine messages that included personal attacks, character assassinations, and veiled threats. I had planned to collaborate with two colleagues as consultants to an outside client. But from the comfort and distance of my apartment, I ordered the client by email to write me a check for HK$1,000,000 and in so many words to "get lost."

I finally got sick of myself for making waves, because the Dean of the Business College and the Head of the Department sent me a joint email one day after yet another tirade I had emailed to another one of my colleagues. The Dean and Head both asked me if I needed help, and said that they were standing by, willing to do so, if I would agree to meet with them the next morning. However, I was terrified, in my paranoia, because I thought they were out to "get me." So I emailed to both gentlemen:

> Dear Dean Kwak and Dr. Waite,
>
> Thank you for your email and your gracious offer of assistance.
>
> With this email, I submit my resignation, without reservation, effective immediately, from my post as Assistant Professor of Management in the Department of Management, College of Business, and City University of Hong Kong.
>
> My time is up here. There is nothing more I can do to be of service to the Department, College, or University. I should make way for new blood.
>
> I continue to believe, despite the occasional evidence to the contrary, that China is a great nation, and that the Chinese people are indeed a great people. It is also my hope that, one day in the not too distant future, a United Asia will arise, to one day legitimately challenge, and perhaps overcome, the current worldwide hegemony of the United States. Only time will tell.

I have no idea what I will do next, but chances are my travels will lead me back to the United States. As I tell my students, I say to myself now: Forget about the past, focus only on the future.

In closing, thank you, Dean Kwak and Dr. Waite, for the opportunity to serve, with my small talent, from my humble station, an organization from which I have received so generous a protection.

Respectfully submitted,
Jason Park

Before I submitted this resignation email, I ensured that my bank account received the last HK$80,000 for my monthly salary. It was October 2, 2012, a day after the September payday.

The next day, my now-aberrantly mercurial personality led me to a music store at the Festival Walk shopping mall, a place I had frequented to play the showroom pianos, much to the delight and rapture of the bystanders. But the salespeople would have a habit of interrupting my playing, ostensibly to get me a practice room, but maybe also to get me to stop playing the showroom pianos. In fact, what I didn't like after a while was the fact that they continued to offer me practice room #11, the one with a malfunctioning sustain pedal. I deserved better than this! Everybody should be cognizant of my worth and esteem as an artist! The grandiose thinking and paranoid delusions from mis-medication and ineffective talk therapy started to take effect in the fall of 2012. I felt that I was being exploited for my pianistic talent to bring in clients and sales into the store, and that I wasn't being properly compensated. Not that any of this made sense. If it had, I would simply have left to go somewhere else for my musical adventures.

One day in October 2012, shortly after my resignation at City University of Hong Kong, I showed up at the store. I started playing aggressively on a grand piano, with Grieg's Concerto in A Minor, and terrorized the staff, including the diminutive salesgirl who was trying to help me.

I yelled down at her 4' 11" frame, screaming, "Why don't you give me a better piano to play on? I'm the best pianist here by far! Give me a damn answer, for God's sakes! Let me play the grand pianos!"

"Sir, I only..."

"What? WHAT? What do you know? Why am I talking to you if you're not in charge?"

Then the manager got in my face, instigating me to hit him. I knew who he was, a bespectacled pipsqueak who screamed at me in incomprehensible Cantonese. When I shoved him in the chest for good measure, he fell down backwards, laughing like a hyena, knowing that he had gotten the better of me.

The police were summoned to calm the situation down. The mall security had been called first to prevent me from leaving. I was taken to the police station in a squad car. I had quieted down considerably and even started crying, thinking of my dear mom, while she lived an ocean away, how she had told me that I have to think of myself first before anybody else. I was doing as she asked, standing up to that corrupt music store manager and his cronies.

I was placed behind bars in a holding pen, where they checked my messenger bag for any suspicious literature. They found nothing but some pamphlets of American travel-abroad student programs. I didn't bring any of my medication either; I always counted on myself to show up at my apartment in the evenings to take the bedtime dosages. But the omission had another purpose, I guess, just in case the authorities wanted to incarcerate me as a mental patient.

I had no criminal record, of course, although they did realize I was a professor and that I had some money: HK$80,000 a month, or US$10,000. So after interviewing me with some preliminary questions, they just let me go. I was let into the street, with my belongings, left to fend for myself on my own devices. After this, I grew concerned that they might make a sure legal case out of me if I tried leaving the country.

I also became concerned about the personal income tax that I owed the Hong Kong Internal Revenue Department. In Hong Kong, the government does not deduct taxes automatically from your paycheck. Instead, each citizen has to save enough money to pay their obligation. In my case, that would have been at a 15% tax rate, which is the highest income tax bracket. I knew that the IRD would send the notice, and I was worried, however irrationally, that if I tried to leave the country, they would prevent me from doing so, as if they would actually arrest me at Hong Kong International, or stop me from going to the gate. I needed my money, since I didn't have any savings whatsoever to speak of and all I had in my account was the US$10,000 that had just been direct deposited.

* * *

The next evening, on a Friday night, when I had all the time in the world to calculate inside that busy brain of mine, I snuck into a taxi from my apartment and traveled to the airport while wearing pajamas, with nothing else but my wallet and passport in my pockets. I gave the driver all of HK$500, even though the fare only came out to half of that. Now as I look back on the matter, it didn't make any sense as to what I was doing, although to me at the time, it made perfect sense, since I was grandiose, delusional, and paranoid. There was just a logic to it all, a logic that in hindsight I can still peer into and understand, because I was there the whole time: it all had to do with me. People were out to get me and I was a person of some importance, since I was involved with the police, the Internal Revenue Department, and City University of Hong Kong.

I got to the Cathay Pacific ticket counter.

"Hi," I inquired in a friendly way. The sales clerk met my gaze. "How much is a first-class ticket to Pittsburgh, Pennsylvania, United States?"

"Pittsburgh, Pennsylvania..." she said, looking down and typing quickly. "When would you like to go?" she countered calmly.

"Anytime tonight," I replied.

Her eyes darted up to meet mine, and then fell back onto the keyboard. "Could I see identification?"

Yes, of course, she sure could. I handed over my U.S. passport. She accepted it and put it down in front of her. Her hands were going a mile a minute. There was a pause in our conversation for about three minutes, although it felt like thirty.

"So," she said finally as she heaved a sigh of relief, "to go to Pittsburgh, you would need to layover in Vancouver and New York. The price for a single first-class ticket is fourteen-thousand Hong Kong dollars."

"No direct flights?"

"I'm sorry, no."

Calculating that figure and converting it to U.S. dollars, I realized I was still in the black despite the charge.

"OK, then," I chimed in with a devil-may-care look up into the ceiling.

"Method of payment, please," she half-smiled.

I took out my wallet and offered her my credit card with a US$10,000 limit.

"Here you go!" I said, feeling all big and strong, in a very weak way.

I stood there at the ticket counter for no more than fifteen minutes, although it seemed like twice as long as that, as if the young lady was typing quickly but still not fast enough. My mind automatically concluded that she was looking up my prison record, my tax status, and my employer relationship. I felt the need to show her my U.S. passport, and not my Hong Kong ID, since that could reveal details about me which I didn't want exposed. Despite my anxiety, it was no big issue; she prepared a ticket for me at HK$14,000, which she accepted my U.S. bank credit card for. The transaction processed and was successful.

Next, "How many pieces of luggage do you have?" She peered over the counter.

"None."

She balked: "You have no luggage? Are you sure?"

I replied in the affirmative.

Mystified, she gave me an odd stare, but the moment passed, and I was offered my first-class boarding pass and credit card receipt, and the passport back, too.

The young lady guided me to the entrance to all gates for all flights, and I told her, "Look, miss, they play a tough game, very tough, in Hong Kong. So what's the solution? Get your guard up, WAY up. And don't let it down."

She listened quietly against the buzz and background noise of the airport. Then the ticket agent looked up and said, her gaze meeting mine, "It's not that bad," as she began to smile.

I had wished that what she said were true, but it didn't seem to be the case, and I was so unbelievably unhappy that it wasn't. So with that farewell, I headed to the gate where I boarded my flight.

* * *

## CHAPTER 12

# Back to da Burg

I settled into first-class, just lying there on my side with the seat back, and then a stewardess checked on me to make sure things were all right. My mind was racing as I thought to myself, *Just get off the ground, Goddammit, and then I'll be safe from everybody chasing after me back in Honky!* They finally closed the door and pushed off from the gate. I was relieved that the Hong Kong Police didn't get me, relieved that the Internal Revenue Department didn't nab me, and relieved that the City University of Hong Kong didn't grab me.

Once the plane was off the ground, out of celebratory hysterics, I started howling like a hyena. I was hooting for joy. Everyone in first class turned around, alarmed by the sound. I screamed and yelled and carried on for the Good Lord's Hallelujah! The flight crew was momentarily upstarted, unsure of what to do.

One passenger said, "Jesus Christ, we've got a maniac with us!"

I settled down momentarily until I approached an Indian man sitting across the aisle, and bent over to him and whispered into his ear, "Sir, what do you think of a United Asia?"

And the man replied, "I'll get back to you on that, my friend. Interesting, very interesting."

Yeah right, really interesting. I can now imagine how helpless and out-of-control the crew must have felt with me among the passengers. Fortunately for them and me, I was just lying there most of the flight, even forgetting to eat, which again was a symptom of the mania for me. In that state, I find food repulsive in general. I lose my appetite and I lose weight. When I'm hypomanic, I watch my weight to see if there are any noticeable fluctuations. Weight may not necessarily be the most valid or reliable of indicators, but it may be a signal of something psychological that is off-kilter somatically.

* * *

We had a layover in Vancouver, British Columbia, Canada, where I nearly ran to get off the plane.

A crewmember objected, "Mr. Park, you still have your flight and your seat!"

To this I replied arrogantly, "Give it to someone else," as if I were Marie Antoinette saying, "Let them eat cake!"

I stood in front of the customs official, carrying absolutely no baggage or luggage, and he asked me what my business was as he looked down at my passport.

I said, "To have some fun."

He looked up, unsmiling. He picked up a phone and made a call.

Some other airport personnel approached, about a half dozen or so, and one pretty lady guard asked me, "Why do you not have any luggage with you?"

I replied, "I plan to pick up some supplies in Vancouver, and I want to smoke some Cuban cigars in Canada."

It wasn't working; curiosity turned into suspicion on their part. Another half-dozen personnel joined the party. Meanwhile I was starting to attract a lot of attention. People around me began to stare. Here I was, a bit cold because of the thin pajamas I was wearing, with nothing else on me except my wallet and passport, and I was not answering the questions posed to me by airport staff and security with any degree of rationality.

I was made to stand away from the officials, who huddled up and congregated in front of me.

Finally, one of the male guards, carrying a Glock in a holster which hung at his side, beckoned: "Mr. Park, please follow me." He gave me a reassuring smile.

"Jason is fine," I said grandiloquently back at him.

He was leading me back to the gate. I could only see a plane outside the window, and then I saw the counter, where about half a dozen pretty Asian stewardesses stood. I momentarily stopped in front of them, at the counter, looking side to side, back and forth, as if the sight of so many pretty young ladies could arrest me better than a cop with his handcuffs.

The security guard said good-bye to the stewardesses, and then he shook my hand. I had been taken back to the same plane I had been on from Hong Kong. My request to stay in Vancouver had been denied, but no one even told me that. The guard simply directed me back to the gate where my plane was, and I would head to the U.S. as originally planned.

"Have a pleasant flight, sir. Good evening," he said, with an easy smile. The guy seemed to be really happy to send me on my way.

You see, as in this case, various deviations and twists and turns in the flightpath of a manic bipolar individual are normal, to say the least—and I don't mean necessarily in terms of aviation, either. It may seem just like aimless wandering perhaps, to the rational individual, but to the manic bipolar patient it's not that at all; it's a significance-laden journey. There was a reason why I wasn't allowed into Canada: I was destined to stay in the U.S. and make my way straight for Pittsburgh. No deviance from the true destination would be tolerated, whether from other human beings or from divine intervention.

* * *

I had a layover in New York before Pittsburgh. From the local Internet café at John F. Kennedy Airport, I let Priscilla know by email that I was approaching.

"Hi Priscilla. I am currently in NYC for a layover for my plane to take off for Pittsburgh. The ETA is 9 AM today. Expect an email from me upon arrival into Pittsburgh International Airport. Best, Jason." No nonsense, all business.

I froze in that cold terminal for hours, which seemed like days, and I decided to cool off mentally, trying to think rationally instead of manically. Yet I couldn't really separate the two; they were fused together. I was convinced that my actions were within the general norms of social behavior.

Many people, like me, were standing, since the seats in the airport were full, and I must have stuck out among them because I wore only pajamas. But nobody seemed to mind...

after all, New Yorkers stick to their own business. All the while, the manic thinking kept me busy and soon I boarded the plane for "Da Burg."

* * *

On October 17, 2012, I landed in Pittsburgh International Airport at 9 AM EST, with nothing but the clothes on my back, like an immigrant refugee. It was cold and chilly there, a low-humidity cold that dried you out even in the mostly covered off-ramp. I stood there in my thin pajamas before forcing myself to trudge down the ramp, into the terminal and then into a Pittsburgh sports merchandise shop. There I purchased a Penguins T-shirt, Steelers sweatshirt, and Pirates shorts (waist 36", way too loose for me, leaving me to hold them up with one hand) to complete the look. Fortunately, I still had my Nikes on my feet. I also purchased a bracelet made of crystal and diamonds from Swarovski for Priscilla. And I bought a $300 pair of Bose headphones for Will. So thus equipped, I dumped my pajamas in the nearest trashcan and hailed a taxi.

I don't remember all the psychotic gibberish I was yelling into my taxi driver's ears, just some nonsense about ethnicity that the poor fellow had to swallow to earn his keep. I feel sorry that I did that to him.

"You know, pal, as an Asian, I am a member of an ethnic group, right?"

"Right!"

"But I'm also an American citizen, right?"

"Right!"

"So therefore I understand the plight of you African-Americans everywhere, who are members of an African ethnic group but are also American citizens too! Right?"

"Right!"

I couldn't tell if he got it or not. Of course, he had to agree with everything that this madman said, otherwise he might get distracted and crash his car. He must still be wondering what happened to that crazy Asian dude who wouldn't shut up all the way to Oakland.

* * *

I checked in at 10 AM at the Oakland Holiday Inn Express without a reservation or luggage. No matter to me. It was the best hotel to be in, as it was centrally located in the Oakland campus of the University of Pittsburgh which was adjacent to the South Side, where Priscilla still lived, and a short distance from Troy Hill, where Will was. I had money, so I decided I would get a new wardrobe. But before that would be some food.

I left to have a bite at my favorite Chinese restaurant on Craig Street, ordering fish fillet in spicy red oil with rice. The fish dish would awaken my appetite, and by this time I hadn't eaten in twenty-four hours. The feeling of my stomach gnawing upon itself needed to be addressed, even if I was manic. Within the time I had through the chill grey October afternoon to engorge on the fish dish, I gave the waitresses a $20 bill for a $9.95 meal.

"Keep the change, please."

"Are you sure you want to do that?" one waitress said.

The two girls looked at each other.

"Sure, and remember..." I waved my U.S. passport to them slowly, so they could see the front of it. "...Get your passports as quickly as possible," I admonished them. I figured they were green card holders, but I might have been mistaken.

Feeling that I had accomplished part of my holy mission in Oakland by preaching to these two ladies, I proceeded forth at

11 AM via taxi to downtown Pittsburgh, and the Omni William Penn Hotel.

Exiting the taxi at the awning to the hotel, I spied the nearby Brooks Brothers clothier. Once inside, I showed the salesperson my $10,000 balance inquiry, as if to reassure him that I had the money. Why would I do that? Anyhow, the salesperson, Alex, a British chap, directed me towards beige wool slacks, a wool navy blazer, a blue button-down oxford shirt, a cordovan leather belt, a pair of cordovan penny loafers, and some conservatively grey dress socks. I changed into all of it, put down my debit card, and threw away my Pittsburgh Steelers, Pirates and Penguins paraphernalia in the dressing room.

As I was about to walk out, wearing my new purchases, I heard the manager cry out to me: "Why are you just throwing away your clothes like that, Mr. Park?" She had apparently seen the dressing room.

"Here," she insisted, "take your merchandise in a bag of ours," but I didn't want those street clothes anymore. I was a cocoon in street clothes that had flowered into something beautiful in dress clothes. So I left without the offered bag.

"I'm sorry but I can't afford to carry anything around with me."

Next came a walk around 12 noon down Penn Avenue towards the Harvard-Yale-Princeton Club on Cherry Way. It wasn't that far away but I only vaguely remembered how to get there. Soon I was able to manage to see the colonial red brick architecture. After walking through the entrance, out of the corner of my eye I caught sight of two individuals, a man and a woman, leaning up against a mini-bar, opposite to a grand piano perched in the corner of this entertainment room. Immediately I walked in and laid down two twenties on the countertop, which apparently had the two individuals completely taken aback. They were somewhat stand-offish, and looked as if I had just crawled out from under a rock.

"So why are you here?" the woman spat out, looking askance at me.

"What are you here for?" the man pressed me for an answer.

"Nothing," I replied to both of them in the same breath. "I'm just here to see what's going on."

Little did they know that I was a Harvard Club member from across the continent, and that I knew people at this particular club.

"Do you know who Dr. Esther is?" I shot back at the woman.

"Do you know who Mr. Yadon is?" I interrogated the man.

"Yes," they complied.

I immediately turned my attention to the piano, which was in a state of disrepair. I began playing the "Maple Leaf Rag" by Scott Joplin. I moved forward through the piece and ended on a high note. I heard talking somewhere else in the club, a man's voice, while the two interrogators left the room. I got up to leave, noticing that they hadn't taken their twenty dollars each in tips. I left the money on the bar, as a parting shot to this snooty couple who needed it more than I did, for sure.

I walked over to a woman in the backroom of the main floor office, where she was peering at a computer monitor, and I asked her where I could get Internet access. She told me to go to the local library branch.

I then headed for the Carnegie Library of Pittsburgh, arriving around 1 PM. Once there, I was given rather trivial advice on how to use the computers. I got up on my Gmail account, where I found an email from Priscilla explaining that she had received my email sent when I was in New York.

"Jason, I got your email that you were in New York, headed to Pittsburgh. What do you want me to do now?"

I emailed Priscilla back that I was currently in town and wanted to see her later that night.

"Hi Priscilla, meet me at the Union Bar and Grill at the corner of Craig Street and Forbes Avenue in Oakland, at 6 PM. Don't be late."

I also emailed my dad that I was in Pittsburgh. "Hi Dad. I'm in Pittsburgh now. I should be here for the next couple of days. I look forward to seeing you." But the otherwise innocuous message belied a menacing tone, one which sought satisfaction in a duel, much like Darth Vader and Luke Skywalker. After that I didn't wait much longer for a response from either Dad or Priscilla.

The computer workstation felt claustrophobic. There were people to the left and right of me, and I suspected them of glancing at my emails and stealing my login habits. One man to my right kept sighing as if in relief, at about the same time I successfully logged into the computer. I suspected that he had been watching me fail to log on the whole time, and now he was tracking my progress. Paranoia! The old woman to the left kept shaking her head, as if she had read my emails and was reacting to their emotional content. It didn't occur to me that maybe all she had was a tight neck, which she was massaging. Oh my irritability! I logged out, to conceal my tracks.

* * *

Around 2 PM, I headed past the Harvard-Yale-Princeton Club, continuing onward to the William Penn Hotel, where I asked the bell captain for a taxi. He whistled shrilly for a cab, which sped up right over to the curve in a burst of yellow with black trim.

I got in and told the cabbie, "Roberto Clemente Drive in Oakland, please!"

He signaled his acceptance of the ride right away, "Sounds good, partner!" and we were off! How exciting! Back and forth, crisscrossing the city, every which way! At a red light, approaching our destination, the driver turned to show me something.

"Oh, holy moly," I exclaimed in admiration. It was a large-size full-color high-gloss photograph in a magazine of his favorite model of a Harley Davidson motorcycle, a "hog," all stainless steel chrome, and leather trim, painted with orange, yellow, and black and red accents.

"Yeah, that's the one! That's my baby. I'm saving for it!"

I could tell how much he was in love with Harley's.

"I'm impressed by your passion, man," I said as we settled for the fare together. "Good luck!"

"You too, bro."

I appreciated his well-wishes.

We got to Roberto Clemente Drive just outside Mervis Hall, my old haunt, on time and without incident. I tipped the cabbie generously: thirty dollars total for a twenty-dollar trip. We acknowledged each other's mutual acquaintance, and he sped off to places unknown, while I was stationary, all dressed in my Ivy League sack suit, standing outside in the brisk cold of a Pittsburgh fall.

At 3 PM I went inside into the climate-controlled atmosphere of Mervis Hall to see Abigail in the Doctoral Program Office. I had my hopes high that I would see her, and they weren't dashed: there she was, sitting behind the desk, with her blonde hair, blue eyes, and red lipstick! Abigail was on the phone, however, as she usually was, chatting it up with who knows whom, her hubby, or her daughter. Still, I sat there while she gave me a pleasant look and mouthed, "One minute!" to me. But one minute it wasn't. It was more like five minutes. So I left.

* * *

At the Union Bar and Grill, around 5:30 PM in the evening, I sat down at the horseshoe bar and asked for a ginger ale with ice. I told the waitress to keep the $20 I gave her for the $3 beverage. She complied, smiling all the time. I texted Priscilla on my cell phone to meet me there, as I opened the bracelet case and looked inside, to also attract attention around me to the nifty gift I had bought for a lover. I kept turning around to the entrance of the bar, and looking back behind my shoulders, until it was 6:05 PM. Then lo and behold... Priscilla popped up through the entrance, and took a vacated seat next to me to the right. She seemed cautious and guarded. I had left Hong Kong under mysterious circumstances. *Why is Jason here? Isn't it the start of a new semester at City U?* I slid the bracelet case over to her, and made her observe the brilliantly shiny rocks and stones. She held the box gingerly. I was trying to explain to her how I felt.

"Priscilla, dammit, we have a lot to talk about. I'm just so unhappy with what happened between us. There has got to be a better way. It's not fair to me or to you. What do you think, dammit? I'm so pissed off right now. Can you tell I'm really upset? Can't you?" I wildly gesticulated, as the patrons at the bar took turns staring at me.

One person sat down to the left of me and laid down his credit card at the bar. There was nothing unusual about that, right? But I glanced at him suspiciously. A sense of paranoia began creeping all over me. A sort of master plan emerged half-formed inside my brain: I must talk to Priscilla in private!

"Priscilla," I said, sliding over to her a spare keycard, enclosed within a paper sleeve with the hotel number and hotel name listed on it, "I'll see you real soon."

* * *

I got to my hotel room around 8 PM, where it was nice and toasty warm. I waited for a sound from the door, as I sat in my navy sack suit from Brooks Brothers, at the desk by the warm lamp light. I didn't want to lie down on the bed and crumple my new clothes. I waited and waited and waited. *It doesn't take this long to walk from the U Bar and Grill to the Holiday Inn Express!* I thought. But after about thirty minutes, I heard a quiet noise: a whirring sound to the door's unlocking mechanism. The door opened inward, and of course, there was Priscilla.

"Come in." I continued to be harsh in tone with her.

"OK," Priscilla said and entered.

As she sat down on the edge of the bed, I continued to stay at the desk, my back to her. Then I turned around and faced her, not sure how to handle my emotions.

"Dammit, Priscilla," I said as I raised my voice.

She remained motionless, looking at me.

"Dammit, Priscilla!" I screamed this time. "How could you do this to me?"

She looked stunned, as if to say, "Done what?"

I clarified for her, "You left me all alone in Hong Kong! You left me all alone there to die!" I started to scream: "Get out!! Get the fuck out!!!"

I motioned toward the door, as tears started to stream from her eyes. And she left slowly but surely. I watched her reach the door and close it behind her. And that was that. I felt in my mind that a temper tantrum was simply for good measure, but in truth it wasn't necessary. Why would I yell and scream at the woman I had been in love with for the last five years? It didn't make sense. My reality was skewed.

So my next step? Blow off some steam, I guess.

* * *

I headed for the South Oakland underbelly of the campus around 9 PM, an area of land blighted by condemned dormitories and underage-selling beer distributors. I walked into a bar—didn't matter which, they were all the same—featuring a bunch of guys sitting down on their bar stools, all typing away on their phones, while the waitresses behind the counter stood up all night long and poured the drinks. The interaction between the guys and girls was placed in sharp relief: the guys had the liberty of getting drunk off their orders, but only if they tipped the girls well enough to garner good service.

In any case, I got into a tense conversation with two drunk idiots at the bar. After I asked for a bottle of water from the bartender, I said to them: "Where are you guys from?"

The fat one looked at the skinny one.

Then, over the din of the satellite radio, the skinny one yelled out, "We're from around here. What about you? Where are you from? Where did you come from?" He had asked me those questions as if I had just crawled out from under a rock. I thought he was trying to corner me verbally.

"From the good ole U.S. of A.!" I screamed back aggressively, shoving my passport at his face so that he could see the gilded eagle and United States letters.

Their cover blown, the two slinked out of the bar.

I motioned toward the bartender and then said in her ear, "Wow, I'm glad those idiots finally left!"

She giggled nervously, as if unsure of what had happened, even though she was witness to it. Damn, I must have looked out-of-place in that bar in South Oakland, dressed in an Ivy League sack suit. What a strange juxtaposition it was, my looking as if I had just come from a meeting with the Chancellor, and the bar looking as if Mick Jagger and the Rolling Stones would suddenly pop out of nowhere and do a mean rock n' roll gig. I sat there with my bottled water, with nothing to do except examine my passport and look at a bunch of guys at the bar, with the exception of the pretty waitress. So it wasn't long before I ventured elsewhere.

* * *

CHAPTER 13

# Free Fallin'

I was riding in a taxi on Pittsburgh's South Side around midnight, where the Smithfield Street Bridge connected with Carson Street. I decided to go to Mario's, a premier hangout in Pittsburgh, and sat myself down at the bar, which was sparsely attended by guys sitting on stools. The waitress, a heavily tattooed young lady, asked me what I wanted.

"Bottle of water, unopened, please," I stated as if I hadn't said anything unusual. Who asks for their bottle of water unopened, as if there were a contamination going around? For some reason, I was concerned that alcohol might be laced with the water if it were an open bottle of water. Geez...

I went momentarily to the ATM in the front entrance of the bar and withdrew $300, the maximum, while I checked my account balance: $8,000. I showed this to the same waitress.

"I just want you to know that I want to open a tab with this debit card with this allowance," I said matter-of-factly.

What was I thinking? If the bartender knew the excessive balance on my account, wouldn't that motivate her to overcharge me for everything I purchased? But it didn't matter to me. In fact, I started ordering cigars from the humidor, buying drinks for everybody at the table, purchasing their food orders, selecting "La Bamba" on the jukebox to sing along to a newfound Mexican amigo sitting a couple stools to the left of me... Soon I was puffing away on the Cohiba stuck in my mouth, chomping on chicken fingers and downing bottled water, and chumming it up with a million new friends out of anybody and anyone who happened to walk in to the establishment.

Pretty soon, 2 AM was approaching, and the bar was closing, so I got off my tail, and told the tatted up lady: "Hey, when I look at you, I don't see a waitress, I see a very beautiful lady. How about it? Can I buy you a drink, maybe?"

"Well, I'm already in a relationship, I'm so sorry, but thank you." I think she was scared of me.

But I smiled. "OK, sure." And I walked out of the brightly lit bar to the dark, chill night.

Now that I think about it, what business would I have with a heavily tattooed woman who works in a bar and is up at two o'clock in the morning? I guess I dodged a bullet on that one...

* * *

I then went to a Holiday Inn Express at 3 AM on the tail west end of Carson Street, and asked for a room. I was exhausted, but even in my room, I couldn't sleep. I kept lying there in my sack suit, penny loafers off, jacket on, for I had been freezing in the October chill. I don't think I even bothered to turn up the heat, because I wanted to do something, be where all the action was, and not be held up in my room.

I put on my uncomfortable penny loafers and went downstairs back to the lobby and walked inside the computer room to do some emails. I found some peace in reading emails, even though I had no sense in writing them. Dad had emailed. He stated that he was in Pittsburgh at the Holiday Day Inn Express in Oakland.

I immediately caught a taxi for 1700 Harpster Street in Troy Hill.

The cabbie asked, "What business you got in Troy Hill at 4 in the morning, man? Sounds like some serious shit."

I repeated to the cab driver what I had learned about Hong Kong, but only modified it for the current city. "They play a tough game in Pittsburgh, very very tough. So get your guard up, way up. And don't let it down for a single instant."

"Jesus Christ," the driver reacted, a black guy with dreads. "Sounds like you got a pistol on you, huh?"

"Oh, just keep driving, that's all I've got to say..." I kept him in suspense.

He rounded up the hill slowly, now just a block and a half short of 1700 Harpster.

"Hold it, this is good," I told him. I didn't want the driver to track my movements close to my destination. I didn't want him to know where exactly I was going.

"Don't worry, I'll take you all the way there," he said, seemingly worried.

"No, I got it," I insisted.

"Dude, you got a murder-suicide on you going on or what, man?" he beseeched.

"I'll be all right," I assured as he slowed down to the 1600 block of Harpster.

I remembered from memory where I was going, and knocked on the door of 1700 Harpster. Nobody answered, although the door was unlocked, and moved upon touch. Surprised, I swung open the door and walked in, to find Olivia, Will's wife, lying asleep on the family room couch, covered by a red, heavy wool blanket.

"Olivia," I called out quietly, "Olivia."

She replied sleepily, "Yeah... what?"

"It's me, Jason."

"Oh, hi..." she murmured, rising from her deep slumber.

"Hey, uh... is Will here?"

"What?" she woke up quickly.

"Will," I repeated. "Is Will here..." It was now more a statement than a question.

"I don't think so."

"Um, that's not good."

So it's 4 AM or so, and my boy wasn't there. So I went out to hail a cab once more, and was off to the races again, this time back to the Holiday Inn Express/Oakland, where my dad was.

* * *

After arriving I started joking with the staff at the Holiday Inn Express, tipping them a hundred dollars each from the two trips to the ATM that I made for a total of six hundred dollars.

I told the young black lady at the front desk: "You know, hon, if you're African-American, life is hard. And if you're a woman, life is hard. But if you're an African-American woman... Life's a DAMN BITCH!!!"

To this, we both cracked up hilariously.

I went back to my room and I lay there on the bed until about eight o'clock in the morning, when out of the blue the phone rang.

"Hello?"

"Jason!"

"Hi, Dad!"

"How are you?" Sounded all upbeat.

"Good, Dad. Where are you?"

"I'm in the hotel and do you want to do breakfast in the hotel restaurant in thirty minutes?"

I said, "Sure."

Nothing seemed to be amiss; breakfast with Dad was simply the next thing to do on my busy schedule. So I soaked in a hot shower for fifteen minutes, patted myself dry once I got out, brushed my teeth, put back on my sack suit, and went to greet Dad at the lobby. It didn't occur to me a bit odd that he was in the same hotel I was in, in Pittsburgh. Anyhow...

Priscilla and Dad were both there for breakfast in the lobby level restaurant. I made sure to sit on the outside of the booth, sliding in next to Priscilla. The conversation seemed to go well enough. Both of them were amiable and didn't seem to act as if anything inappropriate had happened...

"So now I remember the Pittsburgh weather!"

"Me, too," chimed in Dad, with a smile. "Very different from Southern California."

"Haha," Priscilla demurred, "I remember Hong Kong and Los Angeles. But I like Pittsburgh weather. It's got character!"

After my third trip to the buffet, I said, "Excuse me, but I have to use the restroom." I got up to leave. But instead of relieving myself I rounded the corner and beelined straight for the front entrance where the taxis were.

"Quick, take me to the Marriot out near the airport!" I yelled to the taxi driver, a culturally refined, professionally groomed Bangladeshi man.

After the forty-minute drive, and once we had stopped at the hotel entrance, I exclaimed, "Thank you thank you thank you, sir!" as I reached out my hand and handed the driver a $100 bill, and insisted he take it for a $50 trip, even though he initially refused. Silly, silly, silly... but I wouldn't take it back from him.

I asked for a room once I got there. It was $250 per night without a reservation but I took it, and without any luggage. I noticed a grand piano in one section of the lobby. That's when I knew they had planned for my arrival! There was a conference in the nearby ballroom, outside of which the piano luxuriously reclined. My interest was piqued. I went to the Internet room and made copies of Jean-Philippe Rameau's "Musette en Rondeau," a slow graceful piece. Armed with this information, I returned to the piano. I sat down, placed the sheet music on the stand, and commenced to playing.

This attracted the attention of the guests, now outside the ballroom, where a gourmet breakfast stand had been placed: yogurt and granola parfaits, breakfast cereals, hot cereal and oatmeal, Cream of Wheat, muffins and rolls, sausage and bacon, breakfast potatoes... you name it, they had it.

But I wasn't interested in the food. I was more intent on securing the approval of the conference participants moving this way and that around the eatables. And there was seeming enjoyment from the music. Even staff momentarily took a break and traveled away from the front desk to hear the lilting melodies and harmonies. But then the doors to the ballroom eventually closed, the staff resumed their posts, and I moved on to the Internet room again. Given the opportunity, I downloaded Rameau's "Fanfarinette," a mid-tempo piece. I nearly ran to the piano again and commenced playing.

At this point the staff came up to me and asked me to stop playing. I complied. Apparently I was disturbing the guests inside the ballroom. I purposely left the sheet music on the piano, went back to my room, and sat on the edge of the bed, trying to figure out what to do next. I decided to order room service, which was delivered promptly.

It wasn't long after when I heard a knock on the door. Opening it, I saw the police.

"Hi, are you Jason Park?" one officer asked.

"I am. Say, I ordered room service, would you like some?" I asked out of courtesy, and rather earnestly.

"No, that's OK," one answered, laughing.

I smiled, "All right, man." They left.

Then about five minutes later, another knock. It was the police again, a dozen strong, and this time they were with Dad, a grave frown on his face, and with Priscilla, openly weeping.

"Come on, Jason, let's go," Dad said seriously, way too seriously for the amount of fun I was having.

"I don't know what you mean, Dad," I angrily objected.

"I don't want any more nonsense from you, Jason. Let's go," he repeated.

"OK, fine," I said, knowing that the game was over.

And so I left with the police, Dad and Priscilla, all out of my own free will.

I only found out many years later, from Dad, that the police were there specifically to interject in the case that I were to become violently uncooperative with Dad's instructions that I be committed. Thank goodness that didn't happen. But then again, bipolar patients can be rational and talked with. The question was: *Would I be ready for hospitalization?*

* * *

I remember sitting silently in the back of the squad car, while the officers sat in front and the police radio squawked.

"Unit 2, please be advised two suspects in the area."

"10-9, I didn't copy."

"Two suspects seen in the area."

"10-4, 10-4..."

After the elation of my mania had worn off with my capture, I told myself that I should leave the officers alone. And so I did... for a while. But I wanted to connect with them, so I eventually reached out to them.

"Officers, there's something you should know about my situation."

"What's that?" inquired the officer in the passenger seat.

"You can choose your friends, but you can't choose your family."

"Yeah, you got that right. I think of my own family, too. I'm thirty-nine and my own family is messed up."

"Something else, too."

"Go ahead."

"Friends come and go, but family is here to stay."

The same officer breathed a sigh of understanding. "Well, that's true, too. You got to use what you have to get what you want."

But then, although I felt that the police officers and I could have talked more, I went quiet for the rest of the trip. I was tired, and I even felt like crying, because the enormity and severity of the situation had started to appear before me, like a ton of bricks and mortar falling from the sky onto me. But I didn't want to cry in front of the officers.

I could be charismatic when I was manic, and perhaps there was a kernel of truth and a rooting in reality to what I had said as well. But I was also charming in a manner that was superficially self-justifying, and more than a little manipulative. Ultimately, my manic communiques were psychotically skewed rather than internally consistent, and cynically self-serving rather than honestly objective.

* * *

During the police car ride, I helped the officer who was driving to locate the University of Pittsburgh Medical Center's Western Psychiatric Institute and Clinic.

"Where exactly is this place?' the officer wondered out loud. He had a sort of gruffness in his voice that belied his senior tenure.

"I think it's on O'Hare. 3711, I think," I guesstimated. The officer was silent, so I wasn't sure he was taking my advice. But we got there in the end.

I was interred at the Western Psychiatric Institute and Clinic, around the middle of October 2012, from the back of the police squad car. The cuffs were taken off, and I was hustled past the security guards, who were all surprisingly well-dressed in navy sack suits themselves. I had no idea what guards wore in "maximum-security" loony bins. But I was still taken aback by the Ivy League get-up. I had gone to Harvard, but they dressed the part. "Must be a uniform, I guess," I muttered quietly under my breath.

The last guard in the sequence spread my legs and raised my arms in body-search mode. There was nothing on me, except for my wallet. I must have left the passport in the hotel room. But no worries, Dad would find it. He had arrived in one of the other squad cars, went standing and spread-eagled, too. He had a tough time taking off his jacket, for some reason, which the cops found amusing. "Hey, this guy can't even take his own outfit off, ha-ha!" I found some grim satisfaction from their comments, as if I wanted others to deride and demean my own dad.

After the body searches, the police began to leave. Interestingly, the two officers who drove me to WPIC stopped to shake my hand before they took off, even though I warned them, "I'm sorry, but my hands are sweaty." But they still shook my hands: "Good luck, Jason." I guess they presumed that I was a good crazy, not a bad crazy, and a smart nutjob, not a dumb nutjob.

Then Dad and I were directed to a waiting room. To my astonishment, Priscilla suddenly appeared! She had been a team player herself, behind the scenes, unbeknownst to me until Dad told me years later. Priscilla had volunteered to help me be in a much safer and better position by working with me. She had also helped with logistical conveniences for my dad. She basically played the role of go-between between me and him. This was all done on her part because she knew the ins and outs of Pittsburgh better than Dad did. For example, where the Medical Center was located compared to the Holiday Inn, how the Pittsburgh police could be called closest to the point of need, when the traffic would be most congested so that a shortcut could be used, etc. All this, too, because Dad would have to be called back to Los Angeles. Pittsburgh was not his stomping grounds, but Priscilla's.

She also tried to work with me for getting medical help. Priscilla spent two entire fateful days away from her work and her family to help me, all the way from the beginning to end, at Western Psychiatric Institute and Clinic, despite all the ups and downs incurred. When a hospital staff member asked her the question: "Did Jason ever physically abuse you?" she answered no. To this day, I am still grateful to her for telling the truth. It was at that point that the hospital staffers decided that I needed long-term care.

That first day, we waited in a greyish white room, Dad and Priscilla sitting next to each other at the far end of one row of chairs, I at the near end and one row up. One black guy sat in the front row with his daughter, waiting for help for his child. He kept looking up toward the idiot box at Judge Judy, as he hatefully blared out that she was a white bitch who didn't know the meaning of justice, and commenting that the white bitch and the system which supported her "needed to go." He was full of hate and anger for society, and impatient for his daughter's treatment.

I got up and told his daughter, "Young lady, right now, your dad is the only man in the world who cares for you and loves you."

Then I gave my debit card to her dad, and said, "Sir, I want to give this to you, you can use the balance on it for your own treatment of your daughter."

He was startled, and after a pause said: "Oh, I really appreciate it, please pardon my language from before..."

I knew from my last account balance check that I had about $850 remaining, and although I had blown most of it in the last forty-eight hours, it was still a valuable parting gift.

Soon afterward, he and his daughter left the waiting room, only for my debit card to pop up in the hands of the staff member on call. Apparently the dad had given it back, or the nurses had confiscated it from him. Who knows?

Meanwhile, I saw Priscilla look down, with her hands in her lap, and she seemed desensitized, as if nothing were under her control and she had stopped resisting. But she was clearly terrified. How could she not be? Priscilla had never been inside a locked facility ever in her life. After about fifteen minutes, Priscilla whispered in Dad's ear and got up to leave. She had nothing to say to me.

Then it was just Dad and me, with a bunch of other crazies in the same room carrying on. One man got on his knees and put his elbows and hands on a chair seat, and started praying. Then all the aggravation and hatred I felt towards Dad, all the rage I could think of, came gurgling forth from deep in my gut and went all the way to out of my mouth, spewing. I screamed at the top of my lungs, "To hell with you, Dad, TO HELL WITH YOU!" while I gestured defiantly with my clenched fist.

One of the nurses, a bespectacled young lady who had apparently heard my outburst, came to me, pointed a finger and scolded, "Young man, can't you see that you have a wonderful family who cares so much about you?!"

To which I replied, "Oh my God, lady, you just lied straight to my MOTHERF—CKIN' face!"

Her eyes glazed over with shock behind her spectacles, and a dead fear darkened her glassy features. She disappeared into the labyrinthine maze of doors and rooms, never to reappear on the ward during my stay there.

* * *

CHAPTER 14

# Committed!

Within minutes of my last outburst, intake was ready for me. Dad and I went our separate ways, whereupon he returned to Los Angeles, and I remained behind for treatment. I was escorted out of the waiting room via elevator to the seventh floor, where they put me in the east wing of the corridor. There I met my treatment team, primarily consisting of Dr. Zachary, a psychiatrist, and Mr. Trevor, a LCSW. There was also a pharmacologist as well as Registered Nurses and other technicians. I appreciated Dr. Zachary and Mr. Trevor, although I wasn't sure they liked me. I got a good feeling from talking to them, and realize now that they must have suspended judgment about me. They were good-natured, and it was at WPIC that I learned of what they called the "therapeutic alliance" between patient and treatment team. "Therapeutic" since the goal is wellness. And "alliance" because the short-term interests of patient and treatment team converge.

I asked my friend Will from Troy Hill to pay me a visit and bring calling cards so I could call Mom in Los Angeles. Will very nicely agreed, and as I greeted him with a handshake, he had a strange gaze in his eyes. It was like a quiet, even stare. I stared back at him, as he peered fixedly into my eyes, as if he could see something in them, maybe even see my eyeballs quiver from side to side, up and down... a symptom of psychotic mania, maybe? He was looking into me and almost through me, it seemed.

"How are you, Will? Thanks for coming," I said as I cast my eyes downward for a second.

"Sure, Jason, no problem. Here, your calling cards," he told me as he extended his hand with the offering.

"Thank you very much," I said to Will as I pursed my lips. "So how's your family?"

"Well, Isaiah was involved in a car accident. He's recovering," Will explained about his son, who had been hit by a vehicle. Apparently there might have been some head trauma, but he was recuperating in the hospital. I was to find out later that Isaiah would be OK. Whew!

Realizing that Will's time was not my own, I suggested to him, "Will, how about if we use their conference room and I'll pray for Isaiah and you can pray for me."

So we headed to a small side-room with a rectangular table that could fit six people maximum: two on each side, one on each end. The room was painted a kind of wan strange yellowish-white, and the fluorescent lighting on the ceiling cast a pall over the table, which was a chipped wooden thing. Behind the closed door, which had a small window in it, we sat down opposite on the long sides of the table and clasped each other's hands.

Will began, "Good Lord, hear our prayer. Hear me ask of you that you remove my friend Jason of his illness... and that his treatment helps him recover... and that the doctors take care of him while he is here... let his family know that he is well-loved and that you, Jesus Christ, Our Savior are looking over Jason. In The Lord's name, Amen."

"Thank you, Will," I told him as we continued clasping hands. "Now my turn. Dear Lord, may your loving kindness and benevolence come to Will and his entire family, including his son Isaiah. May his afflictions be properly cured by his treatment team and good physicians. May you, blessed Jesus, keep the Devil and Death away from Isaiah. Bring life and prosperity to Will's family. Bring life and prosperity to Isaiah. In Jesus's name, Amen."

"Amen," Will followed.

"OK, now I have to get that $300 pair of headphones for you." It was the pair I had bought at the airport, with Will in mind.

At first the nurse-technician on call was reluctant to comply with my request. I had simply asked nicely, "May I have that pair of headphones of mine for my friend Will to take with him?"

And the nurse said, "Sorry, but we can't allow gifts to circulate between patients and visitors," which was a bunch of bunkum. It simply meant that he didn't want to get off his tired ass to look through my box of belongings. I sighed.

Then Will jumped in with some rough verbal prodding: "Hey, man, what the hell are you talking about, that Jason can't give me a damn gift? I have never heard of patients prevented from giving gifts. If it were a visitor giving a gift to a patient, that's one thing, but what you said was a straight-up lie. Now go find it!"

And with that, the nurse-technician, open-mouthed and pale-faced, left and within a minute returned with the object of interest. The tech handed it to Will, who said a simple, "Thanks," and then turned to me, ignoring the tech, who waited outside to escort Will downstairs to ground level.

I gave Will a loose hug and slap on the back. "Ha, good 'ole Will. Take it easy brother, and thanks for stopping by."

"See ya, Jason."

The nurses escorted him to the elevator, and to the ground floor, and I was happy to see him go with his gift.

* * *

What was intriguing to me personally, however, was my attitude towards the hospital confinement. In the beginning, when I first got to Western Psychiatric Institute and Clinic, I abhorred the possibility of being committed to a mental hospital. I just didn't want to be there. The surroundings were alien, the fellow patients were disagreeable, and the food service was always late. But as I progressed through the rehabilitation, things became much more agreeable. The doctor-patient relationship became less adversarial, the food began to taste better, and the patients became more collegial. In fact, by the time of my discharge, I actually wanted to stay at the hospital.

I guess the change in attitude could be chalked up to the fact that I realized toward the end that life was very hard "out there," outside the safety and security of the hospital. The hospital was the "safety net," even though at times it might feel confining. And it was almost as if the hospital staff were the mother hawks, and we patients were the baby chicks, and I was about to be pushed out of the nest in order that I could learn to fend for myself, in a harsh and foreboding environment, after the "pit-stop" of a hospital stay. I inevitably had to meet the whole bunch of patients who had been admitted along with me. We all were getting full and adequate treatment. There was Jessica who slept with a copy of Dostoevsky's *Crime and Punishment* under her bed. She only revealed her intelligence to the treatment team while putting on a show of insanity in front of everyone else. There was Megan, a heavyset young woman with a shock of frizzy blonde hair who liked to swallow toothpaste tube caps and ingest other small bits of plastic refuse. There was "Gabby" who, depending on the choice of outfit on any given day, was either "Gabriel" or "Gabrielle." And finally there was Jesus, the Vietnam vet, who would carry on to anybody and everybody who was in earshot that the Declaration of Independence and the United States Constitution guaranteed his fair right to being honorably discharged.

I myself wasn't any better than they were. The first night I was there, I smeared feces into a Styrofoam cup, out of dissatisfaction with the dinner service. I placed the cup on my tray, left it outside my room for the nurses to take away, covered the tray with my navy blazer, and waited—only to hear a shrill shriek of dreadful disgust: "RRRRRRRR-AAAAAHHHHHH!!!" from one of the staff nurses minutes later. "Ha-ha, I got them, ha-ha, I got them, ha-ha, I got them," I chanted diabolically while giggling to myself like a gagged hyena in my dark room.

In reality, I realize now that the act was not so funny, after all. It reflected a very low level of functioning on my part. But for some part of me then, it made sense to register my dissatisfaction with the "dinner service" in that way, because there was no other outrageously effective way to do so. And that was what I was doing: expressing my dissatisfaction with what people around me were doing for me, in the most grossly offensive manner possible. Obviously this kind of behavior would never be accepted outside the hospital. Even in the hospital, it would not be tolerated.

The next day, during a meeting that included me and Mr. Trevor, Dr. Zachary remarked, "Jason, we noticed some feces on your dinner tray. We want to know if that behavior will stop."

I meekly responded with a yes as I lay spread-eagled on my bed, a barely perceptible smile stuck on my face. *Well, enough's enough, I guess! Ha-ha...*

At first, I did not feel like getting to know any of the other patients, although I was excited to explore my new surroundings and to work on getting out—through my own recovery. With the girls I was more open to the prospect of trying to understand them and their particular problems. I didn't view them as dangerous or devilish—although they could be just as malicious and manipulative as anyone else. But unlike them, the guys tended to be somewhat quarrelsome.

I myself got into a rather violent wrestling match with "Gabriel" when he refused to stop picking on me after I took too many pancake syrup containers during breakfast service. "You motherfucker" this, "You motherfucker" that... He approached me just outside my room without going in. He had an evil grin on his fleshy pale face, and nothing seemed to faze him, as if he were hell-bent on picking on me until one of us were sent to "isolation" He started raising his voice, still snarling at me with that disconcerting grin of his: "What's the matter with you now, huh? Can't you see you're gonna die? I'm going to kick your ass...!" So I picked up my heavy, unwieldy armchair and wildly flung it at his head. The chair careened off the frame of the doorway, bouncing off the walls sideways to come to rest loudly onto the floor.

But that wasn't the end of it. Feeling that my honor had been insulted, and that I needed satisfaction, with a madman's energy I chased after Gabriel, and with all my might, picked him off the ground by his belt, cleared his entire 220-pound bulky body off the ground, and with a scream of white-hot rage, slammed his heavy frame into the dirty grey carpet and onto his side. I jammed his shoulder and his face into the ground screaming, "Say Uncle! Say Uncle! Say Uncle!" over and over again, while he murmured plaintively, under duress, "Get off me, get off me, get off me," over and over again. The staff spilled out of the central office of the corridor, came to me while I raised myself up off of the transvestite, and escorted me to the so-called "isolation chamber."

* * *

After consultation with the pharmacologist, and his own counsel as a psychiatrist, Dr. Zachary put me on a combination of two mood stabilizers, Lithium and Seroquel.

Lithium is considered the "gold standard" for treating bipolar disorder. It is a naturally forming salt, and generates low levels of toxicity for most patients. Still, because of the toxicity, lithium's levels in the bloodstream needed to be monitored closely. I was surprised that I had not known about lithium beforehand as a medication option. No one until Dr. Zachary had prescribed it for me. Even he was surprised by my lack of knowledge about it. I had heard a possibly apocryphal story that when Robert Schumann, the 19th-century musician's moods fluctuated abnormally, he would retire to the public baths in Europe, where the water had high levels of the lithium salt. This exposure is said to have relieved Robert of his mental stress.

As far as the Seroquel, it made sense to Dr. Zachary to prescribe it in addition to the lithium, since they are a common combination. Seroquel is a tranquilizer for psychiatric conditions, and it is often combined with other medications to treat and safeguard against the manias of bipolar type I (my diagnosis).

I myself hadn't heard of Seroquel before Dr. Zachary told me. But my treatment team had earned my trust and I wasn't about to refuse medication. That certainly would be one sure way of extending my stay in the looney bin far longer than I wanted it to be.

With a shrug of my shoulders and a non-committal "Sure, why not?" I agreed to the medication therapy and let the nurse approach me with a small white paper cup with two pink capsules of 300 mg Lithium and one round white tablet of 300 mg Seroquel. I placed them on my tongue, took the Dixie cup of canned orange juice, downed the O.J. with the medication, and off I was, to the races. And this continued for about four weeks, as the lithium and Seroquel levels rose in my bloodstream, and the drugs began to take effect on my mind and behavior. These psychotropic medications require monitoring over weeks, not days. They simply do not react immediately in the patient. It takes time.

* * *

It was approximately for fifty days that I was in WPIC. Towards the last two weeks I began to be preoccupied with a topic of interest to both me and my treatment team.

"So, do you think I'm crazy, Doc?" I murmured quietly, in resignation, somewhat anxious of what answer I would get.

"No, I think you're brilliant, Jason," Dr. Zachary responded, looking me dead in the face.

The man must have been joking, right?

I opened my eyes wide. "You really mean that, Doc?" I was almost frightened by the news, because it seemed as if anything I might say or do afterwards would cause the doctor to retract his statement.

"Yes, I do," he said back to me.

One of the things that had engrossed me as a patient on the ward was the training of the staff. There were doctors, nurses, social workers, administrators... what did it take for them to succeed at a medical center of excellence? This got me to thinking. Each specific staff member had a certain skill set for their particular training. Doctors had the M.D., nurses had an R.N. or B.S.N., social workers had an L.C.S.W., hospital administrators had an M.B.A., marriage family therapists had an M.F.T., and so on. But was it enough to specialize in just one particular branch of knowledge, in order to get ahead? To me, no. You had to have general knowledge and specialist training. In other words, colloquially speaking, one had to be "a jack of all trades and a master of one."

Which was why I couldn't understand why these various degree-holders didn't also know something about strategic management, which after all is a general management topic. Gaining value from every functional discipline seemed to me so important, so essential to doing business. Given the complex organizational dealings that the hospital staff were engaged in, they needed to know how to work in an organization with many different professional types. The education they would receive from even one core or beginning course on strategy would, in my mind, prove invaluable, so that they understood better the vision, mission and initiatives of the organization. I discussed this point with Dr. Zachary and Mr. Trevor toward the end of my stay. There was no easy answer from them.

Boy, did that comment from Dr. Zachary have a huge boost to my self-esteem at that point. Could you imagine? From smearing feces like an infant back to pontificating like a professor again.

I guess the trust issue was resolved—I trusted in the physicians' abilities to heal my bruised psyche, and they trusted in my abilities to be the conscientious patient. This resolution played itself out beautifully when they found out that I could play the piano well. Then came the initially half-baked idea of my playing the piano for the patients. It eventually turned into a one-piece recital for the geriatric ward on the eighth floor.

I was escorted by Mr. Trevor to the elevator and up one floor with nothing but my memory and my stiff fingers, which hadn't been exercised in months. But I sat down in front of the diminutive spinet and practiced a few scales in B-major, and a piano exercise from the "Hanon" instructional manual which I had practiced over the years. Then, after a pause, I began Scott Joplin's "Maple Leaf Rag." Immediately there were awakenings and reactions. Two old white men sat themselves down nearby and started chatting amiably over the din of the spinet. An old black lady who had been idling her time sitting on a bench a few yards away by herself began clapping her hands over her head, rhythmically and to the beat of the "oom-pah" of the left hand part. The nurses and technicians peered from out of the corner of the open space, wide-eyed in astonishment.

About midway through, my coordination of the left and right hands fell apart and I was forced to backtrack and pick up the beat again, throwing off the lady's clapping. I yelled out in upset and frustration for having played less than perfectly. I got to the closing bars of the piece and voila! I heaved a huge sigh of relief, elated that it was over and flummoxed that I had messed it up in the middle. Mr. Trevor, who had been sitting beside me, stood up to guide me back to the elevator.

As we passed by, the old black lady asked, "How many years have you been playing?"

I laughed it off with "Too many!" and she guffawed at my humor. At least somebody at the looney bin appreciated my "Maple Leaf Rag," if not a blueblood at the Harvard Yale Princeton Club!

* * *

On December 7, 2012, the staff decided to let me go. After careful determination, Dr. Zachary and Mr. Trevor decided that my time under their watch was up. Thank God! I had been in there for almost fifty days, and after the feces-smearing, screaming matches and wrestling fights, and what not, I was ready to get the hell out of there.

Mom came all the way from Los Angeles to escort me out of the hospital. So with a plastic bag on me containing a temporary amount of medication given by the nurse-technicians, she and I walked into the grey gloom of a Pittsburgh winter down the concrete streets to the local Holiday Inn Express.

"So where would you like to eat for dinner, Jason?"

"Oh, just the lobby restaurant is fine, Mom."

"Are you sure? We can always go somewhere nicer, you know."

"You know me, Mom, I'm not that picky."

"OK, then! Oh, and I brought some clothes for you."

"Thanks, Mom." I was gratefully delighted for this, since Mom knew that for me, clothes make the man.

It was nice to get a change of pace and scenery, to put it mildly, away from the government green walls of my hospital room and into a queen-size bed, a big improvement over the twin-sized ones at WPIC. However, it was the same Holiday Inn Express where I had been a manic psychotic for twelve hours prior to my hospital internment. I shuddered inwardly at the sight of the ATM tucked away in the hotel foyer corner, where fifty days ago I had withdrawn thousands of dollars for the hotel concierge and staff. But I soon brushed off such memories in a deep sleep, the first away from the lunatic asylum. After a night's stay, Mom and I took a taxi for the airport.

Interestingly, even though everybody else around me would soon register a big change in my character and personality, I didn't quite notice any palpable difference in myself at all. Yes, it was true that I was calmer and less temperamental. And I no longer felt grandiose (like in my manic moments), as if I were "chosen" with God's mission. But nevertheless, I wouldn't have stated in any measure that my recovery was complete. The hospital stay, despite the high quality of treatment, was simply a temporary reprieve, and I was still very fragile and frail. In other words, it was just a beginning. I needed a lot more help than what was given me during my fifty-day sojourn at WPIC.

* * *

CHAPTER 15

# The American Nightmare

I don't remember the plane ride to Los Angeles, other than it was calm for the full five hours or so, and that I was glad that Mom was with me. The last thing I needed was an explosive, full-blown temper tantrum, and in my newly medicated state, with a strong parental figure by my side, a tantrum was not about to happen. Even that little devil inside me that was my bipolar disorder knew that I wouldn't get away with it in an airplane probably populated with a few U.S. Marshals. So I wasn't making a thousand new friends, starting with my seat row or across the aisle. Nor was I intent on serenading the stewardess to join the mile-high club with me. Mom sat next to me, reading the flight magazine or just dozing off, then waking up to get some water from the flight stewardess. It was a very normal, low-key, even-keeled flight across the continent. And as it should have been, since I had been given a fifty-day temporary reprieve to work on my recovery.

Mom and I arrived at Los Angeles International Airport, and Dad picked us up. As I went to hug him, I saw how careworn his features had become. We went straight to Bel Air, under the setting sun of a chill, Southern California winter afternoon. It was while staying at their home that I learned Dad had moved quickly to secure an apartment for me. There had been debate as to whether Torrance or Koreatown would be my next stomping ground. Ultimately the latter prevailed. In Dad's estimation there wasn't much going on all the time in Torrance and it was geographically spread out, without easy access to anywhere without a car. However, K-town was geographically speaking much more centralized and compact, and people and places were more accessible by the public transportation.

In a matter of days, by mid-December 2012, I was situated near the intersection of Wilshire Boulevard and Vermont Avenue. My parents had chosen a small studio on the second floor of an old house turned into apartment quarters, with a common bathroom down the hall for each floor. The walls of the apartment had been slapdashed in a hurried manner, as if any color so long as it was white was fine. There was ancient, marked wood-paneled flooring in my studio, with a twin-size bed furnished with those traditional Korean-style thick and fuzzy wool comforters of a synthetic red-pink color. A rusty-rimmed, paned, grimy faux-French window led out to a tiny balcony with a view of the nearest Yoshinoya restaurant on the corner block, a view partially blocked by the adjacent house.

I quickly got in touch with my surroundings and made a general survey of the area. I learned to walk to places. For example, a thirty-minute quick-step would take me to La Esplanade, a convenience store with walk-in cigar humidor. (I had taken up my cigar habit since my move, but even bargain-basement cigars can add up to be an expensive habit.) Mom and Dad gave me a stipend of $200 a week. Rent, utilities, and the cell phone bill came out of my parents' pockets. With the $30 a day I was expected to feed myself, and with what little remaining, to find entertainment. I could even eat meals supplied at the apartment, but I grimaced at the thought of eating the piles of side dishes that sat all day long in the fly-infested kitchen. Besides, the food was mostly vegetables, like cabbage kimchi, white rice with beans cooked inside seaweed leaves prepared in soy sauce, and the like. But I didn't want to ask for more money. I knew my situation and I wasn't in a position to negotiate. I accepted my financial limitations and tried my best to work within the constraints.

Although at the time I didn't mind the roughness of the area, today I cringe at the thought of having lived there. It was a place strictly devoted to commerce, not a place for the finer things in life. From the corner mall liquor stores selling *soju*, whiskey, and Korean beer, to Mom-and-Pop restaurants serving B-grade all-you-can-eat *bulgogi* for $9.95 a head, there was nothing championing cultural refinement. I didn't go to the all-you-can-eat places. I guess it was because I was busy chatting it up with the young Latina cashier working at the nearby Yoshinoya fast-food joint. Of course, there was no real connection there. Or was there?

At this time, I was seeing a certain Dr. Sutton in his downtown Los Angeles office for psychotherapy. He was recommended to me by Dr. Iovina, who I was also seeing again at this time for psychiatry visits. Despite the change to Dr. Sutton, there was nothing particularly inspiring about my visits to him, other than the chance to dress up in my Hong-Kong-tailored three piece suits to visit his office's snazzy downtown Los Angeles neighborhood. And as far as returning to see Dr. Iovina again, she did not make any changes to my medication, other than keeping the levels of Lithium and Seroquel pretty much the same. And again, she would talk and talk and talk and talk until my appointment ended and I had grown weary of listening to her.

I had managed to get a year's worth of free Seroquel from a leading pharmaceutical firm, as part of its "good-faith" effort to not always only show concern for their bottom-line return on investment. It was not easy, though. I had to constantly send in fax requests for medication, and they would just as constantly renege on the promise until I got the occasional on-call manager to look into the situation. It was their way of screening out applicants, I guess. It was fairly unethical. I mean, "Don't break it out if you're not going to share" is the lingo I would use.

And let's face it: there were no real connections I was making in K-town. Whether at La Esplanade for a cigar, or Yoshinoya for a bite, the interactions were completely superficial dead-ends. So as I stayed longer and longer in my K-town apartment, I felt more and more isolated from family and friends. In fact, I felt my family had left me behind—had left me for dead. And the country I was raised in, America, had similarly thrown me out to the wolves. Between country and blood, I was starting to fall through the cracks.

I descended into yet another manic high in May 2013, six months after I had arrived in K-town. I started sending strange emails with semi-threatening overtones to Mom, Dad, and Gerry. Not long after this, I heard a knock on my door. After voicing my consent for the person to come in, I saw a tall, trim, red-haired police officer dressed in a dark blue uniform with a pistol in his holster stroll into my apartment with a ho-hum demeanor and ask, "Are you Jason Park?"

I nodded.

"Please stand up and spread your legs and put your hands behind your back."

I complied gracefully, saving my anger for later.

Another police office escorted me down the narrow winding staircase out to the sidewalk. I saw Gerry standing on the parkway up a little ways, pressing a phone to his ear. I muttered a litany of bad language specifically at Gerry: "You worthless motherfucking cock-sucking bastard." I hated him for calling the cops on me and restricting my freedom. The officer who was leading me away commented, "Awwww, don't be like that, c'mon now..."

In any case, the handcuffs were not taken off, and the officers and I made the short trip to the K-town police station. Once there, I was helped out roughly into a holding cell, with nothing but a knee-high metal shelf to lie on and a sink with push-down levers for water.

I lay down on the shelf, my head spinning. There was a strange buzz in the air, but it was more inside of me, not in the room. I couldn't get the buzzing to stop. I cradled my head in my arms, begging for relief. It was not an alcoholic buzz, like when the room starts to spin as you lie down to sleep. It was more of a heightened sense of awareness, a hyper-awareness that shone inside of me. Electric flashes of lightning lit up my skull from inside.

Suddenly, in a moment of clarity, I got up off the shelf—which was becoming uncomfortable anyway—and scanned the room. I noticed the camera lens in the upward corner of the ceiling. Sensing danger, I walked over to the sink and crouched down, looking for signs and signals. I peered into the sink closely, as if I could read fortunes from the dripping of water. It required great effort and concentration: I peered even more closely. Then I heard a noise behind me. The police officers had made their assessment and the cell door had swung wide open.

* * *

My family decided that I would be taken to Treatment Facility B in North Hollywood. It was a sad outfit, and I would soon be one of the veterans of this besieged institution. Dr. Miles was my attending psychiatrist. He bore the brunt of my bad behavior. To him I was rude, abrasive, quick to anger, and sullen. But there was a reason why I gave my physician hell. He was my only worthy adversary in the ward.

I treated the staff gingerly, even when my laundry went missing for the better part of a week, until I approached Miguel, the heavyset Latino working there.

"You know me, Miguel... just the laundry, NO QUESTIONS ASKED."

He got it right away, and after an hour my laundry reappeared. So maybe Miguel realized that maybe deep inside me, underneath all the layers of hurt, sullenness, and symptomatic abnormality, was actually a good person, trying to stay put.

Madeleine also received my best behavior. A blonde lady in her thirties, she was the RN on the ward, and although she caught me in a screaming match with Dr. Miles, she was always nice to me, and I in turn was very polite to her.

I remember telling her toward the end of my stay, "Madeleine, can I take you with me?"

She smiled and giggled good-naturedly at that bashful query.

The other patients, however, were... forgettable. There was another Korean-American, in fact, who was younger than me by twenty years or so. He was combative, manipulative, disagreeable, and antisocial—like me, I suppose, twenty years ago. I once passed to him an unopened juice carton out of good will, only for him to dismissively bat it away with the slap of his hand, unceremoniously sending it to the ground. Patients and staff kept their distance from him, and whenever he entered a room full of people, conversation died. He had no dignity or manners while scarfing down his breakfast, lunch, or dinner from the meal trays, and his face cast off an evilly ugly pall below his punkish shaved head.

Another fellow, Dalton, was seriously ill; he couldn't stop babbling. I couldn't understand what he was saying: "Ah-ee font-a font-era mar-ko bram-bee-lin hera-toko mar-eh..." I think he was mis-categorized as mentally ill and really should have been considered brain-damaged. To this untrained eye he was a dunce, and deserved gentler care in a hospital, not in a mental ward. At times he seemed to divulge hints of intelligence, as if he knew that his speech could affect others in ways that he could manipulate to his benefit.

I, in the weak state I was in, constantly barraged by Dalton's ongoing verbal drivel, would run to the hallway in my shorts and T-shirt, and yell, "Dalton, shut the fuck up!"

Sometimes he would stand just outside my bedroom door, going on and on about who knows what, as if to tempt me out of my quarters, and he would be there in the hallway wearing my clothes. How did he get my clothes? Obviously, the staff was playing games with me.

I would rush out of my door and challenge him to a duel: "All right, Dalton, let's go right now!"

But then I would feel ashamed of myself. Dalton would look genuinely terrified of me, rather than express the dunce's courage he would portray to me otherwise. And that's when I knew he had me, because I had lost my self-control, and I was really better off than him. Besides, I wasn't about to retake my clothes by jumping Dalton. For that, I simply asked very nicely and calmly for my clothes from the staff.

But staff and patients aside, it was Dr. Miles who I couldn't stand the most, because he was the one I was closest to the most, intellectually speaking. From his M.D., his black groomed hair, to his rainbow-patterned socks from Neiman Marcus, I couldn't stand that this guy had power over me. To my way of thinking, my dimmed and obscured Ph.D. was more impressive than his M.D. My once finely pomaded cranium had given off more wonderfully perfumed scents than his did. And my wardrobe had once dwarfed his... if only I had access to mine. But the fact of the matter was, I didn't have access to the finer things in life, and if I didn't comply with his wishes, then there was no way out of the hospital.

* * *

Things came to a hilt when there was a need to determine whether or not I should have a Conservator. It was a late September afternoon in Sylmar, outside the Courthouse, with a heat that wilted plants and sent animals into a motionless haze, unlike the stormy rainy tempest inside of me. I felt nauseated, as if some little leprechaun inside me was churning my insides with a paddle and forcing bitter bile and remnants of my past meal up through my esophagus. I was just waiting at a moment's notice to spew forth the putrefaction out of my mouth. And yet my head was surprisingly clear, as if during great stress there would always be "grace under pressure."

I sat next to my lawyer, an African-American bald male in his fifties, at a table which faced the judge's bench. My dad sat at the back of the room where the audience seats were. It was shameful of me what I did next: I rudely told my lawyer off, not once or twice, but a number of times.

For example:

"So what are you going to do for me?" I asked defensively.

"Well, I am going to explain what you're going through and how the judge can best help you," he replied, rather matter-of-factly.

He seemed to know the drill, as if mental patients were a dime-a-dozen to him, and that Conservatorships were things he churned out mechanically, as if on an assembly line, like widgets. But that perception of mine devalued my attorney's worth in my eyes.

"Then what do I need you for?" I demanded abrasively, and feeling despite the sick nausea in my stomach, that I had control over my situation.

"Hah, ahem, well..." the attorney sputtered, taken aback by my coarseness.

The bailiff called the court to order, and the judge, a blonde-haired young lady, sat on the bench. The proceedings began and I became lost in the shuffle of details, so I scribbled on a legal pad with a chewed up pencil as Dr. Miles sat down on the witness's chair.

He began: "The patient smokes cigars, and wishes to work as a cigar salesperson back in Connecticut..."

Dr. Miles went on in a pessimistic drawl, picking up the bits and pieces of what I had carried on to him about, and painting a negative portrait of me. He was not on my side.

Then it was the lawyer's turn. "My client is currently incapacitated in the Treatment Facility B in North Hollywood and is on a heavy dosage of medication..."

Again, not a very flattering portrait of his client, me, who just so happened to sit next to him. It was particularly excruciating to hear, but I had by now a thick skin and could handle myself.

I sat there, silent the whole time, carelessly scribbling away my own rebuttal on that legal pad of mine, when, all of a sudden, the judge addressed me.

"So what about you, Mr. Park?" she snarled, bringing me back to attention. "What do you have to say for yourself?" she continued, again, gruffly.

She came across as a woman who spent most of her time in the company of hard-charging men, despite her comely face and youthful good looks. I sat there with an insolent look on my face, as I straightened up my back, squared my shoulders, and cleared my throat.

"Your Honor," I intoned satirically, mocking the justice in subtle fashion. "This is my perception of how I see things, from my perspective…" I picked myself even higher in my chair, then continued: "…my Korean family has thrown me to the wolves, and my American country has left me for dead. Without support of either family or country, I am stuck in the middle, and thus I am falling through the cracks. Your Honor…" My voice rising to meet the emotional peak in the message, and then falling. "…I am falling through the cracks," I concluded quietly, clenching a raised fist, exhausted by the effort but remaining poised in my seat.

The whole court was silent. The judge was completely taken aback. Who was this young Asian guy talking about justice and family and country and about falling through the cracks? What insane clown talks like that? It didn't make sense that a mental patient would have that kind of poised perspective, and moreover, to express it in a packed courtroom. Why would a mental patient say something like that? Why didn't his own doctor see it his way? Why didn't his own lawyer see it his way? He was way over their heads.

"Now hold on, young man, no you won't," the lady judge responded, quickly recovering. "You won't fall through the cracks, trust me. You won't fall through the cracks," she replied, trying to sound matter-of-fact.

Now my dad approached me from behind and murmured some words close to my ear. I couldn't make out what he was saying. I turned around halfway, as if to register his presence but not his words: "Yes, Dad." I nodded and turned back around. I was feeling sick to my stomach. My face fell into a half-lidded gaze, peering straight-ahead, not sure if I were about to collapse or just vomit the remnants of my last meal.

The courtroom silently went back to its business. The lawyer just sat there next to me like a jackass and stared, expressionless, eyes and mouth open. I couldn't make out or read his mind. *Is he supremely impressed by what I said? Or is he completely embarrassed? Did I say something stupid that will put me in last place with the judge? Or did I come across as intelligent, to place me ahead of all the other courtroom cases in her eyes?*

In hindsight, I know now that the terms of the Conservatorship were still being hashed out, and that my dad was trying to be in charge of my finances, as is typical in Conservatorships. But the court decided against that. Things were getting worse for me. I wanted and needed my dad to be Conservator, but it just wasn't happening.

* * *

CHAPTER 16

# The LPS Conservatorship

I had no driving privileges at this time, and if I ever wanted to drive again, it would require being under the strict restrictions placed on me by the Conservatorship—a more restrictive eye exam, more difficult driving exam, stricter written exam, and extra fees for a driver's license. A person named Harry was made my court-appointed Conservator in October 2013. I knew absolutely nothing about the man, and I knew even less about how he was selected by the court. I met him in a Treatment Facility B conference room, and from that point forward, the rest of my days at that facility were in preparation for my departure. The RN, Madeleine, made sure that I had enough medication for thirty days, while the LCSW on call helped me with the exit paperwork.

Harry drove me to the nearest Houston's steakhouse in Pasadena, for trout and iced tea for him and Hawaiian Ribeye with ginger ale for myself. It felt so good to get out of that hellhole full of real lunatics, with me being the only sane one in the asylum—or so I thought. I was still struggling with my inner demons and wasn't really ready for living alone, back into Koreatown.

In fact, it wasn't until we got over there that I realized I had the same street address but a different room within the apartment complex: Apartment 19, not Apartment 15—again near the corner of Wilshire and Vermont. There was even less space in this already whitewashed room, even less character to an already characterless accommodation. Confronted by this grim change in scenery, I felt that someone had to be blamed, and not so much that someone deserved gratitude. Of course my parents, naturally, deserved to be blamed. And, of course, Harry too deserved to bear the brunt of it.

While the Houston's meal had been civil and humane, the relationship between me and Harry deteriorated quickly, with my move into Apartment 19. At a local Denny's bordering urban K-town, a far cry from the Houston's in the hip suburban center of Pasadena, Harry and I had a tense conversation later that day at dinner.

"Harry, I don't think you can handle the pitfalls and ambiguities of the Korean family dynamic."

I was certain of this, that Harry as an American would never be able to understand the enmeshed nature of Korean family relationships: their hidden agendas, their tenacious loyalties, their potentially violent ruptures. How could he see all that?

"Well, Jason, I don't think you have a damn clue who you're dealing with," Harry said rather matter-of-factly, as if he were rubber and I were glue, and that everything I said bounced off of him and stuck back onto you-know-who.

"Well then, I'll say good night to you, you damn jerk," I replied, leaving a plate full of spaghetti in front of me, as Harry tried to grab my hand to stop me.

"Hold on, Jason, hold on..."

But I stood up and went back to my apartment. My stomach was empty, and I was desperately in need of food, but I had made a show of not eating whatever I had ordered, as if I were on a hunger strike. I was battling the Conservator, the very guy who had power over me and who was trying to help me, the guy you wanted to be diplomatic to, not a jerk to.

Later that night, at about eight o'clock, as the sunset was shining blood-red rays into my darkening, unlit room, I heard a knock on the closed door.

"Jason?" It was Harry.

"Yeah, what is it?"

"It's me, Harry."

"Yeah, what do you want?"

"I just want to drop off your spaghetti for you."

"Just leave it at the door."

"You sure? Can't I say hi to you?"

"No, Harry." Emphasis on the last word.

"All right, Jason. I'll leave it for you at the door. Good night."

"Night."

* * *

Well, this situation wasn't going to last very long, as you could imagine, what with a conflicted Conservator-Conservatee relationship, medication non-compliance, and missed therapy appointments. I was supposed to take my Depakote along with the Lithium and Seroquel, and even though Harry had filled the prescription himself for me, from Dr. Miles's script, I simply wouldn't take it. I was willing to take the medications that Dr. Zachary had prescribed from Pittsburgh, but not the Depakote that Dr. Miles had prescribed. I didn't trust the guy because that pompous ass hadn't given me a reason to trust him. In addition, I was supposed to go to Treatment Facility C in Santa Monica as a group therapy adjunct to my private visits with Dr. Sutton, whom I was seeing again, but I was starting to fall off on the group therapy. I mean, I just didn't see the point of waiting outside my apartment to get into the hospital vehicle *qua* church van to travel down Wilshire Boulevard to yet another loony bin on the Westside so that I could engage in uninspiring group therapy three times a week. I can tell you why it was poor and inadequate treatment: because while under the staff's supervision, I became manic.

One day, I approached Bonnie, one of the case managers there.

"Bonnie, I have a girlfriend!"

"Oh, yeah? What is her name?"

"Kacee. She is beautiful."

"Great! How'd you meet her?"

"Oh, she's in the moon, she's in the stars, she's in the earth, she's in the sky..."

Bonnie peered closely into my eyes. Her face went from emotionally open and readily inviting to analytically probing and faintly alarmed. Something was amiss, it seemed like, although I wasn't sure what it could be. But that's me in manic mode. I can't judge or gauge the effect of my words on others. There's also grandiosity in my speech.

Within minutes, Bonnie had me sit down in a chair in another office at Treatment Facility C and talk to a nurse, who then strapped me into a wheelchair. I didn't protest. I was off on an interesting adventure. I didn't want to interrupt the festivities. The tech rolled me into the emergency room of a fully staffed hospital located across busy Wilshire Boulevard. They placed me on a gurney in the corridor of the hospital and gave me a food tray to occupy myself with, and I lay there, still and prone, as I listened to Kacee having surgery after being horribly raped. *Come on, Kacee,* I said to myself, *they're having you in the next room and I'm listening to all the bleep and burps of the machinery, as they put you back together from that most horrible of crimes...*

Of course, it didn't make sense. Why would Kacee be there, and why would I think that something like that had happened? I was manic with psychotic features, and it was getting worse, with my thoughts getting more and more skewed from reality.

Then, all of a sudden, Harry appeared!

He said, "Jason, what's up, buddy?"

Apparently the staff had been notified to contact him in the case I became incapacitated. He stood there, in the same corridor of the ground floor of the hospital, and I lay there in the gurney, as he and I conversed. I clasped his hand in mine to shake. But something was amiss. I immediately forgot about Kacee in the next room.

I began to bulldoze all over him verbally. "Harry, what the fuck do you want from me?"

"All right, Jason, calm down or otherwise I'm going to take you to a real hospital!"

"Here, pick it up!" I yelled at Harry after I tossed a bread bun from my food tray toward his chest, and it bounced harmlessly off him and onto the floor.

"Now eat it!" I screamed at him, pointing at the bread bun lying on the floor.

I saw out of the corner of my eye a young child apparently being led away by his grandmother as a result of my bellowing, coming out of the other side of a draped curtain, out of the corridor and out to the parking lot. Well, if you can't take the heat, get out of the kitchen!

Harry wandered off to the physicians' desk, where some nurses and doctors seemed to be conferring with him. *What could they be talking about?*

But soon after, there was some movement. I was placed on a different gurney, one more solid and painted yellow and red, and I was strapped in this time with my upper body tilted forward. I was rolled away slowly from the standing-room only crowd, who all seemed to be mesmerized and gossip-ridden by my situation. I was carted into an ambulance, and an ugly "dark night of my soul" began...

* * *

Via a three-hour ambulance ride, I was taken to Treatment Facility D in San Pedro, California in October 2013. I lasted seventeen days there. For some reason, I continued to refuse half of my medication.

I said to the nurse technician, "I have bipolar, which is a mood disorder, so I'll take the Lithium. But I don't have a thought disorder so why do I have to take the Risperdal?"

But that meant I only had half-solved the problem of correct medication therapy. Indeed, I had bipolar disorder Type I *with psychotic features.* So I remained psychotic and off-kilter while there. I also kept vomiting, and I soon couldn't hold any food down, even though I so wanted to eat. I went from 165 pounds to 140 pounds in a span of seventeen days. Smoking made me sick, so I gave my cigarettes away (although I suppose I made some friends at least). The smoking area was lousy: open to the cold air and chill Southern California winter rain, fenced in as if for wild animals, full of characterless concrete and old, rusty benches with the green paint falling off the wooden sections to reveal the nasty splinters underneath.

One time, I walked into dinner, covering the naked lower portion of my body with only a bed sheet which I held in place with one hand. For some reason I didn't want people to know my gender, so I treated the bedsheet as a dress, even though my upper body, which was covered, was a male torso of course. Strange. I used one hand to hold my dinner tray in place, while I used the other hand to hold up my dress. What an awkward situation!

My roommates' names were Sam and Kyle. Sam was a young man who was somewhat effeminate. He kept asking me to help him get out of the facility and to provide information that would allow him to do that. I decided to call him "Samantha" because of his weeny-whiny demands. Kyle kept saying that he was married to the American Olympic skater Kristi Yamaguchi, so I called him, "Mr. Yamaguchi." It was all I could do to keep myself going with some comic relief.

I even got into a fight at one point. There was a beautiful black girl at the hospital, a patient like me, who couldn't have been more than twenty-one or so. One time, during coffee service, a big black brother with dreads sat next to her, shoving her and slapping her, cursing her and cussing her out: "You damn bitch! You should be in here! Damn cunt! What, do you want a piece of me?"

To which the lady put up her bravest and most desperate defense: "Don't touch me! Leave me alone! You should be in jail! Someone help me!"

Everybody in the conference room cleared out towards the other side; nobody was coming to her aid. Realizing that I had to do something, if no one else would, I screamed out, in a sudden access of daring, "Hey, you jerk! Don't you dare talk to her like that!"

The big black guy with dreads, enraged, aroused by the easy pickings of my skinny frame and boyish features, sprang up and screamed out, "OK, let's go, you punk!!!"

He approached me and I leaned forward and put my head down, as he delivered five or six blows to my downturned nose. I heard a commotion and the nurse technicians flooded into the room, separating me from my opponent. A crowd of techs walked me down the hallway, half on my own willpower, half with the techs' help, while the 20-something girl walked along the hallway, pointing at me, and sobbing, "He was only trying to protect me!"

I blabbered through Kleenex given me by a tech, and affixed to my bloody nose with one of my hands, "I'm sorry, I just didn't like how he was talking to you like that..."

She vouchsafed for me to the nurses and doctors. And with that I was led away to take some X-rays of my nose. I returned eventually to my original surroundings. But the big black brother with the dreads was nowhere in sight, and I didn't see him again after our altercation.

There was a particular nurse technician who I didn't like. I thought I remembered seeing him showing off to a female RN a hidden medication which I assumed he had taken from the pharmacy. After that, it was no holds barred dueling and wagering.

One time, I asked him, "When is dinner served?"

Harmlessly enough, he replied, "6:30."

When it became 6:33, I started spitting in his face, constantly, over and over again, never-ending. Immediately the other nurses leaped into action, corralling me off into the Time Out Room.

They demanded to know, "Why did you spit on the tech?"

"He said dinner would be served at 6:30 and he was wrong!"

Then one of them commiserated, "Well, we do have problems with that, all the time, sometimes the meal service is late."

I replied smartly, "Yeah, it's a management problem of course."

So they let me eat in peace, without taking my food away.

* * *

I had had enough, when I realized that I could shit on everybody I wanted to, but like it or not, for better or for worse, I needed my family. So I told the staff I wanted to see my parents. Mom and Dad were called, and they dutifully came to the hospital, not sure what to expect.

They, along with some therapists, who were there at my parents' behest, sat in a large room to listen to what I had to say.

Dad started with introductions, then said, "My wife and I feel that Jason needs to show some willingness on his part that he wants to get better. We are trying the best we can to make sure he gets the very best care."

My dad was speaking from a rational, formal, arid place, and I was placed in the hot seat to show that I, too, was serious.

We were in close proximity to each other: me, Dad, and Mom, with our hands resting on a round white plastic table. In a sudden desire to connect, I reached out my hand and grasped Dad's in mine, as if to say symbolically, "Dad, I love you. And I need you." Mom saw this simple but significant gesture, started weeping, and murmured, "Oh, Jason." Dad seemed astonished, and his face softened (although he didn't cry... the man never cried). Then I reached out with my other hand and held Mom's hand in mine. Thus, we were unbroken, unified, a family trinity: Mother, Father, Son. And then the wheels began turning in my recovery. Hopefully. Happily. Healthily.

* * *

Dr. Sager, a psychiatrist, took over my treatment upon the end of my stay at Treatment Facility D. He met with me in person shortly after the one-on-one meeting I had with my parents. He told me he had traveled over four hours from his hospital office in Ventura to see me in San Pedro, so I realized, even in my agitated state, that he deserved my undivided attention. But I had butterflies in my stomach; I kept hopping up and down, pacing the floor, back and forth, sitting in my chair, then catapulting off of it, all the while begging Dr. Sager, "Please, Doc, won't you please let me go?"

And he would jovially remark, with a wry smile on his face, "No, Jason, we're not done yet."

In any case, I was able to get through the two-hour interview all in one piece.

Thus, at that end point, I asked, "Doc, so what do you think is next?"

He smiled and told me, "I think we're going to have some fun," and he cackled drily, while I did so good-naturedly, too.

That was it for Treatment Facility D. I was off to bigger and better things. The same nurse that I had spit on told me that I was heading to Calabasas for treatment at Dr. Sager's brainchild, Balance Treatment Center. In a final show of reconciliation, I extended my hand to the jerk nurse; he took mine in his own and we shook hands, as if to say good-bye to a mutually forgettable chapter in our lives. My departure was met with quiet fanfare. Either everybody at the hospital was simply relieved to no longer have to deal with me, or perhaps everybody was genuinely happy to see me graduate onward to the next stage of my recovery. Probably a bit of both.

* * *

CHAPTER 17

# Balance Treatment Center I

I can sum up the daily schedule of Balance Treatment Center in one word: *intense*. Here I provide a general outline of the everyday goings-on there:

| | |
|---|---|
| 7:00 AM | Morning wake-up call |
| 7:15 AM | Personal hygiene |
| 7:30 AM | Morning walk at Gillette Ranch Park |
| 9:00 AM | Morning medication regimen |
| 9:15 AM | Breakfast |
| 10:15 AM | Group therapy |
| 11:30 AM | Individual therapy |
| 1:00 PM | Lunch |
| 2:00 PM | Outing (to the mall, beach, park, or farm) |
| 3:30 PM | Physical therapy |
| 4:30 PM | Cognitive Behavioral Therapy |
| 5:30 PM | Laundry & sundry miscellaneous items |

| | |
|---|---|
| 6:00 PM | Dinner |
| 7:00 PM | Music therapy |
| 8:00 PM | Emails & Phone calls |
| 9:00 PM | Evening medication administration |
| 9:15 PM | Bedtime preparation |
| 10:00 PM | Lights out |

As you can see, the daily schedule was fifteen hours long—and there wasn't much deviation from that length. There were downtimes interspersed with periods of intense therapy. Three square meals were provided, although the kitchen's central location to the other rooms allowed patients to snack quickly on, say, cookies and milk between meals and sessions.

However, the components of the daily schedule were not permanent and unchanging, but underwent certain changes as I progressed through "stages" from Day 1 to Day 90. I will refer to these stages by thirty-day periods, demarcated more or less by various holidays of the year: (1) Days 1-30, from approximately Halloween 2013 to Thanksgiving 2013; (2) Days 31-60, from Thanksgiving 2013 to Christmas 2013; and (3) Days 61-90, from Christmas to the end of January 2014.

* * *

"Residence Induction" characterized the nature of the first thirty days of my stay at Balance Treatment Center, from before Halloween to Thanksgiving. I struggled mightily with everything that was placed before me. For one, I was highly symptomatic with anxiety, insomnia, fatigue, depression, mania, and psychosis. I was a hot mess. I would be tired during the day, and have trouble sleeping at night. My thoughts were scattered and my cognitive functioning was impaired. I was quick to anger and yet I was languorous most times. Meanwhile, Dr. Sager worked hard to regulate my medication regimen.

"So how do you feel?" he would ask during our thrice weekly medication sessions.

I told him honestly, "Like crap, doc. I feel like throwing up all the time, I feel weak, I feel down and depressed, at night I can't sleep and I'm tired all during the day. I can't sit still and I'm nervous, sir." As I leaned on the banister or railing, I nearly fell at this point from a highchair by the wet bar that was built into the living room. Regaining my balance in the seat somewhat, I continued, "The numbers 42, 52, and 62 are vital to my existence. I want to have a girlfriend more than anything else in this world. That is my goal."

Dr. Sager looked down at his notes, completely expressionless during my self-report. "What do you mean by 42, 52, and 62?"

"Well, 42 is the age I will succeed at anything. 52 is during the Korean War. And 62 is retirement age for some Social Security recipients."

"Hmmm. And you want a girlfriend. OK. Anything else, Jason?" Dr. Sager asked.

I pondered his question a minute, then added: "No, other than I just feel like crap."

I sometimes wondered if anybody was listening. But the Good Doctor was listening, very closely in fact. But still, to this day, I have absolutely no idea what he was listening for, or catching up on. It is a mystery, his art and science of psychiatry. But unlike some previous psychiatrists who had dialed down the medication, he amped them up, both in number and dosage. For the first time since my initial diagnosis, I was placed on two mood stabilizers simultaneously. No psychiatrist had ever done that for me before. At first I was concerned. *Isn't that dangerous? Isn't that too much medication?* But apparently not, because apparently I was a very severe case.

Dr. Sager put me on an "atypical antipsychotic," which targeted the scattered thinking and the psychosis that he first noticed that went along with the bipolar moods. Unlike a typical antipsychotic, an atypical antipsychotic has less chance of creating side effects in the patient. In addition, he added an anti-anxiety agent, to help me calm down and stop jumping all over the place. That horrible feeling of restlessness which didn't let me sit down began to recede, slowly but surely. And finally he put me on a medication specifically meant to counter the side effects of the other medications. That was very helpful, since the "restless leg syndrome" began to go away, slowly but surely, too. And Dr. Sager amped the dosages up considerably. I credit him with that, especially because despite the possibility of deleterious "interaction effects," where the ingestion of two different medications creates an unnecessarily stronger effect within the patient, he was still in command of his skill and knowledge in helping me avoid that.

* * *

During those first thirty days at the Center, in addition to the visits with Dr. Sager, individual, group, and Cognitive Behavioral Therapy were to play a very important part of the recovery process. I liked all types, I admit. We had the best therapists that money could buy at our disposal at the residence.

But I liked individual psychotherapy the most, simply because it provided direct attention to my problems the most. With my individual therapist Barbara, I tried to talk about my experiences with bipolar mania, specifically the one that triggered my flight from Hong Kong to the U.S. But there was not much time for discussion, because I kept interrupting my own meetings to get a drink...

"Excuse me, Barbara, but do you mind if I go get some water from the kitchen?" I pleaded, exhausted by my own strange antics.

"Sure! I would not mind," she agreed.

Or: "Of course," she chimed in.

Or: "Go for it!" she would approve, at least on the surface, as I would return to assume a reclining position on the floor, or to sit in my seat for about fifteen seconds before leaping out and into the corner of the room. Poor Barbara! But she took it in stride, and we continued this way only for the first thirty days, before the meetings became more productive.

Meanwhile, the group therapy meetings also provided some of the heavy-lifting for recovery. But they were embarrassingly uncomfortable in the beginning. I was constantly in movement, as in for example the following:

"Sorry, guys, can you excuse me?" as I rose to go to the kitchen to get a Styrofoam cup of water (but always closing the door quietly, at least).

"I apologize everyone, I hope you don't mind..." as I lay down on the carpet floor on my back by the sliding doors, to smell the greenery outside and get a whiff of fresh air.

Or, "Hey, I'm back, sorry about that," as I sat down on the comfy couches with my cup of water between my legs.

"Heh, um," as I paced up and down the length of the room. Very disruptive, but entirely unintentional! I just couldn't help my symptoms. This was obviously going to take some time...

And this was while the other three patients attending the session were quietly seated, listening to the therapist. At times, the therapist seemed more miffed by my behavior than the patients were. But I tried to make my actions as discreet as possible. I said sorry as honestly as I could to my compatriots, and that's how I spent the later part of the month of October going into November.

And we also practiced Cognitive Behavioral Therapy (CBT) as a group. CBT was a form of therapy that assumed that dysfunctional moods were generated by faulty thoughts, and that therefore to fix dysfunctional moods required changing the faulty thoughts. We did this exercise periodically, each one of us patients volunteering a dysfunctional mood and a faulty thought that influenced that mood.

It was a helpful exercise, although I thought out loud to Barbara: "If a mood is dysfunctional, why not take a shortcut and change the mood directly, rather than go in a roundabout manner and attack the thought?"

I never got a straight answer for that, other than: "Jason, a mood can't be changed unless the cognitive schema upon which the mood is anchored is changed."

Go figure. I was left scratching my head at that one. But perhaps my questioning was a sign that my innate intellectual curiosity was coming back.

While I was somewhat skeptical of it, Cognitive Behavioral Therapy turned out in the long run to be a boon. But while Barbara explained the CBT exercises to the group at this phase, all I could say was: "I could use a drink," and then I would hurriedly run out of the group room to the kitchen, and grab a chocolate milk carton or other drink from the fridge, only to rush right back to the group room and lie prone on the floor.

* * *

Learning how to get along with troublesome patients who brought their own issues to the table was what you would call "character-building." Even though Balance Treatment Center was only a six-bed facility, all it took was one bad apple to ruin it for the rest of us. For some strange reason, there was always one oddball who wasn't on the same page as the rest of us patients, and disorder would ensue. For example, there was Patrick, who physically threatened bodily harm on a fellow patient one time during group therapy.

"What exactly did you mean by your last comment?" Patrick asked while approaching fellow patient Neal in a menacing manner from behind.

Neal replied almost helplessly, as if he had to point out the truth to a hoodlum despite the chance of bodily harm, "I think that you are really in need of therapy and a lot of psychological help."

With that, Patrick shot off a chopping right upper-cut to Neal's face, just barely missing it. Everyone in the room picked up on that, including the psychologist Walter, who immediately ended the session and escorted Patrick out of the room to the nurse's station.

Even though Neal was willing to forgive the attempted bashing, Balance Treatment Center was not. Not only that, but Patrick's departure coincided with the disappearance of my nylon green laundry bag, which was given me by my family, the only laundry bag I had, and was of a nice quality. I fumed at the loss, but I preferred seeing him go than querying him about the disappearance. Maybe he would bop me on the nose, too. Patrick only lasted three days, and even he seemed to realize that he did not want to be reformed.

He said in our final group meeting with him: "I think that I don't belong at a place like this. I have my life to live first before I would fit in a place like this."

So after the near attack and with this attitude, Patrick was permitted to leave. He took his surfboard (and my laundry bag, I suppose) out of the residence and took off.

* * *

But opposite to people like Patrick were the visits from family, who were crucial to my recovery at Balance Treatment Center. They gave me a sense of belonging and harmony with family and with the larger community at a time when I really needed to feel that. The first visit from my parents was Thanksgiving 2013, about thirty days after my "residential induction" into BTC.

"Hey, Jay!" Dad effused as he got out of the car and saw me out on the porch, beckoning.

"Hi, Jason!" Mom cried out, as she closed the passenger-side door, smiling.

"Hello, Mom and Dad!"

The three of us embraced outside on the dry concrete driveway. We headed into the residence as the nurse-technicians watched us approach.

The chef on location provided the Thanksgiving meal. Everything was prepared. I couldn't have asked for better company, or for better food, especially when my parents had traveled all the way from Bel-Air to Calabasas, and the cuisine was transported piping hot from the kitchen adjacent to the dining room.

We sat down to eat. But physically I was still very frail, less than a month into my stay. I felt nauseous to my stomach, as if the seventeen days I had spent in Treatment Facility D beforehand had really done me in. At that place, in seventeen days, I had stopped eating, was throwing everything up, and had lost more than twenty pounds, down to about 140 pounds. And I am 5' 9". One hundred and sixty-five pounds should be my normal weight. I had not been 140 pounds since as a high school freshman. At BTC, my parents noticed my vastly diminished appetite.

"Aren't you hungry, Jason?" Dad asked with a smile. Mom smiled, too. Their smiles may have belied some concern on their part. I thought maybe they would be cross with me because I was not taking advantage of the opportunity to eat well.

"No, Dad, I just want to make sure you have more to eat," I joked with a weak smile, too.

I kept pushing around at the mac and cheese, the aromatic slices of turkey breast carved straight from the bird, the pile of mashed potatoes with rivers of gravy, the steaming cornbread stuffing coming straight from the oven, and the mountain of bright orange candied yams. It was so frustrating to be ravenously hungry with an empty stomach, but prevented by my own body from taking part in the feast laid before me. It was all a big tease, it seemed like.

But I was very happy to be with family. What if the holiday had passed and nobody had bothered to see me? I cannot think of a more demoralizing, lonelier experience than that, to blow the wind out of the sails of a recovering patient. Being with family meant that I had a meaningful place in this world, that I was esteemed and recognized in others' eyes, and that as long as I applied strong effort toward my recovery, I was going to make it. And I was happy that at least my parents were enjoying the meal, if not myself.

After the meal, our plates were taken, and my parents spoke with me briefly for fifteen minutes.

"So things are going well here, Mom and Dad," I assured them.

"Good!" Mom said. "Are you getting along well with the other clients?"

"Yes, Mom," I said, "they're good people. A little eccentric, I'd have to say, but still nice."

"Well, Jason," Dad said, as he and Mom got up to go, "we'll see you for Christmas, in a month's time."

"Great!" I said, already missing them, "I look forward to seeing you then."

We said as much by silence as we did with words. I watched their car exit the parking lot, and waved to them one last time.

* * *

Days 31 through 60 contained episodes of steady progress characterized by intense conditioning. Dr. Sager continued to meet with me three times a week, charting my progress each time and taking copious notes during my self-report, asking me questions, noting any detours or steps backward in my progress (which does happen with psychiatric disorders). I began to feel significantly better according to my own self-report by the sixtieth day. And I believe he noticed that improvement himself in his notes, based on what I said to him, and how I acted around him.

"42, 52 and 62 don't mean anything to me. I don't know why I said that those numbers are important. But they're not. All that matters is getting better. That is, after all, the only way I am going to get out of here, right?"

"That's correct, Jason, I am glad you see that."

Because Balance Treatment Center was a locked facility, I needed the approval of the attending physician (i.e., Dr. Sager) before I could leave into the general public. And that gave me a real strong impetus to put my best foot forward regarding the Good Doctor.

* * *

Psychotherapy, whether individual, group, or cognitive-behavioral, continued to have perceptible, though marginal, effects through Days 31 through 60. It was not as if it were not working. The metaphor I would use is "throwing as much stuff on a wall until finally something sticks, until the light bulb goes on inside the patient's head." In other words, there is a cumulative effect that is felt, but neither initially nor midway.

During individual therapy, I was now able to sit down in a chair comfortably for the full fifty minutes. This made conversation a lot easier, as you can imagine. Still, although perhaps I was not overly psychotic, I was still quite sick. Barbara and I would talk at times about nonsense things.

"I remember taking an Abnormal Psychology class in college, Barbara. I remember that there were five different schools of psychology that existed: biological, psychodynamic, cognitive-behavioral, humanistic-existential, and sociocultural. How many are there now, since that was the mid-90s when I studied them last?"

Barbara replied, "Well, when I went to school for my Marriage Family Therapy degree, there were eight."

I nodded. "Interesting." *No paradigm consensus, I guess,* I thought to myself.

Group therapy became more interesting as well as more constructive.

"Hi everyone, can I get anybody something from the kitchen while I'm there?" I'd chime in before exiting to where the food was.

"No, Jay, thanks, though!" other group members would pipe up.

At this point, I was capable of processing some simple thoughts and feelings, by way of listening to the problems of the other group members.

For example, Bryson was upset that his son had cut him a check for $10,000. I replied, "Bryson, what kind of son does that for his own father? A great son, because he loves his father!" Bryson began to cry, and we consoled him.

Then there was Octavia, who was in her thirteenth year of depression after the loss of her father. I let her know, "Octavia, you know that he is in a better place now. Don't grieve. He would have wanted you to get on with your life. Honor his memory and do that." And Octavia felt the emotional warmth in the air.

Cognitive Behavioral Therapy also started to make inroads on the process. It first required my sitting still for long enough periods of time until I could process the thoughts. Barbara tried to introduce the concept of "black and white thinking." For example, "black or white thinking" was a patently dysfunctional cognition that nevertheless mentally ill patients got caught up in. To further the metaphor, "shades of grey" better characterized the world we live in.

"Jason, can you come up with a thought that represents black or white thinking?"

I sat there opposite to Barbara, with the others in the group room, trying to focus my thinking.

But I couldn't do it. My cognitive functioning wasn't up to the task.

"I can't. I'm really sorry. Can you go to the next person? I'll think about it for now."

The process exhausted me, and as much as I might strive, I couldn't figure it out. But at least I could sit still in my seat!

* * *

Again, learning how to get along with other difficult patients was a lesson in distress tolerance, and might I say, character-building. There was Vincent, a seriously disturbed young man who had a habit of manipulating his environment and the people in it to his own self-benefit. He and I had to share the same Room D on different beds, and the association was not to my liking. First of all, he'd fall asleep with the windows wide open to the frigid mountain air. I simply closed the windows at night while he snored away. That was simple. But then I had put up pictures and drawings of Chinese calligraphy over the walls of the bedroom. Vincent apparently took it as an imposition on his personal space, so he threw his dirty wet underwear into my closet, on top of my shoes and on top of my own pile of laundry. One night, he suddenly rustled himself up from his space, wearing only underwear and tank top, and in a sleepwalk, posted his body at the foot of my bed and began urinating on himself. It really spooked me out. I ran downstairs to the nurse's station.

"Hey, uh, Vincent started sleep-walking and then he peed on himself at the foot of my bed," I said to the alarm of the nurse-technician.

I remember the tech departing for Vincent's and my bedroom, while I made small talk to the other tech in the nurse's station. By morning, this even had caught the attention of Dr. Sager right away, and the room cleaners noted a significant stain on the carpet next to my bed in the morning (evidence to corroborate my story). And that was all we ever saw of Vincent. They took him away the next day.

* * *

However, the family get-together during Christmas break was *much* better than Thanksgiving's! Same type of food, in general, but with an extra thirty days of recovery under my belt, I was ready to chow down. There was a whole turkey (probably 20 pounds), mashed potatoes with gravy, mac and cheese, stuffing, beans and rice, beef pot roast... ah, heaven! Mom and Dad were there, making the meal very special. There was nothing quite like seeing your own folks, seated next to you, talking quietly and meaningfully to you, all the while breaking bread with them. And again, other family company joined in on the table to make things civil and polite.

But my parents and my brother Gerry also focused on getting down-to-business: in family therapy. At first, Dr. Sager would facilitate these meetings, in the presence of Dr. Cave, a psychologist, and Barbara, a marriage family therapist. These meetings were not scheduled in advance, but rather on an "as needed" basis, as well as depending on the availability of my family members.

"Jason has proven to be well-motivated to engage in his treatment here at Balance Treatment Center," Dr. Sager would begin.

I would nod in assent.

"That's good, Ron," my father would express, while Mom would nod quietly.

Indeed, my brother Gerry threw himself in my corner, saying, "As long as the treatment is benefiting him, I think that is a good thing."

So far, so good, right? And it didn't seem possible that our progress could cave in at any point.

* * *

CHAPTER 18

# Balance Treatment Center II

The time after Christmas 2013 and into January 2014 was one of "preparation for departure via accelerated progress." And although the excellent care I received at BTC continued to the final days, I also realized that BTC would only take me from negative territory up to nominal baseline. If I really wanted to get from mental illness to mental health, I would have to shoot for positive territory. In fact, it would not be enough simply to deliver the moon. I would have to shoot for the stars.

My psychiatry visits with Dr. Sager continued to be progressive and therapeutic.

"Hey, Ron, how the hell are ya?" I would rather bombastically ask of the doctor, as if this were a drunken get-together at a bar. I shook his hand vigorously. There was a smirk on his face, as if the rather silly humor of this patient left no indelible imprint on his character.

"Good, good, um, excuse me," as he left temporarily to consult with one of the therapists, almost out of my earshot.

"So how do you feel, Jason?" Dr. Sager asked as he returned to my case.

"Pretty damn good," I chirped. I was in good spirits. "I haven't felt this way in a long time," I murmured, and truer word was never spoken.

"All right, I'll talk to you again later," he growled, with a smile.

I took his hand in mine, remarking, "I kiss your hand, Don Sager."

He pulled his hand away. I guess my sense of humor was returning.

Individual psychotherapy allowed the patients at Balance Treatment Center to expound on matters that were of a personal nature, in complete confidentiality. I got lots of positive unconditional regard from the licensed clinical social workers and marriage family therapists. Of course, it was not that my family could not provide that unconditional regard, but rather that the therapists had a degree and a license to practice therapy, which made them professionals in their trade.

I talked about my family's interpersonal dynamic: "You know, Barbara, my mom and dad, brother and sister-in-law, and my two nieces mean a lot to me."

There were more free-flowing conversations between me and the therapists, who were trained to give advice and offer counsel on family matters.

"My relationship to my family was always a big deal to me. Or rather, I made a big deal of it, and sometimes unnecessarily so."

"Do you often wonder, Jason," Barbara asked, "how you could doubt your family's love for you, after all the trouble, time, and money spent on your recovery?"

"Yeah, my treatment has been I'm sure really expensive, and I know it. Still, for some reason, I am angry, for some strange, unnerving reason at my family."

Dr. Sager wanted me to process this anger, nip it in the bud, and have done with it. He thought he had it well-medicated with the atypical antipsychotic. Yet we would see where the anger would take me, whether it would extinguish itself, or need further medical treatment. It turned out that this anger would continue to haunt me after my graduation from BTC.

"One of the reasons that I've needed unconditional regard from my family is the distress from the break-up of my engagement."

"How do you mean?" Barbara said.

"Well, the thought that things should be a certain way, but they are otherwise, the feeling of having a strong heart, yet still am heartbroken, the realization that I am by myself and that things did not work out... these were issues I needed help on."

"In other words, a general sense of deep imperfection."

"Right!"

There were also conversations I'd had with friends, who may have misunderstood the nature of my illness, and with whom I desired to redress grievances. Suffice it to say, individual therapy was exceedingly helpful for giving me my own "space" and allowing me to "stretch out" with my feelings, such as about those relationships.

Group therapy also got significantly more productive after Christmas. I was able to sit down for long periods of time, without disruption, and moreover, I could focus on the subject matter.

Sharing our personal stories in the company of others was a big contributor to the redeeming qualities of group therapy. There was apparently a lot of trauma in our lives, directly accruable to our families. One constant refrain for me was my troubled relationship with my father and sibling rivalry with my brother. Everybody on the planet complains of their childhood, I suppose, but it seems apparent to me now that bipolar patients really market this about their backgrounds. But the complaining and "getting it out" was only one part of the process of group therapy. The other part was the feedback obtained from the other group members. And the group members provided empathy by relating themselves to what I had gone through, while the facilitator, if he or she was good, would re-direct the conversation should it veer off course.

So, for example, I'd say, "I get so angry about my brother. The injustice, you know? He never had to deal with what I have. Good luck for him, but bad luck for me. He's building a house in Manhattan Beach for his family, while I don't even have a place to call my own."

A group member spoke up: "Jason, think about how large the mortgage payment must be for that house. And has your brother ever told you that you are not welcome at that house?"

"Well, I guess not," I thought out loud. "Yeah, he didn't, actually."

And another group member named Megan reminded me, "Who says you have to have kids, Jason?" She smiled at me, as if she were pointing out something so obvious it should have remained unspoken.

"Yeah, I guess," I said again, in an obtuse sort of way.

"All right, let's back on track," the facilitator chimed in at this point in the conversation.

So these sorts of quiet fireside chats did a lot to encourage psychological healing.

Also, during this part of the rehabilitation, Cognitive Behavioral Therapy started to pay dividends.

"Well," I said, "let's start up black and white thinking again, shall we?"

"OK, do you have any thoughts about what constitutes a black and white style of thinking?" Barbara proffered.

"Well, what about my mental illness?" I blurted out, after a furious attempt to come up with a coherent answer. "I think it's black or white, but it's really not. It's sort of shades of gray, right?"

"Yes, Jason, you could put it that way. What you're saying—and please correct me if I'm wrong—is that you're a high-functioning bipolar patient, perhaps because of your illness, not despite it. The illness actually gives you a competitive advantage as well as a disadvantage," Barbara went on, unperturbed, apparently not minding my change in bodily position, from sitting to reclining.

"Yes, that makes sense. So it is a veritable shades of grey... grey matter, in fact." I laughed out loud, gazing at Barbara.

* * *

A rather disruptive experience for my last thirty days at BTC was the appearance of Camille, a young lady in her 30s who screamed bloody murder every day at the nurses for some alleged imposition on her autonomy: "You liars! You liars! I hate you! You bloody liars! Thieves, every one of you!"

According to the grapevine, Camille had spent her whole life bouncing around from psychiatric ward to psychiatric ward. Apparently this was nothing new to her. And her father was a rich businessman who could afford the very best facilities for her daughter. But it didn't matter! In my opinion, she needed more than healing inside a psychiatric ward. She also needed to spend time with her true family, and to have her father do some of the real parenting.

She came damn close to shattering the glass windows separating the nurse's station from the rest of the kitchen, and that station was where "Central Command Headquarters" was located. Camille also took a strange liking to me, which scared me but also introduced interesting drama into the third thirty-day portion of my stay.

"Hey Camille, let's go steal a car and then head on down to Mexico," I joked, an absurd statement coming from an absurd patient—myself.

But the staff was not amused when they heard this talk. In fact it caused enough warning for the nursing staff to establish a "line of sight" authorization between me and Camille, so that she didn't sneak into my room, let alone my bed... something I myself hoped wouldn't happen. Fortunately nothing happened. But I learned not to joke around like that anymore.

* * *

In the last thirty days of my stay, a final option for recovery, though not a necessary one for getting out of BTC, was physical exercise. It was an opportunity for thirty minutes in each afternoon for Days 61 through 90 to work with a physical trainer to strengthen our bodies and get our heart rates up. I was the only one out of the three patients at this stage who volunteered to work with the trainer. As you could imagine, I wouldn't even think of doing something like that any time before Christmas of 2013, because I just didn't feel up to physical exertion up to that point. I still felt weak and nauseous. But starting in the New Year, I began to exercise, just a little bit at first, but gradually more and more.

I worked with different trainers, who gave me different exercises to do. One exercise involved tossing back and forth with a trainer a mid-size rubber kickball. Then I jogged behind the trainer around the backyard in a circle at a slow pace. Then there were isometric exercises, where I lifted my own body weight, by doing push-ups, sit-ups and pull-ups. It wasn't pleasant, and I felt almost silly doing such exercises. Didn't only kids do these things?

"Only one more to go, Jason," chided my trainer, as I pulled up on the bar over my chin.

"I—CAN'T—DO—THIS!" I huffed and puffed. Boy, was I out of shape!

"Yes, you can," corrected my trainer.

"HUH! HUH! HUH!" I pulled up on the bar. "OK, I did it! Now leave me alone!" I cried in a joking manner, as I grinned at the trainer. She grinned back.

Another trainer got me to do "steps," or in other words, elevating my body with one leg on top of a waist-high ledge, and then bringing up the other leg, so that I was standing on the ledge. The ledge was to be found bordering the garage driveway. It wouldn't be long before I was huffing and puffing doing these steps, and it only took a dozen ledges before my muscles were screaming in pain.

"I—CAN'T—DO—THIS!" I yelled at my trainer.

"Oh, yes, you can," the trainer smiled.

"OK, OK, you win!" I blurted out as I completed the third set of three.

"See, I told you," snorted the trainer, smiling to herself.

Nobody else wanted to do physical education with me. I didn't really mind. After all, it was up to every patient whether or not they wanted to do it. But I could have used some company. Still, physical therapists say that endorphins are released in the body and brain when one does exercise, so at least I got my fair share, even though nobody else could say that for themselves.

* * *

You would think that by the end of my stay, things would be smooth sailing. But things would hit a bump on the road toward the end of my stay. A perfect chance to practice my skills! It came up in therapy involving family and therapists, and I was participating in it, with less than a week left to Day 90. In a meeting with Dr. Cave, Barbara, Mom, Dad, Gerry, and I, Barbara outlined the agenda to my parents stridently, "We believe that Jason should spend six extra days past the 90-day mark, to make sure he has full measure of progress."

Mystified by this about-face, Dad asked, "Why? Why does he have to stay longer than the maximum stay? He should be ready to leave by now."

Of course, he had the power of the purse, and it did not fit any logic on his part for me to stay any longer than what was contracted originally.

Thinking that I could negotiate a compromise, I countered to Dr. Cave, who sat opposite from me in the circle, as I tried my best to appease the warring factions, "Dr. Cave, what about three more days past the 90-day mark, as a compromise between zero and six?"

My feelings at the time involved separate and competing loyalties to my treatment team and my family: in other words, the doctors who took care of me and the family who funded my recovery. There should have been uncompromising unity.

Dr. Cave asked, "What exactly would that accomplish for you, Jason?"

He had said this with what I sensed was arrogance, but wasn't really. It was an innocent question that I took as a sly barb—which it wasn't. I started to fume, but I tried my best to keep my cool. After all, the idea in processing information was "it's nothing personal!"

"Wait, guys," my brother Gerry asked with a frown, putting up his hands, "why don't we make sure that what we do helps Jason, above all else?"

I think he also picked up on the palpable tension in that living room, as Barbara made her case on behalf of Balance Treatment Center, while Father stonewalled. But perhaps Gerry could say that easily, because he was not paying for my treatment. I do not recall whether he had any financial skin in the game.

The meeting teetered on disharmony, before it was decided that my original 90-day leave date would remain as it was, no ifs, ands or buts.

In a separate meeting with Dr. Sager after my discharge, he apologized: "Jason, I am sorry about the confusion surrounding the end of your stay." This was shortly after Day 90 had passed, during one of my office visits. I realized he was being gentlemanly about the whole mix up.

"No worries, doc," I said amiably. "But do you think I'll be OK?"

"Yes, you will," he replied without hesitation, and I was OK with his verdict.

But to go back to session with the family and therapists, it was Dad's decision ultimately, not mine, not my brother's, not my mother's, not Barbara's, not Dr. Cave's, and not Dr. Sager's.

Dad said, "All right, it's time to wrap things up."

And Dad, Mom, and Gerry got up to leave back for their respective environs.

Those family therapy meetings didn't always leave you feeling happy and skippy, of course, but they needed to be conducted. Otherwise the competing interests surrounding me would not be able to coalesce around me. As for me, again, I learned to govern my passions, "keep it cool," and not take things personally, after a potentially disruptive experience. I was actually glad that I got out of that particular session about the potential extended stay scot-free. It showed the progress I had made with individual, group, Cognitive Behavioral Therapy, and yes, family visits. Balance Treatment Center really got me out of a black hole and back to baseline. I am glad I had a chance to go through their program. And by the way, my weight began to stabilize around 180 pounds towards the end of my stay. I was perhaps a little pudgy by then, but at least I was no longer emaciated! And after a while, some of the excessive weight would come off in the wash, ultimately. Onto other things...

* * *

CHAPTER 19

# Houses Forever

After Balance Treatment Center, a very special apartment space opened up in Sherman Oaks. The organization was called "Houses Forever." Dad was a good friend of the CEO and Founder. Apparently Dad had been active behind the scenes to get me a spot at this place. It was an apartment building that offered permanent housing for the chronically homeless and the mentally ill. It was a nonprofit organization funded by HUD (U.S. Department of Housing and Urban Development), a federal agency, as well as the state of California and the city of Los Angeles.

I moved in on my thirty-ninth birthday, June 17, 2014. It was a beautiful new building, built in a semi-hacienda style, with California stucco accents, and all compliant to the latest building codes. A light canary yellow colored the outside, while the dark wooden door and window trim accented the building perfectly. A cobblestone walkway led up to the entrance, with its gracefully solid, heavy double doors. Inside, down the hall, solid steel doors opened to an elevator, adjacent to the mail slots and a comfortably cushioned, leather chair sitting in the corner just outside the community room. Three floors of apartments led upwards to a rooftop which allowed access to a brilliant view of the L.A. skyline miles away to the east.

My own apartment was a tastefully furnished one bedroom, replete with a living room with a comfortable, lush, dark-brown toned couch, black flat-screen TV with basic cable, ceramic ivory-colored lamps, and separate kitchen and bathroom. I liked it right away. It was a compact living space with all the necessary amenities, a perfect hideaway for a single man to be alone or bring over his significant other. And, what's more, the rent was very reasonable: no more than 30% of my total income.

As far as my finances went, my family and I experimented with Supplemental Security Income, starting from before the move to "Houses Forever." The monthly amount was not much—maybe $900 per month—although there was a significant amount of back-pay—maybe $3,000—that the government awarded me. It was important to note that the Social Security Administration had denied my claim for SSDI, which was for *permanent* disability. I had thirty-seven credits, when I needed a minimum of forty. That might have had some serious ramifications, if I had received it. It would have meant that I could not work for the rest of my life if I still wanted that government support, and that I would have to remain a low-income individual. Well, if I were religious, I suppose God had looked down on me while the decision between SSI and SSDI was being made, and had decided, "No, Jason, not now. I'm not going to put you out to pasture just yet!" And so I received SSI, or *temporary* government support. And I think today that the government made the right decision.

But one thing that really got my goat was the fact that my Conservator held the financial purse-strings. In other words,

Harry received the SSI checks. And, boy, it didn't take much for him to start dangling those resources in front of my face, for any slights, real or perceived, that I committed against his person. I suppose I could be difficult at times, without proper therapy and proper medication. But did that make it appropriate for Harry to turn into a jerk? I guess I shouldn't bite the hand that feeds me. That's the only reason that I can think of for such treatment.

I still also received a couple hundred dollars a week from my parents, to supplement the SSI income. Still, it wasn't much overall and I felt unstable. I kept thinking to myself, *my parents owe me, big! I did everything that they asked me to do. I was a good son to them. And here I am, penniless and stuck on government support. It is unfair, it is unjust, and it is wrong that I am forced to grovel like a peasant.* And this was despite all the money and resources my parents had thrown in to get me to feel better again. Well, I would have to lean on my physicians in the future: Dr. Sager as well as Dr. Cave. Meanwhile, all I could do was sit in my apartment and fume over supposed injustices committed against me.

* * *

## August 10, 2014 – 10:30 PM; Houses Forever

It was Sunday, the dog days of summer, and a full moon to boot. I was lying on my apartment sofa, trying to stay cool under the arctic air shooting from the ceiling A/C vent, when I heard eight thudding beats. From the door. The noise boomed through the clear, dead-hot space of my apartment.

Sitting up, ramrod straight, my heart thudded as I cocked an ear out for more ruckus. But there was just silence. Then I heard faintly the squawks of a walkie-talkie. Squawking, talking, static, silence... again, squawking, talking, static, silence. Footsteps. Quiet conversation. I sensed what this was all about. The timing wasn't coincidental.

But still not completely sure, and desperate to solve the mystery, I jumped off the sofa and rushed to my front door to unlock it. Not even bothering to look through the peephole first, I opened it a crack.

"Yes?"

There were at least eight boys in blue. *Holy moly*. This meant at least four squad cars parked outside. What was I, trouble?

There was one in charge, a real jerk, who started the dialogue: "Jason Park?" He was very curt, very hostile, and very rude.

"Yeah? What's this all about?"

"Los Angeles Police Department. Step outside."

He motioned with his arm, and his voice breathed no nonsense. With a heavy heart, I cursed under my breath. Resigned to Fate, I faced this fellow through the door crack, and began to go through the motions. *Here we go again...*

"Face the wall. Spread your legs. Place your hands on the wall," he barked.

I complied unquestioningly, knowing this was serious trouble. I decided not to object, but to just follow instructions.

The radio crackling continued, oblivious to my presence, sounding out in code.

Two Hispanic guys felt me over, from top to bottom. I was wearing boxers, board shorts and a tank top. Nothing else. No socks, no shirt.

My personal space had been violated. I suspected the cause was a text I had sent to my mother an hour earlier. A threat of manic violence. I had become enraged because she casted doubt on my romantic relationship with the assistant manager of a nearby Mexican restaurant.

"Now put your hands to your sides."

I could tell this jerk was enjoying his hold on power over me. Again, I complied without saying anything. I sneak-peeked a sideways glance at him. The officer looked cruelly at me, as if he were sure that he had this one in the bag, as if my case were just par for the course.

"What is this all about?" I asked in a weak warble.

The jerk did not give an answer. One of the other officers, a white guy of slight build who didn't fill out his uniform, explained matter-of-factly, "You're being detained for a 5150 hold."

I knew the drill. In the state of California, a peace officer in a 5150 case is given the authority to put you on a confinement of seventy-two hours in a psychiatric ward if you are a danger to yourself, to others, or are "gravely disabled." A 5150 is an involuntary hold. In other words, I wouldn't have a choice in the decision when someone called that on me.

I'd been 5150'd twice before in Los Angeles County. And I really didn't want to go back into those circumstances. The indignity of being shoved, handcuffed, into the back of a police cruiser was beyond belief. And the affront to my personal freedom in those psychiatric wards was nonpareil.

"Put your hands behind your back."

Again, I acquiesced. The slight white boy in blue held me by one elbow and then clumsily traipsed me back into my own apartment, while the jerk officer followed. The living room was lit by the single fluorescent light in the ceiling, which cast a dull moon-like pall over the proceedings. Everybody and everything was illuminated in harsh relief by it.

Spying one of my director's chairs in the living room, the skinny officer dragged it across the floor with one hand, scraping it unceremoniously over the linoleum. With his other hand, he perched me on the edge of the seat, with my hands still behind my back. That's when he busted out the handcuffs and...

"Lean back farther in the chair." Then he chained me to one of the wooden posts in the back of the chair. *Oh, brother.*

I was unnaturally bent backwards, while the more-unnatural frame of the cuffs ground into my wrists, making them increasingly uncomfortable with every passing minute. I have never felt so undignified, so vulnerable, so naked, as I felt at that moment, when my civil liberties had been taken away from me.

There was a lot of moving around and shifting by the officers. The jerk officer gave me an unadulterated glare, before going outside, I suppose to gloat about how I was easy pickings. Two officers—an older Asian with a gut and moustache, and the previously mentioned skinny white guy—made themselves comfortable on my sofa, right where I had lain earlier, right where the air-conditioning was strongest. Meanwhile the two Hispanic officers paraded around, back and forth, leaving dried mud tracks and clay-like droppings on the floor.

"How could my parents do this to me?" I cried out rhetorically in anger and pain, as if I had just caught my long-time girlfriend cheating on me behind my back.

"Look, kid," said the Asian officer, shifting himself on my couch, as if he thought he was my uncle doing me a favor by giving me some old-time advice, "there are no bad parents."

Oh yeah, as if what he had just said justified any parenting style whatsoever; or as if what he had just said justified how he parented. Still, I didn't want to reply to his comment.

"I can't believe I'm being 5150'd again," I pined out loud instead in a half-moan.

From my sofa the skinny one replied, "Hey, you're not being 5150'd, you're being detained. OK?"

Then all of a sudden, fifteen minutes after the initial pounding on the door, a curvy female officer, who I will call "Girl in Blue," entered my apartment, approached me, and said, "Jason, I want to see your cell phone."

Her radio chattered as I studied her. For some reason, she commanded authority naturally. It was neither her badge nor her gun that moved me. It was her sophistication in taking control over *information*—in this case, from my cell phone—that commanded respect. So I complied, only this time, with uncontrived assent.

"It is in my bedroom in the upper drawer of the nightstand," I replied.

Thirty seconds later, she emerged from the bedroom, with the flip-phone I was using at the time in her hand.

"What's the password?"

"4109."

She went outside to the hallway, and for about five minutes I didn't see her. The radio chatter continued in irregular cadences from the other officers' walkie-talkies.

Meanwhile, the jerk officer came in to check on me. He stood over me as I sat chained to my director's chair, and he looked sadistically pleased that I was helplessly handcuffed with my hands behind my back. He still had that cruel smirk on his face. I looked up at him, helpless, with dark fears clutching at my throat.

He asked me: "Do you have any drugs or drug paraphernalia on you, Jason?"

"No." It was all I could do to give a guttural, phlegm-choked reply of surrender.

My answer initiated a search anyhow, as the two Hispanic officers went into my bedroom, and through my line of sight, I saw them checking out the bottom drawer of the nightstand. With light-blue rubber gloves on their hands, they began riffling through my belongings.

But then, just at that moment, Girl in Blue walked in briskly, my cell phone in hand. Her radio wasn't gawking.

"Take off the handcuffs," she ordered.

The Asian officer and skinny officer got up from the sofa and obeyed her command.

Still in the chair, I rubbed my sore but free wrists. I felt like crying. How was I going to justify my threatening text to my family? Boy, I really screwed up this TIME! The feeling of contrition was an ocean wave crashing over me and taking me down deep until I hit—ow!—rock bottom, all while I suffocated before it let me go and brought me back up, gasping for air. Top of my mind was the question: *How am I going to explain what I said to my mother?*

But it seemed that the LAPD was letting me go. What had compelled this move? Were they playing games? Maybe not. After all, I had complied with their instructions, I hadn't caused a ruckus while being detained, and I had been completely cooperative with the officers. That was for certain.

But I didn't know what Girl in Blue had seen, or not seen. Or divulged, or not divulged, to the commanding officer. I mean, the threat text was there, in the sent messages folder. Did she and the others disregard it? Or could they not find it? I guess I'll never know.

The jerk officer had treated me roughly, as if he were playing the role of "bad cop" with gusto and relish. But now that I was being let go, his cruel smirk turned into an open-mouthed, frightened stare.

Girl in Blue said, "Mr. Park, we are releasing you from detainment. Are you aware that you are being let go on your own recognizance?"

I replied in earnest, "Yes, ma'am."

And then everybody started clearing out, including the bad cop. They all left. I was in the room all alone. I remained in my director's chair, my wrists throbbing in pain,

After that experience, I was much more careful about respecting my parents, and I had no more 5150s.

* * *

I remember that it was months later, on a cold night in October 2014, when I got fed up with my whole situation. Now real despair began to rain down upon me. I felt helplessness, hopelessness, and worthlessness blanket me and smother me up in their clutches. I choked upon the dark fears that were drowning my sense of self, and targeting my suffering mortality. I couldn't stand being me anymore. No contact with family, lack of physician support, financial distress, no friends around me, no job, no girlfriend, ineffective medications... *This is too much to bear! No one can deal with this heavy burden of existence!*

Desperate situations avail themselves of desperate measures. I had lived almost forty years on Earth, and I had nothing to show for it. I was worse off by that point than I was when I first started my life, at Day 1. *I am never going to get out of this cesspool! The solution is obvious! I must take my own life!*

But I was too much of a coward to hang myself or slit my wrists. Hanging seemed too effortful, and I couldn't stand the pain of cutting skin open. I would do it in a way that would cause minimum pain on the way out. I would go meet my maker easily and without harm to myself. Death became a cowardly act! The way I knew was the way I had heard of from others: overdosing on medication. *Yes, that's it!*

I found that the 750 mg Depakote pills were the ones I had most recently filled up and that I had the most of. With lots of water, I started chugging them down, all 180 of them, until I felt so waterlogged and so full that I couldn't keep anything else down.

*I feel sick.*

I proceeded to lie down in my bed, on top of the covers, and folded my arms, half-crying, waiting for the end to come. Every now and then, I would check the time on my watch, as I lay in the chill of the November night in my room, windows open to the night, which was punctuated by police sirens, rumbling engines, yapping Chihuahuas, and the occasional yell or scream underneath or next door. The only light in my entire apartment was the bedside lamp, which cast a brownish yellowish pall over the bedroom's white, characterless walls.

Then suddenly, and involuntarily, the light turned in my mind's eye from a warm welcoming brown to a sickly yellowish pall, more nauseating than ordinarily comforting. And inside me, I felt the most overpowering retching and vomiting, as if I were a dog who had eaten too much overly rich, beef brisket. I leaned over and threw up the Depakote pills, one by one, in a big gush, rapid fire-like, as if it were a poison my body was trying to eject out of itself. It was so painful, so utterly uncontrollable, that it frightened me. There was a brief pause, as I looked down on the floor, the nearby vicinity spattered by half-digested pills surrounded by a pool of stomach acid. I turned over to my other side, as if to equalize the distribution of pills on the floor, and narrowly missed the covers in the process of transition. The gushing continued on the left side of the bed, the dark side that was unlit by the lamplight, and this time, it wasn't so clear where and when the vomit was landing. All I knew was that the process was only half-finished when I switched sides. Then the noise of spattered puke quieted down a bit until it ground to a halt. Weakly, I put the back of a hand to my mouth to clear the remaining drool.

*So now I tried to kill myself, failed, and to add insult to injury, I have to clean the whole mess myself!*

No need to add anything else to that evening's work detail! I cleaned the mess up, slowly but surely, and quite miserably, weakened, half-sobbing, not just badgered by grief but also angry at my futility. Unfortunately, the bedsheet covers trailed the floor, so the stomach acid was soaked up in the fabric. I had to take the whole cover to the dry cleaners, and its large stain in honor of my effort. I remembered something I had read about Joseph Stalin, when he had heard of his son's failed suicide attempt: "He can't even *kill* himself properly!"

I was at a real all-time low: "I can't even kill myself..." There was real bitterness in my mind now that I couldn't honorably give up my life even if there wasn't anything worth hanging around for. The botched suicide attempt put my self-esteem in a deep well, impossible to extricate from. I had tried to show others what I could do. Now it was clear I couldn't do anything right.

* * *

In December 2014 Dad agreed to lease me a car. It required his credit score and my lease payments. My Christmas present was a silver Honda Civic coupe, one of the last ones off the lot for that year, the same make and model as the Honda Civic coupe given to me as a college graduation present seventeen years earlier. Money would come from the Supplemental Security Income for me to make the lease payment and insurance premium. I got the 15,000 mile-a-year package, with roadside assistance for emergency situations. Gas wasn't factored into the equation, but that's not how I was thinking. I just needed a way of getting around more comfortably and less dangerously than via public transportation. Besides, Civics weren't gas-guzzlers, but fuel-sippers. And as long as gas prices were reasonable, fuel costs wouldn't be an issue.

In 2015 my mood began to spiral out of control, because I had tried a medication for bipolar disorder that had generated a lethal side-effect and needed to be discontinued. Without a replacement medication, I began to express the classic symptoms of psychosis: paranoia, delusions, and grandiosity. I lashed out through text messages at the resident case manager at Houses Forever, simply because she was there and I hated her position of authority above me ("Fat, ugly, and stupid: that's no way to go through life, my dear"). In addition, I went after the administrator, a British gentleman, also at Houses Forever ("Dragged through the streets by horse, strangled but not hanged, emasculated, eviscerated, bowels burned before you, quartered and drawn: that's justice, English style!"). The attack against the British gentleman was explained by the brutal killing of a medieval Scottish knight who fought for Scottish independence against the English. I felt that both of them were out to get me, that they were not good people, and that I had a mission or was chosen to "valiantly" attack them. Obviously, none of this was even remotely true. That's when a telltale rapping came at my door on a sunny, warm, late October day in 2015.

"Who is it?"

"It's Tom and Rachel, please open the door." Tom spoke in a British accent.

I opened the door. "Yeah, what do you...?" I began aggressively.

"OK, stop!" Tom held up his hand.

I paused momentarily.

"Rachel and I want you to go see your psychologist and psychiatrist now," he told me. "Take your car."

"I don't have gas money."

"Well, make it anyhow. Find the way to get some cash, otherwise we will call the police for a 5150 hold. Understood?"

Even in my psychotic frame of mind, I knew the implications of losing my freedom. So I drove to my psychologist's office, whereupon Dr. Cave and I walked next door to Dr. Sager's office.

At that point, Dr. Cave began to ask me questions. I answered, seemingly fine. Then certain questions began to annoy me. Dr. Sager watched and observed.

"So what did you think of your piano teacher?"

"What about him?"

"Didn't he have two sons who got into Harvard?"

"Yeah, so?"

"Well," Dr. Cave began to twist the knife, "didn't they abuse their power once there, engaging in nepotism?"

"Look, Doctor, we've been through this before, why do I have to answer these crappy questions?"

"They're just questions, they're not meant to upset you..."

"Yeah, but they are upsetting me!"

"I'm just asking whether they make you feel a certain way..."

"Yes, they make me feel like I want to kick those bastards' asses..."

End of story. Dr. Sager raised a hand, and Dr. Cave and he began to converse, in range of my earshot, but without backstabbing me or twisting the knife.

"Loxapine, at 25 mg initial titration would be good..." Dr. Cave.

"Titrated up to 100 mg, ultimately..." Dr. Sager.

"Let's check for side effects along the way." Dr. Cave.

So over the course of six weeks starting from October 22, 2015, that's ultimately what I needed—a proper "typical antipsychotic," not an atypical one, to take care of the psychotic features of the bipolar disorder, taken from 25 mg daily slowly to increase to 100 mg a day. Although at various times other antipsychotics had been prescribed for my condition, only this one, Loxapine, was the one medication that put the psychotic fire out cold, rather than inflame it or let it simmer. The only reason why my physicians had hesitated to put me on this particular drug is because of the concern over severe side effects. That might have sidelined my recovery significantly. But it turned out that this was of no significance. Besides, we could simply have discontinued the medication.

Over a longer period of time, let's say, from six weeks to six months, it became clear that this medication at this dosage did a much better job at putting a tight lid over the delusional statements, grandiose feelings, and paranoid thoughts that before had leaked out in anger. And over a longer period of time, Loxapine did not just put a lid on the psychosis, but rather extinguished the anger and permitted me an unskewed view of reality. In other words, it was no longer the case that my reality was different from anybody else's reality, and moreover, it was no longer the case that I demanded that others correspond their reality with my own. The administration of Loxapine coincided with an uninterrupted path of psychological progress and emotional stability that continues to this day.

It was amazing how that was all it took, just another medication added to the arsenal, for things to begin to settle down and normalize for me between friends, family, and employer. Dr. Sager and Dr. Cave also agreed that my full and complete diagnosis would be "Bipolar Disorder Type I with psychotic features." Well, if that's what it says, then that's what it is. And that's why I am still with Drs. Cave and Sager.

* * *

CHAPTER 20

# Commerce & Culture

2016 was a good year, ultimately. It started with the basic, fundamental components of recovery in place: 2 mood stabilizers, 1 anti-anxiety medication, 1 anti-psychotic, 1 sleep agent, 1 med for side-effects, and 1 med for bipolar depression. Starting from 2016 and onto the present day, there would be little to no change in this medication regimen, in terms of types and dosages. And my biweekly visits with Dr. Sager in 2016 began to focus more on how to fashion a life worth living rather than revolving around mere alleviation of symptoms.

"So are there any side effects that you feel from the medication?"

"No, but I would like to get a job now. I think I'm ready for it," I said.

"Hm-hm. Where do you think you could work?"

"Well, I have a Ph.D. in management. Maybe I could teach at USC or UCLA?"

"Yes, that is a possibility."

And I continued to see Dr. Cave on a regular basis, twice weekly.

Dr. Cave noted, "Jason, you may be destined for greatness, because I have never met a patient who put this much effort into their recovery!"

I laughed out loud, and was heartened by the doctor's words.

So far, so good. However, the Supplemental Security Income from the Social Security Administration was really crimping my style. It was difficult to make ends meet on just SSI. Besides, it made for an unpleasant get-together with my Conservator, who was given the checks and had the authority to hand them over to me or not. That was stressful, but the money was still coming in. And my parents increased their allotment over time to $300 a week, which allowed me to get out of some small-time credit card debt.

In other words, financially speaking, I was starting to stabilize, while my mental health also started to take a turn for the better. Although this was just the beginning, it was a good start to the year.

* * *

While time passed by, I was also able to reflect on what I had been missing. For one, I had lost precious and irreversible opportunities to bond with my nieces. It was a sad state of affairs, not being part of my brother Gerry's growing family. And by this time, the gap was largely self-imposed. Willfully pushing people away was, by far and large, the only way I knew how to deal with people who elicited my emotional vulnerabilities.

Yet Gerry would tell me at times, "Jay, won't you stop by sometime? Drive on down and see us. We simply want a relationship with you and for you to have a relationship with the kids."

So on my niece Sarah's fourth birthday in July 2016, I mailed a birthday card to her and a "Hello" card to her sister Victoria, who was younger by two years. A few days later an email came to me from Gerry. It included a link to a video featuring both Victoria and Sarah facing a poised cell phone and together expressing an effusive "Thank you Uncle Jason for the cards and we miss you!" At first, I didn't know what to say or how to react. It was so utterly disarming, the way the kids were obviously just so happy to offer good tidings and good cheer in their greeting.

I actually started crying in my Van Nuys apartment—quietly, to myself, so that no one could possibly hear. They were tears of sadness and joy. Sadness because I lost so much in four years, viciously struggling with my recovery and also being conflicted with my family. Again, it was this feeling that "I am owed one. I did everything that my parents asked me to do. I was a good son. It is so unfair and wrong that I am worse off now than I was before. I want justice!"

But now I felt joy, too, because I knew that reconciliation and bonding were in store for me. So I then quickly dried my tears. That innocent children with the most virtuous of motives were letting me know I mattered to them and that they cared about me was more than I could bear without breaking down. All the conflict among the adults, who had seemed at times to lack the capacity for unconditional regard and positive love as the kids had, made me wonder who was more self-adjusted, adults or children.

Adults tend to do things for more than one reason at a time, as in for themselves as well as for others. Children, on the other hand, could be much more single-minded of purpose, so from my experience I knew that my nieces' sentiments were sincere. I had felt for the longest time that people were out to get me and that loved ones around me did not have my best interests at heart. These feelings had twisted my heart and had made me savagely angry and ready to pounce, like the mongrel that snaps its jaws at the friendly human benefactors who are trying to treat it. But my nieces cut to the core of my soul in such a beguiling manner, to let me know that I still had skin in the game, and that their love for me was pure and pristine.

So as a step up in closeness to my brother's family, I visited them in their rental house, which was their temporary residence while their brand-new home was being built next door. I remember the period because *Finding Nemo* had caught the attention of Sarah, while *Finding Dory* was catching the attention of Victoria. You could tell that Sarah was ahead in development because she could form full sentences with meaningful impact. Victoria was still working on developing her personality, which her pretty face did not register, at least not yet.

It was fun going outside to the driveway and lugging around Sarah in her plastic car-mobile, one of those contraptions that are easily tugged via a plastic handle by an adult.

"Did you like that?"

A nod of her cute head.

"Want to go again?"

She nodded hurriedly, in excitement! So I obliged happily.

She wasn't heavy in weight yet, so it didn't take too much to drag her around on the concrete enclave.

But Victoria was different. She liked to throw things! You could tell right away that she was the more rambunctious of the two, just like her father (my brother)!

After they moved into their new house in December 2016, which was quite a mansion, the kids continued to grow and develop their separate personalities. They were capable of some rather embarrassing questions, such as: "If you're older than my father, Uncle Jason, how come you're not married yet?" After asking something like that, Sarah would squeal out with peals of laughter. From out of the mouths of babes, if you will.

And Victoria would query me: "Uncle Jason, how come your teeth are white on the outside but yellow in-between?" I was more shocked than angry by the question. I guess kids don't have filters between their brains and their mouths.

But the point of this questioning was to show that I was a part of my nieces' lives, and my brother's and sister-in-law's, too. I was not absent from their upbringing. Uncle Jason was not a creepy old recluse who they should keep their distance from. Rather, he was a living, breathing human being with lots of love to give.

* * *

When I think back to the summer of 2016, I know it was truly memorable. In addition to my taking the time to reach out to my nieces, there was a reaching out from my dad's side of the family in Atlanta, of Uncle Frank and Aunt Maggie, who came to attend a Christian Fellowship conference at a major university in Los Angeles, and to see my parents and me. My Uncle Frank and Aunt Maggie were both devout Christians, born-again, in fact. They took religion very seriously. Meanwhile, my dad was basically the only one in his family who did not take to religion, and he had raised me and Gerry to avoid the topic of religion from conversation. Nevertheless, years earlier, in 2009, after I had traveled to Atlanta from Pittsburgh during the doctoral program to be at the funeral of my great aunt, Uncle Frank and

Aunt Maggie had accepted me as part of the family. Me, the abject sinner!

During their visit to California, Uncle Frank, sitting in the passenger seat, and I, driving on the 210, 101, and 405 freeways, talked about various passages of the Bible during the trek from the university campus to my parents' house in Bel Air. It was a bruising hot day for the Lord's discussion in the car. *Why did the Lord make the day so hot?* I wondered. Perhaps it was not the Lord, but rather the double-breasted suit I had on for the conference, having outrageously overdressed. But at least now I could converse with my uncle two feet away from me, in the passenger seat, rather than through impersonal emails.

"Well, Jason, we pray for you, and we know that you are blessed by God. But we also pray for your father. We hope that one day he too will accept Jesus Christ into his life." So that was what this visit was about. Interesting. I mean, they knew that I had introduced faith into a life that had otherwise been structured by *common sense*. But my father apparently was a different story. He was an intellectual who had no room for "faith against all odds." It just wasn't in his character, although he would admit, if cornered, to being mildly superstitious. So I suppose there was hope for him, too!

We got into Bel Air in three long hours' time, around dinnertime. I saw my dad and mom and we embraced. Dad was giggling and he had a funny look on his face. *Why the laughter and grimace?* I wondered. *He doesn't usually greet me like that...*

"Jason, Mom and I have decided on something big for you. OK? Just get ready."

I said, "OK?" rather bemused by their mysterious plans. *What's going to happen? What have they decided for me?* Oh, let me guess: They matched me up with a nice girl! I sincerely hoped it wasn't a case of them setting me up with someone. I couldn't stand their doing that. I felt the desire to freely choose whomever I wanted to go out with.

Nevertheless, I went out with my parents and our two out-of-town family guests for a very nice Japanese dinner in Torrance. I still couldn't figure out what was on my parents' minds. I guessed it was good news as well as news that was important to me, too. At least it wasn't bad news!

I played it cool over dinner, while family caught up with each other.

"So, Jason, we know that our Lord and savior Jesus Christ loves you. We hope you read your Bible every day and pray for the Holy Spirit to enter into your life," Uncle Frank told me.

"Yes, Uncle Frank, Aunt Maggie. I think about Him all the time. I know he is looking out for me. You are right, he has opened his life and love to me. I am forever grateful. Thank you."

In life, I have learned that any aspect of human endeavor, whether politics, or accounting, or psychology, has its own diction and terminology that must be learned in order to participate in any conversation about it. I figured that religion was no different, and it was important to learn the vocabulary, along with its syntax, grammar, pronunciation, and the like, before entering in friendly chit-chat with others.

I said good-bye to everybody after dinner—Mom and Dad, Aunt Maggie and Uncle Frank—and headed back up to the San Fernando Valley, so that my relatives could converse closely with each other. I felt it was not my place to stay any longer. I knew that Aunt Maggie and Uncle Frank had a son who was severely autistic, and the tragedy had hit everybody in their family hard. I think they understood what my parents were going through with me, even though I had a mood disorder that

I recovered from, while their son, Alex, had a developmental disorder that mired him in dysfunction. I knew they probably wanted to talk about me and Alex, so that was why I felt uncomfortable and felt the need to leave. But I was sure I would hear from Dad in the near future. In fact, we had scheduled a family therapy session together the following weekend.

So I found out in a session with Dr. Cave and my parents that Mom and Dad would provide me with financial support in perpetuity. It would do away with the Supplemental Security Income I was receiving from the government, and the amount already being given by my parents would increase significantly. *Hallelujah*! I was quietly and inwardly relieved, and I hugged Mom and kissed Dad on the forehead when we returned to their Bel Air house from the appointment in Calabasas.

This was a landmark decision for me. Never had my parents willingly given money to me without conditions or reservations. Of course, there was a general understanding, right from the get-go, that any money willingly given could just as easily be taken back. And that such money should be spent fairly, wisely, and justly. Still I was so grateful, and so happy that I could enjoy some financial freedom and independence.

So I wrote the Social Security Administration in the Fall of 2016, informed the agent receiving the letter that I no longer needed the Supplemental Security Income, and requested that I be taken off their payroll. I thought to myself, *Boy, I'm sure the government will feel very relieved to hear that somebody out there wants to get off of SSI, rather than get on SSI!*

I remember, though, feeling ashamed for taking my parents' money. It was almost as if my pride were wounded because I could not live on my own without my parents' largesse. But I processed this information at a support group meeting and the participants around me basically said, "There's no reason to be ashamed, Jason. Your parents are trying to help you. There is no shame involved here, and they do it because they care about you, not because they think you're damaged goods or anything..."

Well, I remember feeling that way about myself in the early stages of recovery, when I genuinely was damaged goods. It was hard to get that feeling out of me. But twenty years of therapy has taught me not to feel that way. Now I am more like a high-maintenance European Piaget chronograph than a "takes a lickin' and keeps on tickin'" Timex watch. So yes I am high-maintenance, but that's not the same as being damaged goods, which I no longer am.

I can recall a conversation I had with my father about this feeling of shame as an issue.

"You know, Dad, I feel as if I didn't earn the money you give me. Shouldn't I be working or something for it?"

"Nooooo, Jason, you EARNED that money. You paid your dues! There is nothing more that you have to do, other than be good to your family members and be a good person. That's all."

* * *

But not everything in my life at this point was a commercial enterprise. Struggling with life on this earth had led me to contemplate what life was like after this one. After all, we don't really know what happens to people after they die. The scientists claim that once your body dies, then all you're doing is pushing up daisies six feet under. But the religious state that there is a soul or spirit that lives on after death. Who can say for certain that theirs is the right conclusion?

So at Houses Forever, every Monday evening Gus the resident manager, who was Catholic, would hold a Bible Study meeting, for the residents to dine together with him, and then read a chapter or two from the Bible. My attendance, I admit, was spotty at times, but it was enough to read and remember the various portions of the Old Testament: the Torah (Genesis, Exodus, Leviticus, Numbers, Deuteronomy). And we would also read from the New Testament: the Our Father prayer, the Beatitudes ("Blessed are the meek, for they shall inherit the earth") and the parables of Jesus ("The Mote and the Beam").

I also began to delve into Buddhism, which revered a man, not a God, but which was highly spiritual in content. The key was to obtain enlightenment from the suffering felt in this world, an enlightenment the Buddha had achieved first. Mom had brought two Buddha statues over from Korea, and in 2016 she allowed me to have one. There was also a miniature gong and mallet that could be paired with the statue. In the bedroom of my apartment, I made a small table shrine with the statue and the gong along with two electric candles, one placed on each side. I would strike the bell with the metal mallet and then bow to the statue three times, along with an ancient prayer ("Save us o merciful Buddha!" in Korean). I later began to place dollar notes underneath the statue, as if giving money to Buddha was going to help things! But I also donated to Gus's church, and I would occasionally pay for the Bible Study group's food, too, so I guess the practice had some precedent in other spiritual or religious contexts.

There was a lesson I learned from engaging in Bible Study and Buddhist prayers: I was definitely superstitious, in a very real way. My thinking was that if all this prayer and religion were simply superstitious hocus-pocus, well, then, why would so many people take it so seriously? That was my thinking towards the end of this journey. There must be something to it. After all, the financial gift that Mom and Dad gave me was offered at around the time that I began to take Bible Study seriously. Was it possible that my prayers had been answered around that time? Who knows...?

* * *

Throughout 2016, I was also attending support group meetings, an important adjunct to therapy and medication.

There was the National Alliance on Mental Illness (NAMI), a grassroots campaign operating since the 1970s that provided free classes and meetings featuring renowned psychiatrists, psychologists, and government administrators on the topic of mental illness. I often went to the NAMI San Fernando Valley (SFV) monthly meetings, simply because I was intellectually stimulated and also somewhat comforted by them. And the meeting venue was quite nearby. The meetings guided and channeled my energies into a more efficient and productive recovery trajectory.

I heard a psychiatrist at a NAMI SFV meeting once say, "Look, folks, remember that our understanding of the brain today is similar to our understanding of the heart back in the 1880s." Wow. That definitely put things in perspective, for me. It made me realize how little anybody knew, even physicians, of the brain, this organ inside our skulls.

I asked the same individual, "Is there a cure for mental illness, in the same way that bacterial infections have a cure through antibiotics?"

He answered. "Honestly, that might not be the model we may want to proceed. Very few things are curable, actually, in the way that bacterial infections are curable. We may want to pursue a management approach, whereby we manage the illness, but we don't cure it, like diabetes with insulin, asthma with steroid inhalers, cancer with chemotherapy and radiation, a thyroid condition with medication..." Again, eye-opening statements.

There was also the Depression and Bipolar Support Alliance support group meetings. Instead of a speaker and audience, everybody potentially was a speaker, because we could all choose to participate. I often did, especially when I needed a chance to vent my anger—in the beginning, that is. At first, I used to express my rage towards my parents and brother to everyone who would listen at these meetings. This was in late 2015, when the Loxapine was first being administered. By mid-2016, I no longer expressed those same sentiments.

Participants such as Nancy, a young lady, commented, "Jason, you know, when I first met you at these meetings, you were so angry! Now that's completely gone, and you're just like almost a different person."

"How do you mean, Nancy?"

"I mean, you're just so much more happy-go-lucky, all smiles, free of conflict..."

Finally, there was The Stability Network (TSN), which featured about two hundred or so working professionals across the United States and Europe who had a mental health diagnosis. Its founder and CEO, Julia, was a Yale MBA who had her first psychotic break in business school. With that experience, she endeavored to start an organization (i.e., TSN) that would help end stigma surrounding mental health diagnoses in the workplace.

Toward the end of 2016, I interviewed with Julia to become a member of the organization, as a "Stability Leader."

"Hi, Jason. Can you tell me more about your education?"

"Yes. Harvard Bachelor's and Ph.D. in strategic management from the University of Pittsburgh."

"Sounds great! Now what can you tell me about your work history? Your resume seems to have left off in 2012 at City University of Hong Kong."

"Yes, well, I needed some time off to take a sabbatical, for mental health reasons, of course."

"Yes, of course, I understand that. Are you planning to return back to school to teach or do research?"

"Oh, yes. I plan to return in the spring semester of 2017, in a couple of months."

"Nice! Wow! Well, I would love to have you on board. Welcome to The Stability Network."

"Thank you, Julia!"

Yeah, that's what support groups can do to you. They help you build community and connection into your life. Now again, support groups are not a substitute for regular psychotherapy and psychotropic medication. But they can serve as a powerful and effective adjunct, which is why I do strongly suggest getting involved with them for those with a mental health diagnosis. After all, it helped me, and there is no reason to believe that it wouldn't help others!

As for the plans to return to academia, well....

* * *

CHAPTER 21

# Last Stop

While I had the financial backing of my parents, I knew as well as they did that I wouldn't be happy just sitting around and doing nothing. Soon the prospect of employment in my original line of work, in academia as a professor, began to bud again. Dad knew a professor in the business school of the university he worked for who had known me in my first year on the job market when I was just a lowly graduate student. She was in a position to do me a huge favor: get me a teaching post at the business school at the research university my dad worked for.

I met with her in the fall of 2016, and over lunch we talked.

"Dr. Moran, it just occurred to me something about the management field, about doing research in that field."

"Yes, go ahead, I'm listening," Dr. Moran said before going back to munching on her salad.

"Well, it seems that back in your day, it was all about small sample sizes and large effect sizes. Whereas in my day it is more about large sample sizes and small effect sizes," I said between bites of my steak, juicy and done medium.

"Excellent point, Jason," Dr. Moran declared. "We seem to be going the wrong way, in other words. It means ultimately that we're peddling useless advice to business practitioners."

Not to get technical, but this was a subject of great significance, the connection between sample size and effect size. I knew it would impress her, because I sounded already like a senior scholar, focusing on more philosophical aspects of the field, such as "p-hacking" and the like. So the meeting went well, and we enjoyed our respective meals of meat and potatoes and vegetarian salad.

About this time, my parents had begun to support me financially, and I had announced to the Social Security Administration that I no longer needed the Supplemental Security Income (SSI) payments from them anymore. I also worked out with Harry the terms of ending the Conservatorship. Lately he had been very avoidant to take on calls or meet with me or any member of my family. That practice ended when Mom rather surreptitiously (!) called him from her cell phone and locked him down for a meeting at my parents' Bel Air house. It was a little strange working with him, because at times he could be very available, and at other times he would just disappear. But he had also been very tolerant of me for the longest time. I understood from Dad that he was a good guy in one sense because he never bothered to return to Dad to receive pay for all of his services. I guess Harry and I agreed that I had made enough progress, and ultimately that both of us had had enough of each other. So I received my last SSI check from Harry at my parents', I called up the public defender to send in my letter to the Courthouse in Sylmar to officially end the Conservatorship, and that was it.

Shortly after a perfunctory meeting with the Department Chairperson, which went well, I received a letter in the mail from the Head of the Department of Management and Organization at the university's business school, stating an offer of an employment contract for the spring semester of 2017, teaching two sections concurrently of strategic management to undergraduate seniors. Each section contained forty-eight students to be exact.

I showed the letter to my parents; it was as if I were showing them my acceptance letter from Harvard nearly twenty-five years ago! Mom was quietly ecstatic while Dad expressed demure satisfaction.

I asked my father, "So what do you recommend I do from here, Dad? I'm sure I should thank certain people for putting me in there."

From here on in, Dad began to mention next steps as to what to do in response to the letter: "Jason, I think you should definitely want to thank the Department Head for the offer, offer appreciation to his connection for having pulled some strings on your behalf, thank Dr. Moran for getting you in there, and thank the staff ahead of time for their willingness to work with you.

"Sure, Dad. I'll take care of it." And so I did, and I ended the talk by bowing to my father.

A few days later, I received an email in my personal Hotmail account from Sofia, the Administrator of the Department of Management and Organization. Sofia immediately became an important ally. She asked for my W-4 and I-9 forms, my passport and social security number, and she informed me that I would receive my own email account, keys to an office space in the basement of the accounting building, my own university ID card, a direct deposit of my salary into my bank account, as well as a new textbook with a prepared syllabus. I was delighted. This was getting better and better!

As 2016 drew to a close, things started to fall into place. I became acquainted with my new colleagues, and I found out that the administrator, at my pleasant persistence, had placed me with two sections, back-to-back, on Tuesdays and Thursdays, each section lasting one hour and fifty minutes, from 2 PM to 3:50 PM and from 4 PM to 5:50 PM.

* * *

New Year's of 2017 passed with little fanfare, precisely because I was getting ready for teaching. Of course, the little ones, my two nieces, had all manner of fun, whooping it up with fireworks on the beach in South Bay where Gerry and his wife Tabitha took them on New Year's Eve. But Tuesday, January 10, 2017, was the first day of class for me, and that really marked the beginning of my New Year. And I was not about to get caught with my britches down. I read half of the twelve chapters in the textbook over a period of six weeks, a chapter each week. I also read, at least once, every case study and teaching note assigned up to the midterm examination—just to get familiarized. I didn't want to be "just one step ahead." That was anathema to me; I thought it would be anxiety-provoking, to always worry that I had to keep pace with the students. I didn't have to prepare so far ahead, of course; it was just my own desire to be preemptively over-ready. So Jason-like of me!

* * *

On January 10, I walked into the classroom, a half-hour early... how typical of me! There was nobody there. Completely deserted.

I heard the silent hum of the computer work station, breathing out hot air, stacked in an open cabinet in the far corner, tucked away behind the podium for the professors and instructors. Undeterred, I walked my way to behind the podium, undid the clasps on my dowel-rod briefcase, and pulled out my laser pointer/clicker, the flash drive containing my PowerPoint slides, and my copy of the syllabus. With nothing else to do, I sat in the high chair standing behind the podium, and twiddled my thumbs.

Then, after about fifteen minutes, the kids started trickling in. At first, they only numbered a few, but as 2 PM approached, more kids started arriving: short and tall, red-haired and blue-haired, Asian and white, Hispanic and black, Indian and South American, male and female, heavyset and slender... a kaleidoscope of possible human types, and then some. This was Southern California for you! At first, I wasn't sure how I was going to do a lecture in front of this young, yet seasoned crowd (they were undergraduate seniors, after all). But after the years of teaching at Pittsburgh and City University of Hong Kong, I dove right in and picked up on it right away.

"Hello, everyone, welcome to Course ABCD 101: Strategic Management. I am your professor, Jason Park. Now before we begin with the slide presentation that I have for you, I would like to take the time to get to know each one of you much better than so far. Currently I don't know you and you don't know me. But we will begin to know each other right away. So let's begin with the first person, in alphabetical order: Michael Annis, where are you?"

"Right here, sir..."

I scanned the room and pinpointed where the words were coming from, in the front row, to the far right. A buff kid with heavy, intimidating tattoos on his forearms. He had one arm up as I called on him, and he rested his head on the other arm.

I moved closer and stood in front of him, asking: "So tell us why you're taking this course and one interesting thing about yourself!"

I beamed with a huge, perhaps slightly ingenuous grin on my face.

"Well, uh," Michael began, "I'm taking this course because I have to..." Laughter and giggling ensued. "...and one thing about me, I surf."

*Ah, now that is interesting!* "So you ride the wave, literally speaking," I went on with the conversation.

"Yes, I do, sir," the student replied matter-of-factly. He thought he had it in the bag.

"And," I followed up, "do you ride the wave, like, figuratively speaking?"

"Oh, I see," he began, a little taken aback. "Sort of. But what do you mean by that?"

Now his interest was piqued.

"What I mean is, a wave has tremendous, powerful force, and so your job as a surfer is to harness that energy for your benefit and advantage. So in actual life, you try to use your energy to be creative and not 'wipe-out.' You ride the ups and downs of life without crashing and burning, in other words."

"Yeah... yeah, that's right," Michael said, open-mouthed, a stare in his eyes.

"Good. Now let's move on," I said, and continued with the next student on the list.

Afterwards, I showed them some PowerPoint slides. I mentioned my professional achievements (Harvard BA, Pittsburgh Ph.D. and professorship in Hong Kong), my names (my American name: Jason Whan Park, and also my Korean name: 박 상 준, followed by my Chinese name 朴 相 俊), and my own views about strategic management. And then we went over the syllabus, word by word, section by section, with each student reading a paragraph, and then on to the next student sitting to the right of the student before. It was tedious work, but it had to be done. Besides, it was relatively painless for both me and the students. All they had to do was read out loud a section, and all I had to do was conduct the transition from student to student.

The semester went by slowly but surely. From January 10 to April 27, I lectured every Tuesday and Thursday, twice each day, back-to-back sessions. At times I felt that this was something I could do for the rest of my life, and at other times I just wanted to run to the Administrator and say: "Goddammit, Sofia, I quit!" While I had read the first half of the textbook beforehand, and all of the case studies before the midterm, I didn't have serious time to read everything after the midterm. It was just going too fast, and I felt overwhelmed. I did manage to read all the case studies that were listed after the midterm, but not the book chapters. I just relied on the PowerPoint slides that came with the textbook. But I was still at least "one step ahead" of my students.

* * *

But after a few semesters, it became clear that this job was not the right fit for me. And I'm sure it showed. I had taught Spring 2017 with vim and vigor, Fall 2017 with general aplomb, but Spring 2018 with fatigue and exhaustion. Unfortunately, I had to deal with a handful of unruly, disruptive students in my third and final semester, which made the job very stressful. They made it stressful by going over my head and complaining to my direct supervisor, the head of the department, Dr. Wilson. He then decided to sit in on my class, not once, but thrice, thus squelching my desire to discipline the students whose side he took eventually. Of course, they didn't talk when he was there, but they simply wouldn't stop talking—in the very front row, that is—when he wasn't. That really ground my gears! So Dr. Wilson was a new, ultimately unsupportive boss who did not want to deal with my complaining about the students, who were complaining about me.

"Jason, you gave out to half of the class A's!"

"What's wrong with that, Dr. Wilson? Those kids earned their grades!"

And then he tested me on the material:

"Jason, what is a macro-variable for the threat of suppliers in the Five-Forces Model?"

"I don't know, you tell me!"

"The small number of suppliers, approaching monopoly..."

*I mean, really, is this a pop quiz for professors or something?*

"Yeah, but Dr. Wilson, that's not a macro-variable. That's micro or meso at best!"

And while the money and benefits of the position were good, the teaching job was unfulfilling, because it was the same material over and over, semester to semester. The university as an institution no longer held any special glamor or place for me.

Dr. Wilson ultimately decided not to extend my contract for another semester. I was piping mad, especially when Dr. Wilson told me that in an email, without the guts to see me in person. Well, I guess it saved me a trip down to campus. Although I was pissed, I took the time to write a conciliatory email back, one that cleared out my feelings honestly and also my desire to make the best of an unpleasant situation. Besides, I thought it would be best to be a good sport about the whole matter. As a final rejoinder, I wrote the following to Dr. Wilson's attention:

June 5, 2018

Dr. Joseph Wilson
Department of Management and Organization

Dear Dr. Wilson:
Difficulties in establishing a chosen profession naturally engender feelings of frustration, moroseness, and animosity. It is my duty to divest myself of all such negative feelings; and as far as it is in my power to do so, to cultivate friendly feelings towards those with whom I have perhaps contended, and maybe widely, but also honestly, differed. Local disputes, personal grudges, and private differences should be blotted out; and, as I withdraw from academic life, an honorable, straightforward course of conduct will secure the respect of all parties involved. Whatever my closing responsibilities may be to the department, school or university, I will meet them like a man.

The independent attempt to establish myself as a professor at USC has failed; but the consciousness of having done my duty faithfully, and to the end, will surely, in some measure, repay for the hardships I have undergone. In bidding you farewell, I would like to thank the following individuals for their efforts on my behalf: you, Dr. Wilson, for benevolently supervising my work; Dr. Moran for giving me my start at Prudence; Dr. Purcell for assisting me greatly with my students; Dr. Sedgwick for strongly raising the quality of my syllabus; and Ms. Cavell for kindly ceding to my incessant demands. And I now cheerfully and gratefully acknowledge my indebtedness to the staff of MOR whose zeal and fidelity have been the great source of my past success in teaching Strategic Management.

> I was the best professor I could possibly have been, given the particular constraints on my person; I can be the best I can be in whatever professional opportunity lies ahead, despite the especial limitations on my character. In doing so, I will obey the laws, preserve my honor, and it is my belief that the university to which I have relinquished my position can afford to be, and will be, magnanimous.
>
> Respectfully submitted,
> Jason Park

Actually, tensions had been running pretty high on the part of campus where the business school buildings were located. Three months prior, during the beginning of the Spring semester of 2018, a faculty member had erroneously declared an "active shooter" in the building where the business school classrooms held lectures. What happened next could be predicted: there was a general evacuation of the building which alarmed everyone in school, including students, faculty, and staff alike. The police were called to the scene, and they found nothing. Actually, the false alarm was generated by the same faculty member's psychiatric illness of some sort, perhaps involving psychosis or a mood disorder. She was gone within the week.

Although all this had nothing to do with me, I concluded my stay at the University after collecting my financial savings and strengthening my resume. Afterwards, it took six months—the latter part of 2018—exhausting all of my unemployment benefits, journaling and talking in therapy sessions, thinking in quiet and thinking out loud, and going to support group meetings, before I decided I could move on. In New Year's 2019, I still had no idea what I could do to occupy my time productively over and above obtaining money from my parents. But I kept thinking about it, as I was always writing in my journals, constantly recording notes of my therapy sessions with Dr. Cave, and informing Dr. Sager about my feelings and thoughts.

* * *

I realized that all the *writing* I had ever done, whether philosophical at Harvard or research-based at Pitt, had turned me into a seasoned writer. In fact, everything productive I had done since college was all words-based, not numbers-based. And that was not necessarily confined to philosophical tomes or management articles. In fact, the one thing that I *was* doing the whole time—writing—was the one thing that could make best use of my faculties!

So once I realized that I would try to be a writer, in general, I then recognized that I could apply my writing style to yet other genres. And the next logical step was to find a particular genre that focused on a certain subject matter close to my heart: write a memoir about my struggle with bipolar disorder. Perfect. Maybe it was time to write about something less academic and more personal: about being afflicted with a diagnosis and finally recovering from it.

The memoir was a quest—a hero's journey—from diagnosis to recovery, with recovery being the Holy Grail of mental health conditions. And the quest involved great exertion on the hero's part, the overcoming of many obstacles, and the changed nature or character of the hero And the changed nature of the hero would involve: (A) complete abstinence, (B) lack of betrothal, (C) no issue, (D) assuming the sedentary life, (E) commitment to family, and (F) confrontation of the mental health condition. And a major lesson of the story is: *although currently there is no cure for mental illness, however much we may seek it, recovery is possible, which means that there is always hope.*

At first, when I sat down at my laptop, there was nothing but a blank screen in front of me. That stupid cursor kept blinking impishly at me, daring me to type, in the upper left hand corner of the screen. *All right, I will!* But I couldn't think of anything to say that would hold even a captive audience. But once I could concentrate on nothing but just one thing, that's when I knew I had taken the first step. So start I did. And I started, right from the very beginning of my life, before my adjunct teaching post, before Hong Kong, and before the University of Pittsburgh... before the Balance Treatment Center... and back, even farther back, to Harvard, then to Fox Chapel Area High School, then to Dorseyville Middle School, then to Falk School, and out of Pittsburgh to Los Angeles and then right back to Lawrence, Kansas, where I was born.

I wrote, tentatively at first. But then I felt compelled to write—from the heart, the seat of the passions, the source of one's emotions, the wellspring of one's feelings, the cradle of one's affect. With growing conviction, I let my brain process its memories, then emit its neurochemical signals, down through my arms, into my hands, in coordination through each of my fingers, into the sensitive fingertips, onto the black plastic keyboard, then converted into silicon-based electrical signals, into the computer's own memory banks, from which appeared black strokes on a white monitor, like ink on paper. And this is what emerged...

January 1, 2019
I was born in Lawrence, Kansas. Whenever people ask me where I was born, they inevitably do a double-take

to my response. Or they raise an eyebrow. Most Korean-Americans of my generation (Gen X) were born on the coasts, specifically Los Angeles or New York City. Or they are Korean-born transplants who became permanent residents. I guess my curious questioners never suspected an ethnic Korean to come straight from America's heartland. But it's true, and I have my passport and birth certificate to prove it...

* * *

# Afterword: Advice to Others with Bipolar Disorder

What is most challenging about suffering from mental illness, and for those who care for people like you and me, is the length of the Road to Recovery, even with a favorable prognosis. It would have been so helpful to me to have a rigorous account of mental health recovery to lessen the time spent suffering. My goal of offering this Afterword to other sufferers of this illness and their loved ones is to help recovery begin to move forward with the least delay.

To accomplish this, I have condensed Part I of this book into the essentials needed for recovery—one Pre-condition and three Requirements. This Pre-condition is having the Self-Motivation to Get Better. The three Requirements consist of: (1) Trusting Your Treatment Team; (2) Reaching Out to Your Family; and (3) Engaging with Your Community. When the Pre-condition and three Requirements are present together, they contribute to the patient's recovery most quickly and completely.

There is an accompanying diagram that shows the progress of a prototypical patient from Pre-condition, through the three

Requirements, and finally to mental health recovery. I include this diagram to guide the discussion below. (See page 276.)

## The Pre-condition: The Patient's Self-Motivation to Get Better

The Pre-condition of having the self-motivation to get better starts the process in the center circle of the accompanying Figure.

Having the motivation to get better requires *being open to treatment*. The first and most important part of my recovery was realizing that there was a problem, and that it lay with me. Furthermore, I had to realize that the world did not revolve around me, and any attempt on my part to cynically manipulate my environment would be a useless gesture. When I returned to Los Angeles from Hong Kong, I was not in my right mind. I should have cooperated sooner with those around me. Had I been more open to treatment then, I could have more fully acknowledged the "red flags" emerging, and recovered in time. Resistance to treatment, which is the opposite of the self-motivation to get better, is a sure-fire way of short-circuiting one's start on the Road to Recovery.

But overcoming that resistance sometimes requires external forces, because you are so sealed off from within. That is when the (1) treatment team, (2) family, and (3) society can overcome your irrational objections. Hospitalizations, 5150s, Conservatorships, and even Laura's Law (for court-ordered outpatient treatment) can be used if you are particularly unwilling. I have had my share of these, and consider them part of the past. Do *not* interpret these initiatives as personal slights! Rather, they are for everyone's safety. Learn to embrace these golden opportunities to be motivated to get better.

If you open your door to treatment, treatment will open doors for you. My Ph.D. program at the University of Pittsburgh required individualism and entrepreneurship, and I was expected to continue visits during this time with a mental health professional. I initially resisted seeing a psychiatrist because I thought my ambition was enough for me, and I did not want to waste precious time in the shrink's office. But I learned valuable lessons about personal happiness and professional success from the Good Doctor. Of course, I still had to shoulder recovery and school on my own. But the physician's insights allowed me to see the light of graduation at the end of the tunnel.

## Requirement #1: Patient's Trust in the Treatment Team

Once you are motivated to get better, then the next logical step would be for you to begin trusting your treatment team. That comes first before contact with family or with the community. You need and deserve the professional support of the therapist and psychiatrist.

Trusting your treatment team—and their trusting you—means that both parties *establish a therapeutic alliance*. In other words, the treatment team wants you to get better, and you want the treatment team to help you get better. As a result, each party's short-term interests coincide naturally. In this alliance, the treatment team will heed your concerns about medication side-effects, and use a personalized therapeutic approach for you. In turn, you must follow the therapist's and psychiatrist's instructions, attend appointments faithfully, and take the medication as prescribed.

Any suspicions you harbor towards your treatment team could end the alliance, with disastrous consequences. Also, do not think you know better and self-medicate! While under Conservatorship, I accepted the mood stabilizer Depakote prescribed by my previous doctor at the University of Pittsburgh Medical Center, but I declined the anti-psychotic, believing that I only had a mood disorder. However, the psychiatrist had observed psychotic features in my thinking, so my second-guessing of the treatment team sidelined my recovery for a long time. Also, remain medication compliant! One time I went off my medication against doctor's orders. I ended up rambling all over metropolitan Pittsburgh, disturbing people in the hotels, nightclubs, and bars for forty-eight hours, much to the chagrin of the police, who were eventually detached to sequester me into the local psychiatric ward.

In the final analysis, establishing a therapeutic alliance with mediocre or poor doctors could be hazardous to your mental health. At the same time, there may be doctors that you really like, but your insurance plan will not cover them. Again, this is not conducive to your mental health. My advice, given these considerations, is to find the doctors who are the *right fit* for you, and who are covered by your insurance plan. They may not be what you want, but they will probably be what you need. And as long as they are willing to work with you, and you are willing to be cooperative with them, it could be the start of a very productive therapeutic alliance. So trust your doctors, and they will trust you, too.

## Requirement #2: Patient's Reaching Out to Family

Once you have established a bond with your treatment team, you can proceed to an outer circle on the figure: your family. Reaching out to family means that both parties *feel close belonging*. I remember feeling a renewed sense of close belonging with family through my relationship with my two nieces. Although not my own children, I treated them in some ways as my own. And as their uncle, I *belonged closely* to my family through them, because of my auxiliary but still important role in their upbringing.

Alienation, the opposite of close belonging, destroys the human spirit and the will to persevere. My family's relationship with me changed when I grew from a symptomatic twenty-three-year-old to a stable forty-three-year-old. Even in broken relationships, one can "pick up the pieces," if honest re-assessment occurs. When I brandished a golf club at my father, the relationship on some level ended. But a new one took its place, when I sought amends with him, and he accepted. Ending alienation and cultivating feelings of close belonging should be your *modus operandi.*

Of course, some people don't have families that are supportive and loving, even biological, half-, step-, foster families or legal guardians. But more important than reaching out to family is *reaching out, period!* That can include reaching out to friends, even. At a sober living house where I briefly stayed, the feeling of family was strong, although none of us were related biologically. Our only goal—sobriety—against our common enemy—addiction—gave us all a shared sense of belonging. Even the house's two bulldogs made us all feel loved and gave us a sense of belonging. So from that positive environment came the feeling of close belonging. Thus, reach out to family, whatever healthy form it takes, and your family will reach back out to you.

## Requirement #3: Patient's Engaging with the Community

Once you have reached out to your family and renegotiated lasting bonds with them, you can proceed to an outer circle: engaging with society. That means that both parties *freely associate with the other.* We can only associate freely with those who want to associate freely with us. In other words, "engaging with society is a two-way street." When I texted a Japanese-American friend that she was a "Jap" and that her Irish-American husband was a "Mic," they cut off all communication. My bizarre, outrageous hate-speech elicited the "silent treatment," which expressed their choice to freely dissociate.

The resulting isolation was unfortunate. In fact, *solitary confinement* in jails causes psychological damage to the most intransigent criminals. But I was not a criminal; in my own unwise way, I was reaching out for company and help. So I joined support group meetings, held with others with mental health conditions, and from all walks of life. At these meetings, I voluntarily talked about the racist texts. Though I felt compromised, the group accepted the experience, provided helpful feedback, and moved on, without reservation. My feeling of isolation diminished considerably.

Ultimately, I became a professor at a major research university in Los Angeles. This time, before I began my tenure, I asked myself: *Would I associate freely with myself based on my current behavior?* So I made a commitment to myself to express tolerance to students, collegiality to faculty, and benevolence to staff, all of whom had a stake in the university's future. As I started the job, I made it a point to maintain my composure, keep a sense of humor, and remain emotionally diplomatic, despite the work stress. As a result, people began to freely associate with me. Thus, *engaging with others in the community, regardless of station*, is the key to being engaged by the community in turn.

## End-Result: Patient's Mental Health Recovery

After achieving engagement with the community, the concentric circles outlining the various groups to make contact with end. At this point, we then proceed to the outside space on the Figure: mental health recovery. When we have achieved the Pre-condition and met the three Requirements, the chances for mental health recovery are quite good. But what does mental health recovery look like?

Well, like the area outside the circular spaces, there is a certain freedom from restraint. Mental health recovery can be summed up in one word: autonomy. However, autonomy as a word refers to freedom characterized by *responsibility*. It most emphatically does not mean untrammeled, unconditional freedom, where you can do whatever you want, whenever you want, with whomever you want, wherever you want. No, no, no! Instead, it means that the patient has no longer abdicated responsibility over his mental health, and has now taken over the reins of control over his life. Specific activities in life include:

- the patient makes smart and wise decisions over his care,
- the patient has found a financially remunerative way to support his lifestyle,

- the patient lives free of trouble with the law,
- the patient engages in relationships with happy and healthy human beings, and
- the patient has a place to call his own.

There may be many other initiatives besides that, but this is only a start. In other words, autonomy is "the good life." Don't we all want that? None of these activities are beyond the ken of any mentally ill individual, nor of any mentally healthy individual. However, they require a disciplined, committed approach to life. All the activities I list above take time and energy to realize. Rome wasn't built in a day.

## Conclusion

The statistics surrounding mental illness are grim. According to the Stability Network, people with mental health conditions experience higher death rates resulting from suicide, job loss, unemployment, violence done to them, poverty, and homelessness. And mental health conditions cost approximately $400 billion annually in lost earnings, health-care expenditures, and disability payments.

Currently there is no cure for mental illness, only recovery. That may sound like a death knell, but really it is a matter of framing. Take the remission of cancer with chemotherapy, management of diabetes using insulin, or treatment of asthma via inhaled steroids. These may not be cures, but they are forms of recovery, and definitely can produce positive outcomes. Recovery from mental illness is no different. With the Precondition and three Requirements, there is hope for the future.

The stigma associated with mental illness is fading. Science is tackling mental illness from every possible angle. Therapeutic techniques are becoming more advanced, and psychotropic medications are getting better. So if you are facing the challenge, remember that learning to master a mental health diagnosis (like any other great but difficult endeavor) can be very rewarding.

* * *

**The 1 Pre-condition & 3 Requirements of Mental Health Recovery**

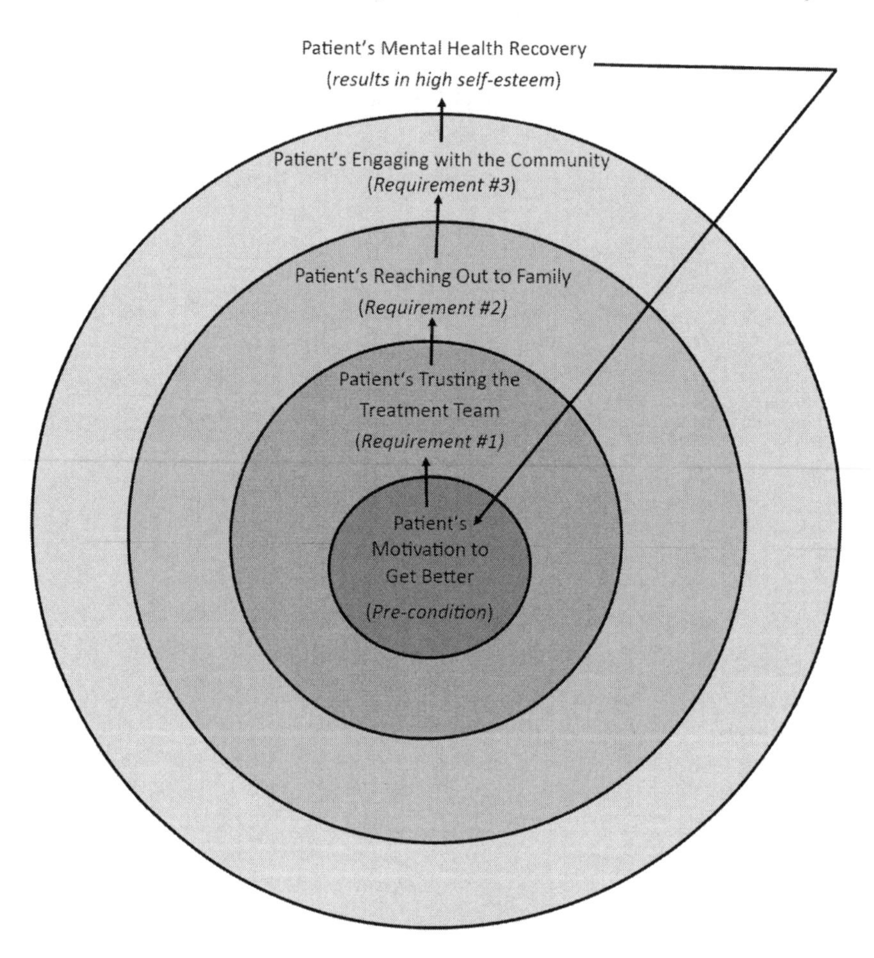


By Jason W. Park

LOS ANGELES POLICE DEPARTMENT

**MICHEL R. MOORE**
Chief of Police

**ERIC GARCETTI**
Mayor

P.O. Box 30158
Los Angeles, CA 90030
Telephone: (213) 486-0150
TTY: (877) 275-5273
Ref #: 8.2

October 29, 2019

Dear Stakeholder:

Please join the Los Angeles Police Department and the Los Angeles County Department of Mental Health for the quarterly Mental Health Crisis Response Program Advisory Board meeting. The meeting will be held on Thursday, December 5th, 2019, from 10:00 a.m. to 11:30 a.m. at the Zev Yaroslavsky Family Resource Center, SEC/JOS Room, 7555 Van Nuys Blvd, Van Nuys, CA 91405.

The goal of the Mental Health Crisis Response Program Advisory Board is to provide a forum for the exchange of information, to identify new mental health developments, and to provide advice and assistance regarding mental health issues. It is through the exchange of information and ideas that we can succeed in finding ways to attain an optimal level of service to the community.

Your participation at this meeting would be greatly appreciated, as your input would help to achieve the goals of the Board. Please feel free to bring your program's literature to share. To RSVP, please contact Senior Lead Officer Jasminka Jurisaga, Mental Evaluation Unit, Detective Support and Vice Division, at (213) 926-3828, or email 36897@lapd.online. Parking is available.

Very truly yours,

MICHEL R. MOORE
Chief of Police

SYNTHIA L. LEE, Captain
Commanding Officer
Detective Support and Vice Division

## Transcript of a Public Address given by Jason W. Park, Ph.D., to the Los Angeles Police Department and Los Angeles County Department of Mental Health

December 5, 2019

Hi everybody! How's everyone doing? Doing OK? OK, I see a lot of nods, and I don't see too many shakes, so I guess that's pretty good, huh? Alright!

You know, folks, when I told my friends and family that I would be speaking to you ladies and gentlemen, they were all without exception very impressed. To protect and to serve, to protect our community and safeguard crime victims' rights, and hope, recovery, and well-being, contain the essential nobility of your respective organizations. Do not lose sight of these, even when it's easy to become cynical and pessimistic.

I am here to talk about my own recovery from mental illness: what helped, what did not help, and what could have been done better but wasn't. In other words, the Good, the Bad, and the Ugly. And I will conclude with any thoughts I may have that might help you when encountering a crisis situation. It's important to note that everyone's path to recovery is different. I will be speaking from my own experience and sharing what has and what has not worked well for me.

So remember: this is not a pep talk; I am not a motivational speaker; and you men and women don't need a cheerleader. I stand here before you today as a mental health consumer who is a member of three mental health advocacy organizations: the National Alliance on Mental Illness or NAMI, The Stability Network and the Depression and Bipolar Support Alliance or DBSA.

I also am a member of the population in LA County that is most vulnerable. In the worst cases they can't pay the rent, can't balance a checkbook, can't avoid the streets, can't access medical care, can't take care of their families...and so on and so forth. So may the same courage, honor and respect you bring to the badge, the DA's office, and the DMH, one day rid our city of the scourge of mental illness.

Over twenty years ago, I was diagnosed with bipolar disorder type I, which out of two types is the more severe. It is characterized by episodes of depression and elevated moods, like irritability or euphoria. My current psychiatrist would also add "with psychotic features." That would include paranoia and delusions on top of the grandiosity of bipolar. So I have a lot on my plate, as you can tell!

**Here's THE GOOD in my recovery – what helped me.**

First, **Medication compliance** – taking the medications, in the right dosage, at the right time of day, day in, day out, according to the doctor's instructions. I take seven different medications to battle my condition. So I am rather heavily medicated. Note that taking medication for mental illness is like taking insulin for diabetes or inhaling steroids for asthma. You wouldn't think twice, right?

Second, **Stress reduction** – Personally, I know some people with bipolar who are married with children. But I am single with no kids, and that's a choice I made in order to minimize the amount of stress in my life. Instead, I simply enjoy playing the piano, listening to Electronic Dance Music, taking long walks, and playing chess with my 7-year-old niece, although I don't like losing at chess to a 7-year-old.

Next, **Self-motivation** – The patient has to want to get better. The change for me began when I first realized that there was a problem, and that the problem was within me. And that my own selfish manipulation of others in my environment had to stop before I could address my own life and what I wanted to do with it. Using my parents for petty cash, groceries, illicit drugs, alcohol, rent money, and cigarettes, with no job made me a leech and halted progress in my recovery right in its tracks.

Fourth is **Trust in treatment team** – I have my psychiatrist and psychologist. It is important that I tell them exactly how I'm feeling. Let's face it, folks: therapy is a luxury. We could all use some therapy at some point. Imagine talking about anything and anybody you could possibly want, without consequences and in complete confidentiality. It's amazing how much better you feel afterwards.

Fifth, but oh so important, is **Family support** – Family is about feeling close belonging with others. Typically a biological family exhibits this, but also in a step-family, a half-family, foster families, with guardians and even friends becoming families. When my family gets together, there's a lot of hugging and kissing going on in a loving way. And the good things you apply within the family, you apply to the community.

Now the last but not least factor – **Community engagement**. When I think of community, I think of the Depression & Bipolar Support Alliance's Pasadena chapter's twice weekly peer meetings. And the National Alliance of Mental Illness's In Our Own Voice presentations have substantial grassroots impact. I also attended my first Stability Network's international conference, where I met working professionals in varied industries with mental health diagnoses.

Community also includes the DA's office, DMH, LAPD/LASD, Conservators, judges, public defenders.... While community engagement is intangible because it can't be heard, smelled, tasted, felt, or seen, it is real, and its influence, while imperceptible, is irresistible. As a once mentally ill patient who is now mentally healthy, I know that engaging the community determines where I ultimately will end up in society.

So I want you to know that in many cases, like in mine, mental illness can be successfully treated and managed. But for me, getting the correct treatment, having family and community support, and having the willingness to work on my own recovery were all necessary to achieve this.

**What about THE BAD – what didn't help?**

First, **Self-medication** – administering your own pills, like drugs and alcohol. I abused all but heroin in college. It pushed back the depression temporarily. But now I have been drug and alcohol free for 12+ years. While sobriety may not contain the sky-highs that can come from self-administered drugs, it certainly lacks the downsides, and my life is much more even-keeled.

Second, **Getting off medications** – Prescription medications should not be stopped without a doctor's instructions. I found that out the hard way when I went off all 7 of my medications, only to sucker-punch somebody by landing a right cross straight on his nose. Today, such violent impulses no longer control me, since I always take my meds.

Third, **Occupational stress** – I wish that I had found the right career early on that fit my lifestyle and instilled in me a passion for what I do. After Harvard, I was a car messenger, a law clerk, a research assistant, a secretary, and a telemarketer. These assignments were all thankless and low-paying with no hopes for advancement. My current vocation as a writer is a big step in the right direction.

Fourth, **Not trusting my treatment team** – I once had an excellent Egyptian psychiatrist, until I started calling him the Egyptian Magician. He was not amused. "No, Jason, there's no magic here," he said. And my therapist, a rather large gentleman, became irritated when I constantly asked him what his waistline was. Behind the humor was the mistrust of both men. I didn't take my own recovery seriously because I was in my first year of a PhD program and I was still in party mode. I had to earn the trust back of both physicians when I became serious about my recovery, because I became serious about school.

Fifth is **Alienating family** – I think family conflicts need to be resolved first before moving on. The one time I got into a fight with my father, I was taken away for simple assault. Years later, I was 5150'd by my brother to Aurora Las Encinas Hospital, to then be conserved afterwards. These days, my family and I always get together on holidays and on weekends, and there is harmony, not discord.

Last is **Fighting the community** – Disengaging with the community was what was next. My conservator called an additional 5150 on me to Cerritos College Hospital. I could easily have fallen through the cracks of society had not the community of Los Angeles been more benevolent in my case, and unfortunately, I still made it very hard on you folks. It's still hard for me to forgive myself.

**Then there's THE UGLY – what could or should have been done, but wasn't.**

I once worked in a top-20 law firm in Century City in the late 90's, straight out of college. I was clearly symptomatic at the time. I was full of outbursts, angry exchanges, grandiose thinking and acting, paranoia, depression, and delusional thinking. And the HR contact person actually reached out to me and asked me if the law firm could help with access to therapists or counselors. And do you know what I did? I refused the help. So in a matter of weeks, I was terminated from my job as a litigation clerk. So here are a few things that could have been done better, but wasn't.

Cultural misunderstanding – lacking comprehension of mental illness

Didn't want to admit – my personal pride was at stake and I was in denial

Short-sighted thinking – just glad that in the first meeting I wouldn't get fired

I thought I could "will" myself out of this emotional problem – and you can't.

Fortunately, these negative behaviors are behind me. I have been very fortunate to get the right care and treatment.

**And finally, some things that might help you folks—law enforcement or providers—when you encounter someone in crisis.**

**Bizarre/outrageous behavior is not the same as (dangerous) antisocial/psychopathic behavior**. There is overlap, but that can be teased out. Smearing feces, dancing at an all-night rave party, buying five BMW's, each a different color, would fall in the first category: diverted from jail. Armed robbery, first-degree murder, and forcible rape of a minor, would be the second category. In other words, go directly to jail!

Indeed, malicious intent tends not to characterize a manic episode. People with mental illness are more often victims of crime, rather, and people with mental illness are not necessarily dangerous. Only a small subset of the mentally ill are violent.

**Try to show empathy**. This is about putting yourself in the other person's shoes. This person you are encountering could easily be your brother, your aunt, or even yourself. Getting through to that person's state of mind is key. That you matter to them, but also that *they matter to you*, moves the process in a constructive direction.

Hospitalization for mania should look like hospitalization for a heart attack. We don't think twice to involuntarily commit somebody for a heart attack. Why then does society view a heart attack and a manic episode differently? We would never say to someone who is having a heart attack: "What's wrong with you? Why are you acting this way?" As a society, we have room to grow in understanding that in both situations, the person is not in control of their own heart/brain/impulses and is therefore in need of help.

**CONCLUSIONS – thanks and praise**

I would like to thank Ms. Jackie Lacey in absentia and the entire DA's office, the LA County Department of Mental Health, the Los Angeles Police Department and the Los Angeles Sheriff's Department, the MEU and SMART units, Homes for Life, NAMI, DBSA, the Stability Network, and Senior Lead Officer Jasminka Jurisaga, and all others who I may have missed, for being a wonderful audience. And thank you again for letting me be of service. Have a great day.

# PART II

# Appendices

APPENDIX A

# Backgrounder from Jason's Parents

It's comforting to know what we should do for Jason now and for the future. My wife Sunhee and I have decided to contribute one section to this book that our son, Jason, wrote with courage and candor. We want to share our retrospective lessons and insights about what we as parents should have done for Jason *to support his speedy and stable recovery.*

We both have agreed that we do not want to delve into how we might have parented Jason differently *so that he could have avoided his bipolar disorder*. Addressing this issue is beyond the scope of our expertise, and we do not know with relative certainty a way that we as parents could have prevented the disorder. In this book we also do not want to offer readers a laundry list of pains and heartaches that Sunhee and I both endured over the twenty years or so during Jason's sufferings. There are just too many and they are too difficult to enumerate. And we do not believe that sharing such information with readers would serve Jason's interest and goals while he is a book author. Instead, we have decided to focus in this section on *what we may have done differently to help Jason recover more quickly after the onset of his illness.*

Jason's book and our introspective analyses of the last two decades since Jason's initial diagnosis gave us renewed and highly informed insights that we think may be helpful to other bipolar patients and their family members who are facing the same difficulties as we did in the past. The question is: What could, would, or should we have done for Jason from the onset of his illness so that he did not have to go through such a long and arduous journey? We certainly do not claim that our introspective analyses and suggestions are the most representative and authentic remedies for bipolar patients. We simply cannot make such a claim because each patient is unique and different from others in the severity and the nature of his or her disorder. However, we also believe that the four key lessons that we offer at the end of this section may have properties general enough to help patients with mental disorders to recover.

Let us start by introducing who Jason was when he was young. This information may help readers understand why we did what we did during his illness. When Jason was in kindergarten through twelfth grade, both Sunhee and I felt blessed that we had what many parents would call the "perfect child" and "perfect student." He was always eager to please us and others, wanting and enjoying the recognition that he so richly deserved at that time. He was a fearlessly goal-oriented child, spending three to four hours each and every day practicing the piano in a Spartan fashion to be the best. His school performance was simply superb, and he excelled in all of his extracurricular activities He graduated as valedictorian of his class and received a positive decision as an early action candidate to Harvard. He always respected us, followed our wishes, and became a great role model for his younger brother.

Simply stated, we were very happy with Jason and felt extremely fortunate to have him as our son. We also felt the same way about his younger brother, who was as gifted and well-behaved. Both children were bright, well-built, handsome, and well-mannered. They both received acceptance as early action candidates to Harvard, which we were extremely proud of.

In his K-12 school days, we missed the early signs of his disorder because he performed so well. Starting from junior high school, there were some signs that we should have not brushed off. At the time, we thought and wished that he would simply toughen up and eventually get through his "trifling" conflicts such as getting bullied in school. When we first learned that Jason had bipolar disorder, we really did not have an understanding about the nature of the illness. However, Sunhee and I thought that we could bring the old Jason back and that it would be more than possible to cure his condition. We believed that Jason had not lost his will to get better with his own determination and persistence. Our interactions and conversations with him were based on this assumption. While we knew that he was not in a normal state of mind, we still expected from him his normal and rational thoughts and behaviors. Hoping and wanting to bring Jason back to his younger days made us refuse to believe that Jason had changed into an adult with a very serious and lifelong illness.

Reading Jason's account made us feel highly inadequate and inattentive to his limited capabilities. He went through so many painful, lonely, insulting, humiliating, and depressing situations by himself. We as parents did not offer him a secure place where he felt comfort and safety. Instead, it appears that we asked him to face such situations on his own. Again, we expected him to toughen himself and be a courageous man. We did not recognize that Jason had not developed his emotional maturity as well as he had developed his intellectual maturity, and that he was unable to function smoothly in social settings, due to his disorder. Discussed below are four key lessons that we learned retrospectively that we would have followed during Jason's battle with his illness if we had been aware of them. They are listed below and are not necessarily independent of each other. We have decided to treat and discuss them separately because each lesson has its own importance and implications on how to prepare and cope with a patient with bipolar disorder.

## LESSON 1: Detect symptoms early and respond quickly and responsibly.

We witnessed Jason's very poor mental and emotional condition when he came home after college graduation, not long before he was diagnosed with bipolar disorder. In order to cheer him up, Sunhee and I took him to the Grand Canyon. We had a great time there together; he appeared jovial and very gregarious. He seemed to be 100% the Jason who we used to know when he was young. However, right after we returned home, I saw him sitting on the living room couch alone in the morning, struggling with sadness and despair. That sudden change of mood baffled me a great deal, to say the least. At that time, I strongly believed that his despondence, despair, and deep sadness was an abnormal, exceptional, and temporary phenomenon that I could ignore. I simply did not pay enough attention to the fact that Jason was becoming a very different individual who had started to suffer from a very serious mental disorder.

In retrospect, we should have responded to this change within Jason and arranged the best possible medical team within our budgetary constraints. We should have examined the background and the qualification of each doctor and psychologist available to Jason. This is because treating a person with bipolar disorder properly from the beginning has a tremendous impact on his or her subsequent prognosis and recovery. In our case we do not believe that Jason received proper treatment at times. It appears that his initial inadequate medical treatment and therapy led Jason to develop enormous anger, distrust, and hatred toward us. It took many years for us and Jason to restore a stable and respectable relationship. The psychological, financial, and emotional costs that we and Jason paid due to this misguided treatment were very heavy.

## LESSON 2: Set realistic goals for the patient's recovery.

When Jason was hospitalized in Los Angeles several years ago, we were notified by the landlord in Koreatown that his room should be vacated for another tenant. Sunhee and I thus went there to clean his apartment room. His room was chaotic and in full disarray. It took several hours to clean the room and we both felt exhausted. While cleaning his room, I asked myself, ***How** on earth could Jason have stayed in such a messy room?* **What** caused him to live in such a chaotic condition did not occur to me. Instead of having empathy and sharing the same pain that Jason must have gone through in his chaotic and messy room, I was trying to cope with my own deep disappointment, numbness, and enormous frustration. Instead of trying to figure out how to reduce Jason's stress level and improve his mental stability, I was busy dealing with my own deep disappointment. I know that Sunhee felt the same way.

One of the key lessons that we learned from Jason's case is that, as mentioned earlier in this section, our focus was on bringing Jason back to his old self, NOT on how to lessen the severity of the symptoms of his mental disorder and how to make him feel better as a person. We tended to emphasize correcting his destructive or provocative thoughts and behaviors based on rules, policies, or arrangements. Whenever Jason experienced an emotional outburst and disrupted his relationship with us, we often imposed a "tough love" rule on him, penalizing him for his inappropriate behaviors. For example, we lowered his monthly stipend, limited the frequency of his visits to us, or refused to talk to him during a certain period of time, trying to convince him that his uncontrolled behaviors had negative consequences. However, from Jason's viewpoint, we were trying to control him, his thoughts, and his behaviors with our financial power. This led him to develop more anger and distrust towards us, which created the basis for the vicious cycle in our relationship with Jason. In retrospect, we were too impatient with Jason's prospects for his full recovery from the illness. We did not even think that it could be a health issue that Jason would have to deal with for the rest of his life. At the early stage of his illness, we should have accepted the fact that we perhaps would never be able to bring Jason back to his old days because he had become a different person with bipolar disorder.

## LESSON 3: Establish the need for mutual communication and vigilant monitoring.

It is very important for one to constantly monitor a patient's mental, emotional, and psychological status without lowering one's guard. There is a temptation to falsely assume that a patient is recovering well and making great progress, and handling himself or herself well without family intervention. This is a very dangerous approach that may spell disaster at a later time. We personally experienced Jason's freefall from a reasonably functioning independent person to an incoherent, psychotic, and malfunctioning individual during his stay in Hong Kong as a university faculty member. We thought that he was doing well and things were moving in the right direction. Jason was also trying very hard to assure us that things were indeed moving along although his research was not going well. It was only much later that we learned from him the poor medical support he received in Hong Kong and the subsequent emotional and psychological difficulty he had endured there.

We truly wish that through more frequent communication and vigilant monitoring, we had recognized his ill health and brought him back to the States so that he could have had the necessary medical support team. It is our belief that the ineffective medical treatment that Jason received in Hong-Kong and his personal and professional difficulties in a foreign land had a compounding impact on him, reinforcing one another to push him in a terrible downward spiral. We believe that this unfortunate period in Jason's life left serious scars on his personal makeup and still slows down his journey to full and complete recovery. We do not, however, intend to make any disparaging remarks about the quality of Hong Kong's medical support toward mentally ill patients. We are sure that it offers first-rate medical help to them, on par with treatment in the States. Jason simply was not able to take full advantage of the medical resources that were available to him in Hong Kong.

## LESSON 4: Immerse yourself with the meaning of unconditional love.

Our focusing on bringing Jason back to his old self made it extremely difficult for us to fully digest the meaning of *unconditional love* and to practice it with him. It took so many years for us to understand the true meaning of unconditional love by heart. At the beginning we thought that it was simply jargon that practitioners in the mental health industry had come up with. To us at that time, it was a meaningless term that was too difficult for families of mental patients to realistically practice. It is only relatively recently that we started to understand the beautiful meaning of this term.

Our unconditional love for Jason should be to accept and care for him with empathy no matter how different he has diverged from our own expectations and wishes. Why is this unconditional love so important to Jason? We know that it definitely reduces his stress and mental anguish, which, in turn, helps him to deal with his troubled mood disorder. Accumulation of stress over time through conflict with family members and others close to them has a very detrimental effect on patients with bipolar disorder. Jason was no exception.

In retrospect, we do not think we offered a place where he felt safe, supported, and emotionally nurtured with unconditional love. One may certainly argue that unconditional love does not cure mental disorders and, in fact, may even possibly lead patients in the wrong direction, by creating a tendency to depend on others without learning to become independent. While the potential of this negative effect may exist, we nevertheless argue that the danger and difficulties caused by the absence of unconditional love seem to be much more detrimental.

These days we simply accept Jason as who he is. We do not dwell on what we would like him to be in the future. This is not because we have given up on him, but because we realize that Jason has already done as best as he could with his condition. He deserves credit for going through an incredibly difficult and painful life, fighting against the enormous odds stacked against him. Whatever Jason wants to do hereafter, we should respect and support him. He should hold his head high and feel good about himself because he has fully paid his dues to become a financially and socially independent person. Despite much adversity, he valiantly challenged many obstacles that his bipolar disorder imposed on him. Jason may no longer be an esteemed professor in a university. He may not ever be a respected judge in a court. But why should this matter in the first place? To Sunhee and me, the most important task is to let Jason feel happy with his life and support him as best as we can to ensure it is meaningful and productive. This is what unconditional love means to us.

* * *

Before we close our section, we would like to write a few words about the word *recovery*. This word may be interpreted in several different ways, and to us it has several different meanings. The first interpretation is that Jason has been very stable and functioning very well without any noticeable symptoms for three years. That is clearly recovery from his darker period. The second interpretation of recovery is his conscious and successful effort to integrate three requirements for wellness into his daily life: (1) trusting his medical team, (2) loving his family members, and (3) respecting societal rules and regulations.

The third and final interpretation of recovery is that Jason has been very active in identifying what he can do to make his life meaningful and productive. Jason's current status aligns with these three aspects of the word "recovery," and he is ready to once again manage his life as a productive member of society.

APPENDIX B

# Backgrounder from George A. Cave, Ph.D., Psychologist

I met Jason about six years ago while he was being treated for Bipolar Disorder with psychotic features at Balance Treatment Center, a six-bed residential facility for those struggling with psychiatric issues. Jason had just been discharged from a locked facility, a hospital whereby the patient is not allowed to leave without being discharged by their attending psychiatrist. Jason had been involuntarily admitted after having manic behavior as well as psychosis. Psychosis, simply stated, is a phenomenon that occurs to some whose reality is skewed. A person who is suffering from psychosis has a false sense of reality but they believe their reality is, or should be, everyone else's reality. I was asked to treat Jason since his regular primary therapist took a week's vacation.

Our first session was quite colorful. Jason asked me, "Of what value are you to me?" He seemed agitated, arrogant, and rude (naturally, psychologists don't generally make such judgments about patients but I now do only for the sake of explanation). Jason was difficult to talk to and wanted to end our sixty-minute session after only a few minutes. I met with Jason every day for the next week and things did not get much better. Regardless, after a week, his primary therapist returned and I thought that to be the end of it.

Jason completed his time at Balance Treatment Center and found housing at a sober living home. Shortly after that, Jason, with the help of his Conservator and family, moved into his own apartment through an organization that provides housing for the chronically homeless and the mentally ill.

Several months later I received a phone call from Ronald Sager, M,D., Jason's psychiatrist, asking if I would consider seeing Jason in my private practice. It seemed that Jason had threatened someone and this had frightened his outpatient therapist. During our first session I assessed Jason to find that he was still symptomatic. Jason and I agreed to meet for treatment three days a week. I had met with Jason's family while he was in treatment at Balance Treatment Center and they also agreed that it would be a good fit.

Jason was a handful but much less so than when we worked together at Balance Treatment Center during his residential treatment. Jason still seemed to be somewhat angry with a skewed sense of reality. His first book had been published and this seemed to annoy his family and many others who were mentioned in the book. The things that seemed to be bothersome to those mentioned were factually correct but the conclusions reached were skewed, much like Jason's thinking.

It wasn't long after we started working together that Jason became more and more stable. Our relationship continued to improve as well. Jason continued to seem pressured by trying to earn money and felt that the first book would satisfy that need. Just the same, he continued to improve to the point that I initially thought that Jason had plateaued. He had written some apology letters and the relationship between Jason and his family had improved somewhat, although his family continued to seem cautious.

After several months Jason developed a rash, most likely a side effect from one of the new medications he was taking. He was told to discontinue its usage immediately and he did. No medication was prescribed to replace the discontinued medication at that time. A couple of months later Jason became more symptomatic with increased paranoia, agitation, increased spending, and more argumentativeness.

Jason saw his psychiatrist two or three times but was able to present himself as stable as he had been previously. Finally, I went to the psychiatrist's office with Jason and was able to question Jason to the point that he started to answer questions whereby the psychiatrist could see that Jason was not as stable as he had presented himself previously. This is not at all uncommon with people who are experiencing a skewed reality. But it takes a great deal of energy to conceal one's symptoms effectively, and cannot be maintained for very long. Also, when the patient is questioned, it is harder to maintain concealment of symptoms, and decompensating may appear quite readily.

After some discussion with Jason's psychiatrist, a "typical antipsychotic" was prescribed in addition to his other regimen of medications. This was a turning point in Jason's treatment. Within the next six weeks Jason became more and more stable to the point that noticing any symptoms at all was difficult. It was during this period when we curtailed our sessions from three times a week to twice a week.

Over the next year Jason continued to improve to the point that it was difficult to see any symptoms at all. He was able to start dating a woman he met online and it seemed to become serious. Shortly after this, Jason secured a teaching job at a very prestigious university. I became concerned that the increase in stress could produce break-through symptoms. That is when symptoms "break through" the threshold that the medication is maintaining. In cases such as this, medication might be changed in an effort to increase the threshold. In Jason's case he had no further symptoms.

Interestingly, just about the time the university job was to start, Jason and his girlfriend broke up. Both of these activities, starting a new job and ending a relationship, can be very stress-inducing and stress can exacerbate symptoms. Regardless, Jason was still able to remain free from symptoms. The job was difficult and every week Jason would talk about not wanting to be a teacher and the stress that it caused him. However, he never missed a day at work and continued for three semesters before deciding that it was not for him. Jason started to concentrate his attentions on writing this second book.

Our sessions together focused on issues that were happening in the moment using a cognitive-behavioral (CBT) approach. Few psychologists use primarily one therapeutic approach and I am no different, as I use more of an eclectic approach. The first, as is the case with most psychologists, is a person-centered-Rogerian approach which accepts the client as is and attempts to give the client unconditional positive regard. CBT focuses on the here-and-now, under the belief that the way a person is currently feeling, thinking, and behaving is the focus of treatment.

Rarely does a client stay in the here-and-now, and it is most uncommon for people who are experiencing current psychological issues to continue to stay in the here-and-now. The mind wanders to other periods in a person's life that are similar or that the client believes had some input as to the way the person is feeling in the present. This is when a more psychodynamic approach might be used. The client talks about what sort of things might come up as he thinks about the here-and-now and where his mind goes, usually somewhere back in time. This might very easily be to a time in his childhood. Very few people have had a flawless childhood. Things that a parent might think are somewhat harmless may very well stick with a child for most of his life. During this time of psychotherapy, the therapist listens and then makes interpretations of the events and how the client felt about the events. As the therapist I would then try and tie that event back to the current situation or topic.

Our therapy sessions have evolved over the years and currently often start with how Jason is doing and how his week has been going. Jason's current life follows a basic routine with his parents being a big part of his life as well as his psychiatrist and this writer (his psychologist) being another big part of his life.

It took Jason many years to develop the structure and routine that is working out so well for him. Jason has come a long ways from those first sessions we had at Balance Treatment Center. He is no longer angry and has developed significantly in nearly every way a person can develop. His relationship with his parents has become quite good and it seems that all of them truly enjoy each other's company and the time they spend together, even taking vacations together. A couple of years ago this would not have been possible.

Jason usually brings points and topics he wants to talk about. He brings his journal with him most places he goes and writes things down as the week goes on so that he does not forget. It is during these discussions when I can see what Jason is thinking about, what his mood is, and what the frustrations and concerns might be. We then process these as they come up. Oftentimes, we continue the topic during the next session.

The human mind is an extremely complicated thing. It stores information as well as our own interpretations of events along with the accompanying emotions. When things become distorted is when many people have difficulty making sense out of their own lives. When a disorder like bipolar disorder is added to the mix, things can get much more challenging. Keep in mind that when a person goes into a manic state with psychotic features, their reality becomes skewed, but at the same time, memories are still being created. When all of this is combined into the person's consciousness, reality testing breaks down and the person experiencing the psychotic episode is no longer in the same reality as those around him. It is the psychologist's job to try to help the client/patient come back to baseline.

Working with Jason over these past several years has been, for the most part, quite enjoyable and rewarding. Watching a patient go from where Jason was to where he is now is uplifting and provides a sense of hope for all patients suffering from bipolar disorder as well as from other serious psychiatric disorders.

Dr. George A. Cave, Ph.D., Psychologist
Author, *Just Be a Dad*

APPENDIX C

# Backgrounder from Ronald D. Sager, M.D., Psychiatrist

I first came to know Jason Park when I interviewed him on a locked psychiatric unit at his parents' request to assess his suitability for the Balance Treatment Center Residential Program. Balance Treatment Center Residential is the only six-bed mental health rehabilitation center licensed by the State of California. As the medical director of the Balance Treatment Center, I would be Jason's attending psychiatrist. As it has turned out, I am still Jason's psychiatrist now on an outpatient basis.

During the past six years, I have treated him in the Balance Treatment Center Residence ninety-day intensive residential program, at the Balance Treatment Center as an outpatient in the Balance Treatment Center IOP (Intensive Outpatient Clinic) in an acute hospital setting, and now I continue in an outpatient program primarily for medication management but also with brief psychotherapy. This emphasizes a major point that the pursuit of treatment for a patient with bipolar disorder is a lifetime pursuit. The patient ultimately has to be committed to continue treatment. There are genetic markers, there are constitutional factors that the person was born with, there is the nurturing environment in which he was raised, and there are many, many life experiences which influence the ongoing treatment. The major factor in Jason's success has been his determination to recover and his commitment to treatment—not only to work with his providers but to accept his family support as well. I really applaud Jason for his relentless commitment, for without that he would never have recovered.

Back to the story of Jason's recovery... When I first met him on a locked psychiatric unit, Jason showed multiple signs and symptoms of a bipolar disorder, mixed with psychotic features, which eventually was his diagnosis. He presented as very scattered in his thinking, quickly traversing from paranoid ideas to grandiosity to intense feelings of depression, making many irrational comments that seemed nonsensical. For example, blurting out numbers 42, 52, 62. He complained of being anxious and fearful of the future. He had overwhelming thoughts about himself and the probability of success. He bordered on suicidality most of the time as per his report.

At the time, I was impressed by his openness and humbleness but at the same time he presented as arrogant and grandiose. Then, in the next breath, he would say he could not believe anyone would come all the way down to the facility from Calabasas to see him. For the most part, Jason was pleasant but did admit to getting into fights at the hospital but claiming of course that he was provoked or they started the fight.

Although assessed to be a very severe case and currently on a Conservatorship, I was most impressed by his motivation for treatment. He indicated that his mission in life was to have a productive job and a girlfriend. In addition, his parents had stepped up by committing to pay for 90 days of treatment in a residential treatment facility.

Jason entered the Balance Treatment Center Residence within days after the interview for a ninety-day period of intensive treatment. This would include individual and group psychotherapy, cognitive behavioral therapy, medication management, and stabilization on medication.

Jason struggled initially. He was hostile, argumentative, indirectly threatening staff but when confronted still showed his strong motivation to listen and succeed. Jason's medications at Balance Treatment Center included two mood stabilizers, atypical antipsychotic medication, and medication to help with side effects, anxiety, and sleep. He started to show improvement within the first 30 days but his progress was very slow. This was indicated by periodic flare-ups during which he in fact threatened a female resident and had to be placed on "line of sight." Family visits were tense and uncomfortable but showed some signs of reestablishing better relationships. Fortunately, while this did not come easily and did not come quickly, it did happen.

By the time of his discharge from Balance Treatment Center, Jason was well engaged in both individual and group psychotherapy. He had many positive interactions with the staff. He was not making any bizarre comments, could deal with redirection, and was beginning to form some positive relationships.

At the beginning of 2014 extending through 2016, Jason's medications had to be adjusted frequently. At first, he was on the atypical antipsychotic Risperdal along with the two mood stabilizers. Then, at some point in early 2014, Risperdal seemed to lose its effectiveness. Along with that, I was concerned with the long-term possible metabolic effects from this medication.

There were several major turning points that occurred around mid-2014 or the end of that year. Jason was very angry and harbored a great deal of resentment toward his parents. This was based on his belief that they had done something wrong while raising him. This is a belief common to almost everyone who has ever been born and raised by parents. But, more importantly, it has been noted that in someone who is bipolar, this belief is intensified and that was true with Jason.

In mid-2014, Jason wrote some very threatening emails to his parents and this led to his requiring a brief hospitalization. His therapist was frightened by Jason's threats and refused to continue treatment with him. Fortunately, we were able to enlist the services of George Cave, Ph.D. who had briefly treated him at Balance Treatment Center. George was a good choice because as a strong parental figure he was direct with Jason and helped Jason contain his anger, directing it towards healthy outlets and resolutions. As part of the treatment that George Cave instituted at the time of the transfer of care was regular meetings with Jason's family, in addition to individual therapy. Again it appeared that Jason moved forward from this point.

Shortly thereafter, Jason was taken off of his Conservatorship. He obtained a driver's license and this gave him a renewed sense of freedom and hope for the future. Unfortunately, as we all know things do not turn around quite that quickly and when still without a job, living away from his parents, not having a girlfriend, few close relationships, Jason started getting very depressed. He talked about feeling morose and hopeless.

At this point, again a medication change was considered. Lamictal was selected, the only true mood stabilizer antidepressant prescribed, which is often the most successful medication and one that has made major differences in people's lives. We were very disappointed when Jason developed a rash. This was a Steven-Johnson rash, the only rash which can actually be lethal. Subsequently, Lamictal had to be stopped. Latuda, another atypical antipsychotic, was started. Latuda had a primary indication for bipolar depression and it was started as a low dose, at approximately 40 mg with food at night. However, by December, when Jason became manic, it was necessary to increase it. Again I am pointing out the fact that with Jason and with anyone who has bipolar, there are these rapid changes in mood that can be very disruptive to their life. However, Latuda was helpful along with the two mood stabilizers but his mood did not fully stabilize.

In October 2015, Jason became unruly with the staff at the apartment where he lived, and it became apparent, along with the helpful insight of his therapist, that another option was necessary. I chose to add a "typical antipsychotic," something generally psychiatrists shied away from because of the increased likelihood of side effects. This is something I learned from working at Vista Del Mar, an acute hospital in Ventura—that a typical can be used to help stabilize the patient's mood. Jason was started on Loxapine at 25 mg, titrated up to 100 mg, and this led to a major turnaround in the beginning of a prolonged period of progress and major improvements in his life. That included obtaining a job, an academic position at a major university, and dating relationships with women he had met as friends or was set up with by family members.

To this day, Jason remains on multiple medications, two mood stabilizers, one atypical antipsychotic for bipolar depression, one typical antipsychotic for psychosis, one sleep aid, one medication for anxiety, and one to counteract any side effects.

Jason has continued to progress and stabilize his life. His relationships with his family, developing a career, and improving his romantic relationships continue to move forward. I truly believe his success is exactly what he claims—a relentless commitment to health, a willingness to trust his providers and the support of his family, and, at this point, the extension of these ideas into the community.

Jason is the kind of patient who works hard at everything he does. He wants to develop himself in all aspects of life, of human development. Working with Jason had been rewarding. It truly was never unpleasant nor complicated and I plan to see him as his psychiatrist in the future.

Ronald D. Sager, M.D., Psychiatrist
Medical Director, Balance Treatment Center, Calabasas, CA

# About the Author

Jason W. Park is the author of two memoirs and a number of short stories and personal essays. His writings typically revolve around the hero's journey: overcoming seemingly insurmountable obstacles, exerting heavy, strenuous effort, and emphasizing the changed moral fibre of the protagonist. His lifelong battle with mental illness, aimed at achieving recovery and wellness, is the constant theme in his second, current memoir. When not writing, Jason volunteers his time as a speaker and peer advocate of The Stability Network (TSN), Depression and Bipolar Support Alliance (DBSA), and the National Alliance on Mental Illness (NAMI).

Dr. Park received his baccalaureate from Harvard and his Ph.D. from the University of Pittsburgh's Katz Graduate School of Business. He was born in Kansas and raised in Pittsburgh, before leaving for warmer climes in Los Angeles post-college. He dabbles in being a Pittsburgh sports fan, and remembers fondly the Super Bowl victories of the Steelers and the Stanley Cup championship wins of the Penguins (but he still waits for the Major League Baseball Pirates to win a World Series—last one was in 1979). With a strong avocation for music, he enjoys listening to Electronic Dance Music and playing classical piano.

# Acknowledgments

My last twenty years have been lived collaboratively and so much gratitude is in order.

First and foremost, gratitude goes to my father, who stuck with me, through thick and thin, from the bitter beginning to the happy ending. I bow deeply to him, who taught me the right values to live by and the wrong ones to eschew. They say that the apple does not fall far from the tree, and I am immensely thankful that this is true in real life.

I would also like to express my love for my mother, who always knew what was best for me, even at times when I refused to admit that. Her firm insistence in abiding by the right way, even in situations that put her in potential danger, is a testament to her love for me. The only thing I can do in this case is to reciprocate her love with this acknowledgment.

My brother deserves acclaim for the way in which he gently treated me during the worst phases of the crisis besetting our relationship within the family. He always acted with my best interests at heart, and always gave wise counsel, which I continue to be amazed by. Indeed, he in many ways has acted as the older brother, not the younger one.

I would also like to thank my sister for being understanding when it was necessary and for introducing me into her own side of the family. One of the highlights of my life was August 2008 in Santa Barbara, as best man at her wedding. I have never felt as happy as I did at that moment, being surrounded by family and friends, and toasting her journey to marital bliss.

And to my nieces: May you both grow up strong in body, wise in mind, and kind in heart. Not having children, I view you two essentially as my own. I am greatly satisfied to be someone who gets to see you enjoying your childhood and later sailing right on to adulthood! Be good to each other and provide good company to one another on the road of life.

My psychologist, George Cave, Ph.D., has been an essential member of my inner circle. He quietly listened to my deepest fears without flinching. And at times hilarity would ensue! But that was the enduring beauty of our working relationship. With his Ph.D. in psychology as background, he and I could talk about things on a very high level. Without that intellectual camaraderie, recovery would not have been possible.

And my psychiatrist, Ronald Sager, M.D., is one of a kind, due to his training in psychiatry and psychoanalysis, and how he applies it. He could work wonders with medication, which stopped my bipolar disorder right in its tracks. Dr. Sager obviously knew what he was doing, and he always kept a very close watch on me, for which I am eternally grateful.

I would also like to thank my friends and colleagues at the Depression and Bipolar Support Alliance, the National Alliance on Mental Illness, and The Stability Network for their support group sessions, mentoring presentations, and coaching conferences, which elevated my recovery over the last five years.

I am indebted to the Independent Writers of Southern California (IWOSC) and the Writing Conference of Los Angeles for helping my writing move forward. And thanks to the Small Business Development Corporation for getting my website off the ground. I also acknowledge the Greater Los Angeles Writers Society (GLAWS) for fostering my collegiality with other writers.

An unsung hero in this whole caper was Mr. Dick Stusser, my court-appointed Conservator. He really shook (figuratively) a lot of order into me when Disability Payments were not entirely forthcoming as expected, or when my Supplemental Security Income dried to a trickle... by the 2nd of every month. The man did me a huge favor managing my finances, which were predictably chaotic to begin with, and bringing them down to a soft landing on Ground Zero, when it became time for me to manage my own finances.

At this time, I would like to recognize Ms. Andrea Reider for engaging in a masterful performance of the interior layout design. And let me offer tribute to my cover designer, Design9creative, for allowing my book to be judged by its cover. I did not realize until the concluding stages of the book writing project, and the initial stages of the book publishing project, how important visual presentation is for a book. Both individuals deserve a round of applause.

And last but not least, a great expression of appreciation for my editor, Ms. Robin Quinn. She knew how to draw out my own independent voice in the manuscript, while she cogently elicited her own views about what direction it needed to go in. She also taught me the important lesson that not everything runs according to my schedule, and thus patience is a virtue. I am lucky to have her in my corner on this enterprise.

Los Angeles, 2021

Made in the USA
Columbia, SC
20 March 2021

34444529R00198